MANAGEMENT-MINDED SUPERVISION

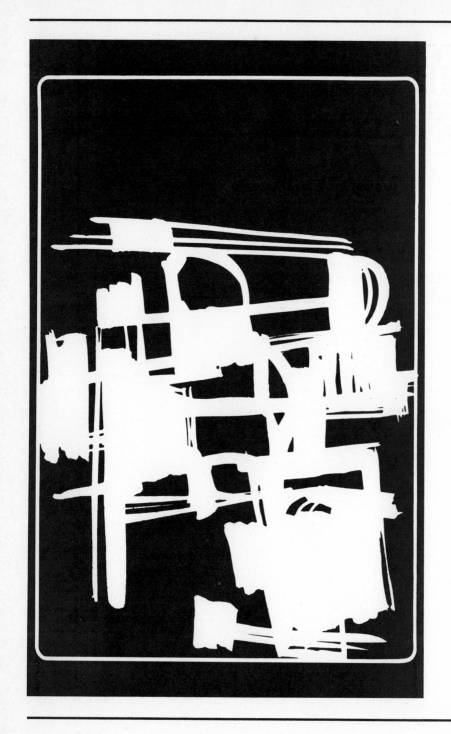

MANAGEMENT-MINDED SUPERVISION SECOND EDITION

BRADFORD B. BOYD

Management Institute
University of Wisconsin

McGRAW-HILL BOOK COMPANY

New York   St. Louis   Dallas   San Francisco
Auckland   Düsseldorf   Johannesburg   Kuala Lumpur
London   Mexico   Montreal   New Delhi   Panama   Paris
São Paulo   Singapore   Sydney   Tokyo   Toronto

Editor in Chief: Edward Byers
Editing Supervisor: Linda Stern
Senior Editing Manager: Elizabeth Huffman
Production Supervisor: Stacy Rosenberg
Art Director: Frank Medina
Designer/Illustrator: Bill Frost

Library of Congress Cataloging in Publication Data

Boyd, Bradford B
   Management-minded supervision.

   Includes bibliographies and index.
   1. Personnel management.   2. Supervision of
employees.   I. Title.
HF5549.B778   1976   658.3'02   75-43751
ISBN 0-07-006941-7

MANAGEMENT-MINDED SUPERVISION, Second Edition

1 2 3 4 5 6 7 8 9 0   DODO   7 8 5 4 3 2 1 0 9 8 7 6

PREFACE

The need for management-minded supervisors in business, industry, and government exists today as it never has before. In the coming decade, several million men and women will be promoted to supervisory positions and will come to understand that the supervisor is management at its closest point of contact with the productive employee. For the executives to whom these newly made supervisors report, a primary question will be, "How can we get our supervisors to think and act like managers?" To this question and to the growing need for capable, management-oriented supervisors, the present edition of *Management-Minded Supervision* is addressed.

ORGANIZATION

Management-Minded Supervision, Second Edition, is built around three major resources of the supervisor—management-mindedness, leadership, and job knowledge. Research and day-to-day work with supervisors from hundreds of organizations have helped define these essential needs. The conference rooms at the University of Wisconsin Management Institute have provided a laboratory in which the techniques of supervisory management could be tested.

Performance Objectives

The text is a supervisor's manual. Its organization places needed emphasis on the major resources of the supervisor. Each part is introduced by performance objectives that highlight the central issues dealt with in the part. The performance objectives also provide a way for the reader to plan individual goals to be achieved.

Burt Hall Cases

The immensely popular Burt Hall of the first edition has returned. Burt is the supervisor of an assembly department in a fictitious manufacturing plant. He provides, I hope, the only fiction in the book. Each chapter begins with a problem, or as an optimist would say, an opportunity, that faces Burt. A composite of thousands of good supervisors across the land, Burt Hall has his strengths and his weaknesses. Often the reader will share Burt's viewpoints; many times the reader will wonder how Burt could be so wrong. Burt stimulates thinking and personal evaluation of the reader's own management practices and attitudes. Although he is a supervisor in a manufacturing plant, Burt faces problems that might confront retail store supervisors, government department heads, or supervisors of white-collar, sales, or technical personnel. He is a first-level manager.

Text

The coverage in the book is wide-ranging and of immediate value to the front-line supervisor interested in a practical approach. The areas of communication, training, decision making, and organizing are among the many aspects of supervision that are dealt with. A chapter, "Getting Along With the Boss," has been added to expand the coverage of the vital relationship between the supervisor and his or her superior.

Highlights

The highlights at the end of each chapter summarize for the reader the main points of the chapter. They help reinforce the key points and provide a handy review for future reference.

Every chapter is followed by questions which can be used for individual review or group discussion. Again, these questions help the supervisor to relate text material to his or her own experience and to focus on ways in which to resolve immediate situations.

Case Problems

A new feature of the text, the case problems appearing at the end of each chapter expand the approach of the Burt Hall cases by giving the supervisory trainee the opportunity to test the principles of management-mindedness as supervisors in government, banks, hospitals, offices, airlines, and retail stores. Each critical incident is carefully tailored to the chapter content and followed by a number of questions designed to prompt the reader to explore alternate ways of handling specific problems.

Suggestions for Further Study

For the supervisor or executive interested in pursuing the study of management, a list of readings is included at the end of each chapter.

AUDIENCE

Employees in business, industry, and government who want to become front-line supervisors or to improve their management skills will find this book helpful in developing an insight into the supervisor's problems, challenges, and opportunities. Others will also find the text of value in a number of ways. The training director who wants to set up a program on the basics of supervision may find it helpful to use the case studies which precede each chapter to initiate group discussions. Members of management interested in orienting the new supervisor to the management viewpoint may find here some of the things they want to say. Personnel departments seeking to develop potential supervisors in presupervisory training programs may find approaches in this book to give direction to those programs. And the student who seeks to understand the role of the supervisor in the management hierarchy will have access to a point of view shaped by over twenty years of working with managers in business, industry, and government.

ACKNOWLEDGEMENTS

It would be impossible to acknowledge individually those who have contributed to this book because I would have to begin with the thousands of supervisors who have attended institutes at the University of Wisconsin and shared their experiences, problems, and opinions. The literature in the field of management has certainly helped shape the thinking reflected on these pages, as have consultants, professors, and managers who have served the Management Institute program so well as discussion leaders. My associates at the Institute also have contributed substantially over the years to the philosophy that is contained in this book. To the many firms who have cooperated in research projects or who have accorded me the opportunity of conducting supervisory development programs in their plants goes a special word of thanks.

Recognizing the difficulties of giving individual recognition, I still feel that three such expressions of gratitude must be made. The late Clayton G. Orcutt, a former associate in the Management Institute, did more than anyone else to keep my thinking and my vocabulary oriented to the supervisor. His common sense and practical approach provided me through the years with an example I have been proud to follow. His counsel helped me greatly to develop empathy for the supervisors for whom this book is written.

Professor Norman C. Allhiser, director of the Management Institute, provided the encouragement and support that was needed to start and complete this book. His direction of the Management Institute, more than anything else, has molded my own management-mindedness.

An especially warm word of appreciation goes to Mrs. Gladys Dahl, who has so capably handled the administrative work of our Supervisory Institutes. Her dedication has contributed immeasurably to the smooth functioning of our section. To an already heavy work load, she cheerfully and enthusiastically added the burden of preparing the manuscript.

Lastly, to the over 100,000 who used the first edition of *Management-Minded Supervision*, my special thanks, since their support stimulated this second edition.

BRADFORD B. BOYD

CONTENTS

PART ONE

MANAGEMENT-MINDEDNESS

Business without profit is not business any more than a pickle is candy.
CHARLES F. ABBOTT

Success or failure in business is caused even more by mental attitude than by mental capacities.
WALTER DILL SCOTT

PERFORMANCE OBJECTIVES

A supervisor will be able to measure his or her ability to function as a management-minded supervisor against the following criteria:

1. To support daily management's philosophies and policies.

2. To have reached agreement with the boss on the major responsibilities of the job.

3. To be able to define three or four quantifiable objectives for the department supervised.

4. To have taken periodic inventory of how well job performance measures up against required skills, knowledge, and abilities.

5. To have developed a personal plan for self-improvement.

6. To be implementing at all times some part of a personal improvement plan.

7. To have communicated all essential information needed by employees in the performance of their jobs.

8. To satisfy the boss that he or she is fully informed on what is happening in the department.

9. To have analyzed each communication failure from the standpoint of what can be done to prevent similar failures in the future.

10. To have established a climate in the department that produces at least five new ideas or suggestions for improvement per month.

11. To mentally ask what's good about an idea before reacting negatively to it.

12. To have carefully planned the initiation of any important management change in the department.

13. To identify specific reasons for employees resisting change when it occurs.

14. To have made the boss understand and agree with specific goals in supervising the department.

15. To have assured the boss of a desire to grow by indicating a willingness to accept delegated responsibility.

16. To have personally expressed appreciation to the boss for each time he has given assistance or support.

CHAPTER 1

DEVELOPING MANAGEMENT-MINDEDNESS

Why is there so much concern for developing management-mindedness? It comes simply from a widely held belief that the way a person thinks determines the way he or she acts and that all supervisors should be concerned with acting and functioning like managers.

We can discount the tendency of some to think that the supervisor's job is declining in importance. A conservative estimate is that six to seven million new supervisory positions will be filled in the coming decade. Consider the words of Edward C. Schleh, author of *Management by Results.*

> If management is to do an effective job in coordinating all of the activities of an enterprise to sound accomplishment of company objectives, its prime approach should be based on the first-level requirements. What is required at the first-level operation is in the long run the final result of the enterprise. All of the planning work along the way is usually of little value unless the first-level people turn out something worthwhile and sell it at a worthwhile price. This emphasis on first-level operation is one of the first

and cardinal requirements of any management approach and should be paramount in the decisions of managers at every level.*

THE CASE OF BURT HALL	Just one more month to go and a decision about Burt Hall, supervisor of Assembly Department B, would have to be made. Burt had been made supervisor on a jointly agreed-upon probationary basis.

He still had an inactive membership in the union and would retain his seniority if either Burt or management decided that he should return to his old job.

Perhaps the phrase "either Burt or management" contributed to the problem, for both Oscar Palmer, plant manager, and Ray Ford, assembly superintendent, felt that Burt just hadn't taken hold as "a member of management." Burt, unaware of their concern, also felt deep down that he was not doing the job for which he had so much enthusiasm just five months ago.

A top producer, intelligent, well liked, and properly motivated, Burt was a unanimous choice when the vacancy in Department B was created. "A natural for the job" is the way Ray Ford concluded his recommendation of Burt. Everyone involved in Burt's selection felt the same way. It wasn't hard to sell Burt on the job. He did, however, express some concern about whether he could take the tremendous responsibility and whether he could boss his old buddies. That was when the probationary arrangement was worked out. No one really thought that it was any more than window-dressing. Now, five months later, this face-saving arrangement provided the basis for the discussion between Mr. Palmer and Ray Ford. Burt was also doing some soul searching.

Things started out smoothly enough for Burt. The people in his department liked him—they always had. He knew the work to be done, and no one minded taking orders from him. While he felt a little uneasy bossing people at first, he soon gained confidence, He demonstrated that he could take production schedules and transform them into completed orders. He knew his job was production coupled with good quality and low costs. This was where he concentrated his efforts. He was rewarded by encouraging comments from Ray Ford on his excellent production record.

*From "Management Based on the First Level," in *Management International*, International Review for Management and Managerial Sciences.

It hurt, then, whenever anything or anybody interrupted the smooth flow of production. Burt was quick to show his displeasure—not by shouting but by scowling and silence. Changes, for example, irritated him. "They can't get production if they keep monkeying around with methods," he complained to several of his assemblers.

Specials got under his skin because they took longer. Burt couldn't see why standard lines couldn't be made to work. Ray Ford told him once that the company took great pride in accommodating customers, but Burt still felt they could sell the customer on adjusting to standard lines. It was important to recognize the company's overall goals and customer demands, Ray told him. Burt agreed, but said that each supervisor had to have individual goals and that his was to make his department the most productive in the plant. Burt's interest in production was commended by Ray with a caution not to lose sight of the total picture.

When the union objected to restudying a job on which a new method had been installed, Burt sided with it. He knew there would be a fuss, and he wanted to avoid anything which might disrupt production. The labor contract permitted the setting of new rates on a job whenever a new method or new equipment was installed. Burt and the steward argued that there wasn't enough of a change to warrant a new study. Management had felt that the rate had been out of line for some time. The new method gave them the opportunity they had been waiting for. Burt reluctantly supported the new study. His reluctance gave Mr. Palmer the first reason to question Burt's promotion.

As time went on there were other occasions when Burt's attitude reflected his feeling that he stood between management and his employees—a part of neither. He saw himself as being fair to both sides. His employees perceived him as a company man—all production and costs. Mr. Palmer and Ray Ford developed the feeling that he was a "loner"—out to set a mark for himself. No one, including Burt, had any doubts that he had changed since taking over.

Burt found it difficult to pin down just when or why he began to feel this job wasn't his cup of tea. He had started out with an overwhelming desire to succeed. There hadn't been any major problems or blow-ups. Relationships with his buddies and fellow workers had changed, but no more than he had expected. Production increases hadn't been spectacular, but he had done better than his predecessor. He did, however, feel under pressure from above and from staff departments who interfered with the smooth running of his department. Riding herd on production seemed to take more and more of his time. There wasn't much, he concluded, to make him feel like a member of management. At least on his old job he knew who he was and where he stood.

"If only we could get him to see the whole job instead of just pushing production, we might still salvage him, Ray," Oscar Palmer stated in discussing the decision that must soon be made. Evidence of Burt's feeling that people were producers only was mounting up.

Once Burt's strengths (and they were substantial) and his limitations (also real) had been weighed, both men concluded that Burt Hall was too good a man to let go back to the ranks. He needed direction and guidance. They needed to know more about Burt.

1.   What were Burt's strengths and limitations?

2.   What is management looking for in a supervisor today?

3.   What are the major responsibilities of a supervisor?

4.   Is the supervisor really a member of management?

WHAT DOES TODAY'S SUPERVISOR NEED?

In considering the case of Burt Hall we see him in a situation that many supervisors have experienced or will experience—eager to do a job, not sure of where they fit in the scheme of things, and debating with themselves the wisdom of the decision to become supervisors. Until the doubts are resolved and new direction is established, Burt will flounder. His concern for production will deepen, his attitudes will harden, and his professional sense of balance will desert him. By a sense of balance we mean the ability to see the whole job in perspective. For this the integration of the company's philosophy and policies with personal goals and ambitions is essential. Recognition of the major responsibilities of a supervisor in addition to production must be clear. Overemphasis of one responsibility to the neglect of others has caused the downfall of many men and women with excellent supervisory potential.

For several years now in researching the problems employees encounter in making the transition to supervisory work, the question has been asked, "What does today's supervisor need?" Contributions from thousands of front-line supervisors, plant managers, educators, authors, and consultants point to three major areas of need. First, supervisors must be *management-minded*. Second, they need the *skills of leadership*. Third, they must possess *job knowledge*.

MANAGEMENT-MINDEDNESS

Here, perhaps, is one of Burt's greatest shortcomings. The supervisor is the front line of management. No matter how the company is organized, no matter what title is used, there is always that first-level management position that calls for the direction of the productive employee. Most men and women at this level are called supervisors, or foremen, but whatever their titles, they are members of management. Identified in the minds of others as managers, they should think like, act like, and perform like the management of their organization.

This involves knowing the firm's aims and what the firm stands for. It means understanding the goals and objectives of the entire organization as intimately as the supervisor knows the standards and quotas that exist in a department. Working in harmony with management, the supervisor becomes a part of this philosophy in word and deed. J. Paul Sticht, when he was vice president of Campbell Soup Company, wrote, "Whenever a man accepts a supervisory position he accepts with it the responsibility of supporting and advocating management philosophies, policies, and procedures—and can expect the full support of management in return."* It's safe to assume that the great majority of members of higher management share this view. Unfortunately much more is hoped for from supervisors than is actually expressed in orienting them for management positions. Many management-minded supervisors carry Mr. Sticht's thought one step further by saying that if a person cannot be wholeheartedly dedicated to the management's philosophies and approaches, it would be better to resign the assignment.

Developing management-mindedness requires among other things adopting constant self-improvement as a way of life. The day when supervisors could sit back and coast is gone. There's no room for the "I've arrived" way of thinking. An effective supervisor personally identifies with the company's struggle for survival in a competitive world. Just as the company must constantly seek ways of improving its products and services, the supervisor must look for opportunities to be more valuable to the organization. Technological improvement, expansion, reorganization—all spell out the fact that unlimited opportunities await the person who is keeping pace through self-improvement.

Supervisors must also recognize that they are the pacesetters for those who report to them. Setting the example is a powerful means of demonstrating that personal development is expected from subordi-

*A.M.A. Encyclopedia of Supervisory Training, Chapter 1, American Management Association, New York, 1961.

nates. Supervisors who rest on their laurels after being on the job and who do nothing to keep abreast of new developments are shortchanging the organization. The same can be said about a company which shows no interest in improving its products, expanding its markets, or updating its facilities.

To be able to understand the vital role supervisors play in communication is also a part of management-minded supervision. Communication is the nervous system of any business enterprise. We can easily see how effectiveness is impaired when the necessary information on which to base decisions isn't available. A manager must be in the know to function effectively. The smooth running of a department or an entire firm is directly proportionate to the communication ability of its management.

We can easily recognize that supervisors occupy a unique position as far as communication is concerned. Orders, rules, standards, policies, and attitudes must all be communicated to the production employee. Since supervisors have direct contact with employees, the burden falls on their shoulders to see that they understand what is expected of them. And it's not hard to see how much higher management must depend on the supervisor to communicate to its members the attitudes, feelings, and problems that exist in the departments. Management policies are formulated in the light of this information. The supervisor's job is to keep management informed.

One of the truly distressing elements of organizational communication is the clarity with which we can see the deficiencies of others. Supervisors from many companies often say that communication is a prime weakness in their firms. "This communication training is fine for me, but the person who really needs it is my boss," is heard repeatedly. Yet whenever higher-level managers plan supervisory development programs, communication is invariably identified as a high-priority need.

Awareness of the need to communicate is the first step in improving communication in an organization. Management-minded supervisors don't complain about the poor communication of others; they initiate steps to get the information they need. They see to it that those with whom they deal understand their objectives. Most of us will find that when we do a good job of communicating with others, it makes others want to communicate well with us. Harmony and cooperation between individuals on a management team depend on communication. Communication between individuals who respect one another is spontaneous and creates mutual respect that continues to grow. All the communications principles and techniques in the world, however, won't help those who dislike each other. Every supervisor has the potential of being an excellent communicator, but first he or she must think like a manager.

Management-minded supervisors are enthusiastic about change and are skilled in initiating it. They feel that it is not enough to accept change but that they must be a part of it, find opportunities to make improvements, and implement with vigor the changes introduced by higher management. Here again Burt Hall gave his superiors reason to question his support of management's way of thinking. Unconsciously he was resisting change because it would interrupt the smooth operation of his assembly lines. Yet Burt would have been the first to deny that he was resistant to change or guilty of the kind of thinking expressed in these words: "We've been getting along fine with the present method. Why change now?"

The expectations of higher management were nicely summed up by Malcolm MacNaughton, president of Castle and Cooke, Inc., when he wrote this message to supervisors about their jobs and the future.

> In looking forward to what the future will bring, there is one factor in management I can feel sure about. That factor is change—change in products, change in methods, change in organization. At Castle and Cooke, Inc., change has been facing us continually and at an ever increasing rate. We feel that change is a necessity for growth, and we intend to grow. When I have meetings with our management personnel, I stress the need for change and growth because to survive we must change, and we must grow. If you, in your job, recognize that we are in a changing industrial world and we have to change and grow with it, then you will be able to continue to do your part effectively as a member of management.*

LEADERSHIP SKILLS

Volumes have been written about the supervisor as a leader. Social scientists have sought to identify qualities of leadership, in the hope that once they found the formula, a mold could be built and each of us pressed into it—to come out an ideal leader. This is nonsense.

Make no mistake about it. When we are placed in positions demanding leadership, as Burt Hall was, we will lead in different ways,

*"What's Ahead for Supervisors in 1966," *Supervision,* Vol. XXVIII, No. 1, January, 1966.

according to the personalities we have been cultivating all our lives. Leadership is not coddling people, as some would have us believe; nor is it hitting people over the head to get what we want. Leadership is getting people to work to achieve the goals of the enterprise. It's giving people something to work for.

Burt Hall started out well enough, but as months went by, a stronger and stronger orientation to the requirements of production put him in danger of losing sight of the requirements of people. He was beginning to see his people as tools—and this is a shortcut to failure. It's universally acknowledged that in any organization people are our most priceless asset. We've heard this so often that we risk overlooking it. Production is a prime responsibility of supervision, but productivity depends on people. The intelligent and successful manager recognizes this. He or she can't afford to take the people who make up the work force for granted.

The management-minded supervisor, then, will know and understand employees as individuals and treat them as such. He or she will realize that motivation is much more than money or a pat on the back and that some of the more commonly accepted incentives do almost nothing to stimulate workers to do their best.

To lead people, one must teach them. Any manager, from the top all the way down, accepts an obligation to train and coach those reporting to him or her. A job at the supervisory level is frequently bigger in this respect because a supervisor has so many more people to guide and direct. So many supervisors delegate this job to their better employees, yet they aren't satisfied with the results they get. Is it because they find it convenient to ignore the fact that a good operator doesn't necessarily make a good instructor? Management-minded supervisors recognize that when they delegate the authority to train, they don't divorce themselves from their responsibility to be sure that they have well-trained employees under them. A supervisor must train those who train others or at least should make provisions for their training to ensure the employee-instructor's ability to effectively handle the responsibility for training others.

Leadership skills not only call for skills in motivating and training; the management-minded approach also calls for creating a positive climate for discipline—training people to make punishment unnecessary. Many an enlightened supervisor will quickly acknowledge that discipline should not be thought of as restrictive, or as a policing operation. Discipline has the ultimate goal of self-discipline. There is a great difference between the leadership approach and the ''bull-of-the-woods'' approach.

JOB KNOWLEDGE

Many executives and educators have declared emphatically that job knowledge isn't a vital concern to them in placing people in supervisory positions. "Give me a supervisor who can lead, and he or she can function in any department or any industry." There is an element of truth in that statement. We can add, however, that new supervisors had better set about learning the methods, procedures, equipment, and machinery in a department if they are going to function very long. When men and women start supervising in new departments they have the extra burden of learning as much as they can as quickly as they can about the work performed. They will not gain their employees' respect until they demonstrate an understanding of the problems faced by the operators in performing their jobs.

As much as we hear about minimizing the importance of job knowledge in supervision, it is still the factor to which management gives the most weight in selecting workers from the ranks for supervisory jobs. In a survey conducted by the University of Wisconsin's Management Institute, 225 plant managers were asked, "What are the most important considerations in selecting a production worker for the position of supervisor?" Ranked number one in that survey was job or technical knowledge, and close behind in the number two position was ability to get along with people.

With automation and technological advancements becoming more and more a part of our business life, job knowledge is likely to remain an important attribute of the management-minded supervisor. The technical knowledge of the department's operations is, however, only a part of the job knowledge of the modern supervisor. Of primary importance is knowing how to manage. Precious few come to the supervisor's job with this knowledge. Rank and file employees have their work planned for them; they are given orders; their work is supervised and inspected. Until they actually become supervisors, they have little opportunity to learn these management skills. In most cases no one knows how well they can perform the process of managing.

The process of management at any level consists of four functions: planning, organizing, motivating (or directing), and controlling. Degrees of difficulty and emphasis vary, of course, from one level of management to another. Top executives, for example, spend a great deal more time and effort planning and organizing. Although at the supervisory level these functions are not ignored, usually the primary emphasis is on motivating and giving orders and on controlling performance.

Inability to plan has put many supervisors behind the eight ball in their jobs. Standards, schedules, goals, quotas are all a part of the planning function. Determining when work is to be started, how long it should take, what materials and equipment are needed, who will do the work, how one job will coordinate with the next—this is planning. A supervisor who lacks skill in planning often complains that there isn't enough time to do everything expected of him or her. Burt Hall is beginning to reach this point in his career, and if he doesn't check this tendency, he will soon become a "crisis manager"—one who spends most of his time jumping from one crisis to another, constantly putting out fires. The planning of personal time on the job can be an extremely satisfying and rewarding first venture into organized planning. We'll discuss this in a later chapter on planning and organizing.

To narrow the gap between what he or she wants and gets when an order is given, a supervisor should know what happens when the order is issued. Why do some orders produce an enthusiastic response, others the blank stares of confusion, and still others a grudging minimum compliance of questionable quality? Spending as much time as they do in directing the work of employees, supervisors need to be sensitive to how people react when they are given orders.

Once the work of the department has been planned and organized, and the orders issued, the management-minded supervisor knows that jobs and activities must be followed up. Control is a key to effective managing. It is here that the supervisor matches performance against the goals and standards that have been set. Modification may be necessary. The opportunity for recognizing a job well done becomes apparent. The control function is intimately related to the planning function. Most supervisors use many forms of control every day—production reports, attendance and time reports, cost and quality reports, progress checks, and performance appraisals. Of these the last is most difficult for many supervisors. To evaluate an employee's performance and periodically review that evaluation with the employee has for many supervisors produced negative rather than positive results. Instead of improving morale, it has lowered it. As a management control properly administered, the performance appraisal and review has the potential for substantially upgrading the performance of the entire department.

Job knowledge for the management-minded supervisor, then, consists of two major areas: the technical knowledge of methods and equipment and the knowledge of how to manage. The first is brought to the job by most supervisors. The second must be learned, for few have the opportunity to acquire it before accepting management positions.

Part 3 of this book will deal in more detail with this aspect of job knowledge. Interestingly enough the management process is very seldom covered in management development programs for the first-level supervisor.

IS THE SUPERVISOR REALLY CONSIDERED A PART OF MANAGEMENT?

Perhaps in considering the case of Burt Hall, we have taken for granted that because Mr. Palmer and Ray Ford wanted Burt to become a member of management, managers in general prefer to promote supervisors from existing employees; and that because Burt himself had doubts as to where he stood, most supervisors feel they are not truly part of the management group. Is Burt's situation—being chosen from the ranks—typical? Let's consider the survey of 225 plant managers from companies employing over 9,000 supervisors to see, perhaps, how managers view the problem of management-mindedness at the first level.

The question was asked, Are supervisors usually appointed from within your organization, or will you go outside the company to hire? Ninety-four percent said they follow the practice of promoting from within. However, there is an increasing emphasis on formal education. Two-thirds of the group considered a high school diploma a minimum educational requirement. More and more technologically advanced companies insist on college degrees for the first management level. An obligation to look first within the organization for those with the proper qualifications will be recognized for some years to come.

Ninety-seven percent said yes to the question, Do you consider your supervisors a part of management? While in many companies the ability of higher management to create this feeling on the part of the supervisor is lacking, supervisors should not ignore the fact that the desire is there. One of the most exciting challenges for a supervisor, it seems, is to demonstrate his or her management-mindedness by taking the initiative rather than waiting to be initiated into the club. A company, like any organization, stands in need of men and women with management and leadership abilities. Sixty-two percent of the plant managers surveyed responded negatively when asked, Do you feel that the supervisor in your plant adjusts easily to the management viewpoint as contrasted with what he or she felt as a worker? Plant managers recognize that the adjustment is difficult and want to see the adjustment made as quickly as possible.

Higher management, even though evidence sometimes points to the contrary, wants and expects the first-line supervisors to feel and act like members of management. But how about the supervisors? How do they feel? In another survey 250 first-line supervisors were asked, Do you feel in your present assignment that you are truly a member of management? Significantly, only 74 percent said yes. Those who felt they were members of management only sometimes accounted for 24 percent, and the remaining 2 percent flatly said no. Those who said no or sometimes gave as their reasons the failure of management to communicate with them and the lack of authority to make decisions in their own departments. Implied in the responses is the fact that supervisors, too, want to feel they are a part of management. Why then the concern?

It is expressed in the attitudes of those 225 plant managers toward their 9,000 supervisors and the many others who at one time or another had come under their supervision. In two widely separated sections of the questionnaire, the plant managers were asked about the difficulties new supervisors had in making the transition and the weaknesses the supervisors most commonly displayed. Bear in mind that these were completely open-ended questions; there were no suggested answers. This makes the responses especially significant. The two questions appear below, with response indicated.

What do you feel are the three most common weaknesses supervisors display in the performance of their job?

1.	Poor attitude	56%
2.	Poor management of their job	50%
3.	Poor disciplining	22%
4.	Poor communication	21%

What, according to your experience, are the most difficult problems faced by the newly appointed supervisor?

1.	Management (planning, organizing, etc.)	43%
2.	Adopting a management attitude	42%
3.	Human relations	25%
4.	Discipline	22%

Now the reason for the concern becomes more obvious. Poor attitude—or a lack of a positive management-mindedness—is either first or second in the response to both questions. The same is true for the management skills we discussed earlier—skills for which there has been so little training. What does today's supervisor need? The survey confirms it: (1) management-mindedness (an attitude); (2) leadership skills; (3) job knowledge (especially of the management process).

**BUILDING A POSITIVE
MANAGEMENT ATTITUDE**

Management is many different things to many people. Here let us think of it in connection with the organization, the company. The excitement employees feel at being selected for promotion to supervisor may have died quickly once they were burdened with the responsibilities of the job. The glamour of managing can fade rapidly into the headaches of personnel and production problems unless something is done to keep enthusiasm alive. The Reverend Norman Vincent Peale wrote of near miracles in transforming people's lives when they found and experienced "the power of positive thinking." Dr. John Schindler used much the same approach in his book *How to Live 365 Days a Year*. Both said in essence that how we think determines how we act. Psychologists stress the importance of participation in winning the cooperation of others. Participation as a part of the management team in the organization is the beginning. But how should supervisors participate? How should they identify with the firm?

Part of the answer can be found in knowing just as much about an organization as possible. The history of the company in which a person is building a career is often fascinating. Who are the founders, and what were their dreams? Many companies started with an invention—the product of one person's imagination. Others started with a needed service and then grew, expanded, and diversified until the original purpose was lost completely.

How much does a supervisor know of the company's total line of products or services? How does the department fit into the total scheme of things? A management-minded supervisor will have some knowledge of how the company is organized. He or she will know where its markets are and what is being done to expand those markets.

If a supervisor were to consider investing a few hundred dollars of hard-earned cash in the common stock of a company, he or she would investigate the progress of that company, its earnings, its growth potential, its concern for research and development, its capitalization, the strength of its management, the diversification of its products, and so on. What about when the investment is a career commitment? Shouldn't a supervisor then know at least these things about his or her own firm? As supervisors learn more about the company's operations, they naturally build a stronger identification with it. In fact, many supervisors testify to having drawn attention to themselves as potential supervisors when as production employees they demonstrated an interest in what was going on in departments other than their own.

The truly management-minded supervisor represents the company both inside and outside the plant. Among the many hats worn is that of public relations. The supervisor is the representative of the firm at professional meetings, in social groups, and in community activities.

MANAGEMENT RESPONSIBILITIES OF TODAY'S SUPERVISOR

Burt Hall was moderately concerned, when accepting his new job, about the tremendous responsibilities it entailed. Unlike most production workers, he was willing to shoulder these responsibilities perhaps without a clear-cut idea of what the responsibilities actually were. On the one hand, he used the word *tremendous*. On the other hand, he demonstrated a limited awareness of the scope of his responsibility when he concentrated almost exclusively on production, costs, and quality, in that order.

A group of supervisors, when asked to enumerate the things they are responsible for, will contribute over one hundred if given enough time. Supervisors can generally reach agreement on seven basic supervisory responsibilities when their jobs are analyzed. These seven cannot be ignored. When one or more of them are overlooked, the supervisor's approach to the job is not balanced. The seven identified here are not in order of priority. At any given time, any one of them might merit a supervisor's prime concern. No one of them, however, can be set aside for very long.

PRODUCTION

Broadly conceived, production is a major responsibility of every supervisor. Production might be a product; a service, such as maintenance; a subassembly; clerical work; or sales. The supervisor's job is to accomplish that production with the resources available.

QUALITY

In today's competitive economy, many salespeople hold that the quality of their products is all they have to sell. Quality is built in where the product or service is produced. The supervisor is the key person in stimulating quality-consciousness and job pride in the work force. The management-minded supervisor knows the company's policy on quality and accepts as a major responsibility the quality of work performed in the department.

COSTS

Most of us work for profit-making organizations. Profit is the reason why people are in business. The profit motive has brought this country to its present economic level. The management-minded supervisor strives through cost control and cost reduction to contribute in any way possible to the profit of the firm. Further, he or she helps employees understand that they, too, have a responsibility to contribute to profit. In government and nonprofit organizations, the supervisor is still charged with the responsibility of seeing that the work of the department is accomplished with the lowest possible expenditure of funds.

METHODS

Production, costs, and quality are all aided by using the most efficient methods. Management-minded supervision is continually seeking easier and better ways of doing work. Work methods which waste time, effort, supplies, materials, and tools should be analyzed and improved. Stimulating employee participation in improving work methods is the mark of an effective supervisor.

MORALE

Morale is people's collective attitude toward work, the company, management, their equipment, and their workplace. The responsibility for high morale and an enthusiastic work force lies essentially with the supervisor. Good morale doesn't happen by chance. It begins with a supervisor who is sensitive to the feelings of subordinates, but who is neither a coddler nor a slave driver.

Today, as never before, that sensitivity to individuals is needed with new elements in the work force. Youth with a different value system, women expecting equal treatment and opportunity, disadvantaged persons from minority groups, all challenge the supervisor's ability to build morale in the department.

TRAINING

Every responsibility we have mentioned is dependent on the employee's knowing what his or her job is and what's expected in the way of performance. Teaching the employee the requirements of the job is important. So is the development of positive attitudes toward quality, costs, housekeeping, and safety. A characteristic of any new employee is eagerness to do a good job. With proper training, this eagerness can be cultivated and maintained.

SAFETY

Minimizing risks and hazards in work areas is the interest and desire of all management, but it falls to the first-level supervisor to see that the safest possible working conditions are maintained. Most industrial firms have safety departments charged with the responsibility of safeguarding the work force and protecting plant equipment. The federal Occupational Safety and Health Act (OSHA) puts a heavy burden on the employer to provide a safe working environment. Employers must, of course, depend on the supervisor to keep the organization in compliance with the act. A supervisor therefore has a responsibility to be familiar with the requirements of OSHA and the company's expectations of supervisory performance under the act. Safety directors are the first to admit that they depend almost completely on the supervisor of the department to enforce safety regulations and to see that safe practices are followed by the work force.

As already mentioned, these seven basic responsibilities have not been listed in order of importance, and at any given time any one of them might demand special attention for prolonged periods of time. During a period of recession, for example, our primary concern is often cost reduction. A series of lost-time accidents might very well produce a concerted emphasis on safety. The announcement of a new product by a competitor frequently brings renewed concentration on quality improvement. Rapid expansion or the automating of production lines may make training the most important part of a supervisor's job. The temptation to let other responsibilities slide during these periods may throw a supervisor's view of the job out of perspective—when the need for a balanced approach is imperative. A balanced approach means a proportionate concern for each of the seven major areas.

Figure 1 shows the job of the management-minded supervisor diagrammatically. The supervisor brings an understanding of the functions of the management process to the job in order to carry out the major responsibilities. Inability to see both people and the work in proper perspective can quickly lead to trouble. For example, a supervisor who can think only of the work to be done, or production, soon acquires the reputation of being a slave driver, a company person, or a bull of the woods. At the other extreme is the supervisor who puts personal popularity ahead of all other considerations. Nothing is more important to this person than being a good guy, and the end result is a wishy-washy approach to management. The need for some kind of balance again becomes quite apparent.

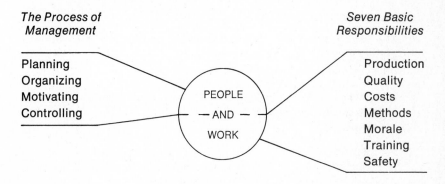

FIGURE 1   The Supervisor's Management Job

How can we describe the *real* management-minded supervisor? How does higher management regard him? Philip A. Coleman, president of Bristol Brass Corporation, expressed the answer to these questions quite well: "A real topflight foreman is the most maligned, most overworked and most underpaid jewel in the corporate crown. He is, at the same time, a man of pride, with a deep sense of achievement who knows full well that he is a substantial contributor to the finest standard of living in the world—the American system of free enterprise."*

*"What's Ahead for Supervisors in 1966," *Supervision,* Vol. XXVIII, No. 1, January, 1966.

HIGHLIGHTS

1. The three basic needs of today's management-minded supervisor are:

    a. To think and act like a full-fledged member of management
    b. To demonstrate leadership skills
    c. To possess job knowledge—both technical know-how and knowledge of the management process

2. Management-mindedness involves:

    a. Knowing and supporting management's philosophies, policies, and procedures
    b. Adopting constant self-improvement as a way of life
    c. Recognizing the vital role of communication in a smoothly functioning organization
    d. Being enthusiastic about change and skilled in initiating change

3. The management-minded supervisor recognizes the need to understand people as individuals and that motivation is the key to effective leadership.

4. Most supervisors come to their job with the necessary technical knowledge but lack an appreciation of the management process, which involves:

    a. Planning
    b. Organizing
    c. Motivating (or directing)
    d. Controlling

5. Higher management considers supervisors to be members of management, but frequently feels that supervisors lack the proper management attitudes.

6. The way we think determines the way we act. Supervisors need to know as much as possible about their organization, its history, its products, its markets, and the company's policies, goals, and objectives.

7. The supervisor's seven major responsibilities are:

    a. Production
    b. Quality
    c. Costs

d. Methods
e. Morale
f. Training
g. Safety

8. In viewing major responsibilities, the employees, and the work to be done in a department, a supervisor must bring balance to the job.

DISCUSSION QUESTIONS

1. In your own words describe the management job of the supervisor.

2. What, in your opinion, are some of the primary reasons supervisors fail?

3. Does a supervisor find the freedom to express personal opinions limited when he or she becomes a "member of management"? Explain why or why not.

4. Why does management put such heavy emphasis on job knowledge in selecting supervisors from the ranks of employees?

5. Do you consider the first-line supervisor a member of management? Why or why not?

6. Why do you think that in over 90 percent of the companies surveyed, supervisors were selected from within their employee groups?

7. Why should it be difficult for an employee to adjust to a management viewpoint when he or she is made a supervisor?

8. What do you think of using college graduates without work experience as production supervisors?

9. Why is a "balanced approach" to the supervisor's seven major responsibilities so important?

10. Elaborate on Philip Coleman's statement that a topflight supervisor is "the most maligned, most overworked and most underpaid jewel in the corporate crown." Do you agree? Why or why not?

CASE PROBLEMS

THE CASE OF HAL ORCUTT

Hal Orcutt, bridge design engineering supervisor with the state highway department, was just about as unhappy as he thought he would be when he took the job less than a year ago. A brilliant young engineer, Hal was identified by his superiors as "a comer" early in his career. To keep him interested in state service and motivated, he was persuaded to take the supervisory job over several older and more experienced engineers.

Hal had never thought of anything in his career planning other than being the best possible design engineer. He didn't like the idea of management. He wanted to design and detail. Somewhat resentful because he was told that this promotion was the only route to getting ahead, he reluctantly accepted.

Now his job seems to be just a lot of petty details, most of them involving people. Training, checking, assigning, correcting drawings and computations, paperwork, listening to excuses, and personal problems were just not his cup of tea. "I'm wasting the most creative years of my life. Instead of designing I'm a nursemaid and paper shuffler," he complained. "Why does a guy who wants to be a professional engineer have to be a manager to get ahead?"

1. Should Hal have been persuaded to take a supervisory job he didn't want?

2. Evaluate his supervisors' pressuring him to take the job, saying it will cause him to grow? How?

3. What could have been done to improve Hal's attitude?

4. How can an engineer progress if it isn't through supervision?

THE CASE OF CORA BENSON

"You just can't trust these young nurses today to do anything right," Cora Benson was telling her husband during dinner. Cora was a supervisor in the nursing service at Claremont Hospital and Medical Center. "If I wasn't after them every minute there's no telling what would happen."

Cora had gone back to full-time nursing when the second of her two children entered the university. Her maturity and genuine dedication to good patient care won her a supervisory position very quickly. Eager to contribute to the training of nurses who in Cora's mind seemed to lack that deep concern for patients, she approached her assignment with enthusiasm.

Now she was wearing out. "Maybe I'm getting older than I thought. Still I can't believe that my 45 years is the reason. I've got to be everywhere. It's ten times more work than I thought. How do you keep up with it? I'd hate to quit when we need the money for the kids' education," she said to her husband.

At the hospital, the nurses under Cora's supervision weren't very happy either. They complained to one another that Cora was smothering them. She redid half of the jobs they had performed both at bedside and the desk. Several felt she undermined the patients' confidence in them. One of the nurses said she knew Cora's heart was in the right place, but her lack of confidence in everyone was hurting morale. "She means well, but . . . ."

1. How do you account for Cora's feeling that young nurses lack dedication?

2. What is the difference between a good nurse and a good nursing supervisor?

3. What role does delegation play in effectively supervising nurses?

THE CASE OF JANET SIMMONS

Janet Simmons, training supervisor for Hagedorn's, a major department store, had just been told she would probably be promoted to buyer of housewares, a position she had worked for so hard. She was an excellent supervisor, well liked by all her salespeople, but for some reason she couldn't define, she hadn't designated her successor.

Mr. Warren, store manager, fortunately hadn't asked her who her choice was. He simply had suggested that she let him know in a couple of days whom she would recommend. He also said it would be best if she outlined the training her successor would need.

Keenly aware that her choice would reflect the quality of her judgment, Janet sat down to write down just what it is that she had been doing so well and so naturally for the past three years.

1. What are the primary duties and responsibilities of a retail training supervisor?

2. What training would be most helpful to a new supervisor in a retail establishment?

SUGGESTIONS FOR FURTHER STUDY

Bittel, Lester R., *What Every Supervisor Should Know*, 3d ed., Chapter 1, McGraw-Hill Book Company, New York, 1974.

Famularo, Joseph J., *Supervisors in Action*, Chapter 2, McGraw-Hill Book Company, New York, 1961.

Ficker, Victor B., *Effective Supervision*, Chapters 1 and 2, Charles E. Merrill Books, Inc., Columbus, Ohio, 1975.

Reeves, Elton T., *So You Want to Be a Supervisor,* American Management Association, New York, 1971.

Steinmetz, Lawrence L., and H. Ralph Todd, Jr., *First-Line Management*, Chapters 1 and 2, Business Publications, Inc., Dallas, Texas, 1975.

Vernon, Ivan R., *First-Line Management: The Foreman's Role in Manufacturing*, Chapter 1, Society of Manufacturing Engineers, Dearborn, Michigan, 1972.

CHAPTER 2

CONTINUAL SELF-DEVELOPMENT

THE CASE OF A
PREDECESSOR'S
ADVICE Burt Hall had just finished going over the day's production reports and was getting ready to head for home when Ray Ford, assembly superintendent and Burt's immediate boss, walked into the office. Ray immediately came to the point of his visit. The company training director was starting a series of training sessions on improving communication skills. Ray thought Burt might like to attend them.

The questioning, almost hurt, look on Burt's face told Ray further explanation was necessary. The series, he told Burt, had been offered last year; he himself had gotten a lot out of it, and he thought that Burt would find it well worth the time. Participation through workshop, rather than a lot of lectures, made the meetings very interesting and enjoyable, Ray assured Burt.

Asking for time to give it some thought, Burt volunteered the opinion that he thought his communication had been all right. Ray sensed that Burt had interpreted his suggestion as a criticism and hastened to explain that none had been intended. He tried to present the idea of Burt's attending as an opportunity to develop himself and broaden his understanding of communication, but there was still no change in Burt's expression. "Look, Burt," he said, "just the fact that I'm having trouble making you see that I have your interest in mind illustrates the kinds of problems we have in communicating. I know what I want to say, but you're getting a different picture. We discussed things like that when I took the course. If you take the course, you might use this conversation for a case problem."

Burt said he was sorry he misunderstood, but said it without much conviction, and promised to let Ray know in a day or so. He also apologized for being in a little bit of a hurry but Wednesday night was bowling night. After a little friendly kidding about bowling scores, Ray and Burt said their good nights and headed for the parking lot.

On the way home Burt argued with himself. On the one hand, he reasoned that if the boss wanted him to take some training that would help him in his job, he should be grateful. There wouldn't be another course like it very soon. On the other hand, he was having trouble enough getting everything done now without knocking an hour off every Wednesday afternoon. To top it off, it had to come on bowling night, which would mean he wouldn't have any time at all with the kids that night. The real hurt, though, was that Ray said he would get a lot out of it. He had always been very careful to keep Ray informed about what was going on, and now to be practically told he needed communication training made him wonder where he had failed. No matter how you add it up, he thought, a suggestion from the boss is the same as an order. If I know what's good for me, I'll take the course.

On the way to the cafeteria the next day, Burt met Harry Gates, the man whose place he had taken. Harry was a popular man whom Burt admired; Burt tried to pattern his own approach to the job after Harry's. Burt always felt that Harry was the one man most responsible for his promotion. It was he who broke the news to him and gave him the most encouragement. Burt was especially pleased to see Harry now. It would give him a chance to voice his concern about taking training to his friend. Harry welcomed Burt's invitation to lunch.

Harry laughed when Burt related his conversation with Ray and explained his concern. "Relax, fella," Harry said, "Ray's OK. He's not picking on you. He probably made the same suggestion to every assembly supervisor who reports to him. Just forget the whole thing." Burt said he couldn't forget it because he had promised Ray an answer soon.

Pushing his chair back and lighting his pipe, Harry said, "Look,

Burt, let me give you some advice. A supervisor's got one job—get out production. You keep your nose clean, meet your production schedules, and you're all set. They can't ask any more of you. Now from what I hear you're doing just that—even doing better than I did. I like that. It makes my last recommendation a good one.

"Now, Ray and Oscar haven't been around as long as I have. They're from what you might call the new school—heads filled with a lot of this management development jazz. Somebody sold them a bill of goods—probably the new training guy who thinks he knows how to run the whole company after a couple of years here. Anyhow, they're both smart enough to know which side their bread is buttered on, and that's with the stuff that's coming off the end of the lines. You keep that coming the way you have been, and you're all right."

Burt asked Harry if his refusal to take the training might not be interpreted as a lack of interest in his job and the company. "I don't think so," Harry replied, "but what if it is? They still can't do anything to you as long as you're pushing out the stuff that brings in the money. You've got enough headaches and pressure keeping those lines producing without going to school. Don't stick your neck out any more than you have to. That's the way I operated for almost twenty years, and if it worked for me, it ought to work just as well for you. With all the new reports they get topside from the data processing guys, you just know they're interested in only three things—production, high quality, and low costs. No sir, if you ask me they can take all these highbrow training programs, throw them out the window, and never miss them."

Back on the job, Burt began the debate with himself all over again. He hadn't expected Harry to be quite so outspoken about personal development. He felt much the same way as Harry did. There's a limit to how much they can expect of a man. Yet Burt knew it wasn't that simple—not that clean-cut. He was bothered by what Harry had said, even though agreeing with him would make his decision easy. He knew there was more to his job than just production. Production is important, but it's not the whole job, he thought. It's fine for Harry to say what has worked for the past twenty years; but times change, and I've got the next twenty years to think about.

The whole problem suddenly loomed much larger than just the communication training program. He knew now that he would tell Ray he'd sit in on the program, but what next? He knew that there would be other requests. Was he opening the door to more of the same by saying yes this time? What would be expected of him in the future? Would raises and advancements be affected by his willingness or refusal to go along on training in the future?

"Ray is a guy you can level with," Burt said to himself. "Maybe I'll jot down a few things I can ask him." Here's what he wrote.

1. Is studying a part of the supervisor's job if he's getting out the production expected from his department?

2. Does management expect a person to put in his or her own time on self-development? If they want him or her to study, shouldn't they set it up all on company time?

3. When does this studying and going to training programs stop?

4. If management wanted to conduct training, why couldn't something be set up that would help the supervisor get out production?

THE NEED FOR CONTINUAL SELF-DEVELOPMENT

From any point of view, self-development is a growing requirement of the supervisory job. It's not just something dreamed up by educators and training directors to make work for themselves. We said in Chapter 1 that continual self-development will be a way of life for the management-minded supervisor. Is this simply academic propaganda? No, it's just a cold fact of management life that is best illustrated by the feelings of a Chicago plant manager.

His firm employs nearly 5,000 people and has over 200 supervisors on the payroll. Electronic data processing had been introduced into manufacturing operations in the past year, they had just completed total automation of one production line, and they were planning the conversion of others to automated processing. His outlook was tough:

> Nearly one-third of our present supervisory force are going to be doing something different within the next year unless they decide to do something to prepare themselves to keep pace with the changes this company is undergoing. Many of them are mistakes we made years ago in selecting our supervisors. Some of the others have picked up the cockeyed idea that they have arrived—that they can just keep quiet and coast their way to retirement.
>
> The day has long passed when we can afford that kind of attitude. It

used to take us six months to know what had happened in a department. Now we know every day at the end of the day what a supervisor has accomplished in his department. Our data processing unit is giving us information on the results we achieve daily. We're finding out who's doing a job for us and who isn't.

The members of the group I'm talking about either don't give a thought to improving themselves or are sitting around waiting for us to spoon-feed it to them. Well, it's not going to happen. If they're going to be managers, they're going to have to act like managers. We'll give them all the help they want, but they're going to have to take some of the initiative. If they want to attend an institute at the university, they only have to ask. If a group wants technical courses set up in the plant, we'll set them up. We'll underwrite correspondence or night school courses, but we don't ram any of these things down their throats.

We're moving ahead fast to stay in front of our competition. There's no other choice. I'm happy to say that most of our supervisors realize the part they have to play in keeping us and themselves ahead. Those who don't are unfortunately going to be eased into early retirement or fall by the wayside.

His attitude is tough but typical of the feeling of many managers who have been disturbed by what they say is the tendency of the younger generation of supervisors to sit and say, "Well, here I am—develop me." Every indication points to increasing technological advancement in both the office and the plant. With those changes will come increased demands for better management, particularly at the first level. The supervisor of today who is content with things as they are will soon find that things just don't stay that way.

Learning is a lifelong process. The challenge is how to direct and channel that learning in order to grow in a job. Formal education—high school or college—isn't enough to sustain managers in their jobs very long. With today's knowledge explosion formal classroom education quickly becomes obsolete. The dean of a well-known engineering school, for instance, claims that in five to seven years the knowledge of a graduating engineer will be obsolete. Medical doctors who are not abreast of the latest developments in their field are cheating their patients. Supervisors have a similar responsibility to keep pace with technical advances in their chosen fields and to understand the new developments in the practice of management.

The West Coast branch manager of a farm-implement manufacturer underscored the concern of many high-level managers when he said while attending a seminar, "I expect my supervisors to have some self-development activity in process at all times. I'm particularly concerned that they read constantly, and I don't mean novels and murder mysteries. I mean a planned reading program geared to their jobs as managers. I expect them to keep me posted on what they're reading." This is an extreme attitude, perhaps, but it is indicative of the interest more and more managers have in seeing their subordinates direct their own development.

We seem to be almost completely out of the era when an organization accepts the total responsibility for the development of its people. Most companies recognize their obligation to make developmental opportunities available and to stimulate an interest in those opportunities. But they are at the same time supporting the principle that in the final analysis all development is self-development. In setting forth its philosophy on management development the Illinois Bell Company stated, "Formal development programs may have limited value unless the individual assumes a major share of the responsibility for training." In further explanation it stated, "The man must feel a strong personal responsibility to plan and direct his own program for self development." In these brief but comprehensive statements two facts emerge clearly: (1) The company is vitally concerned with the development of management personnel. (2) Initiative for planning and directing self-development should come from the individual, not the company.

WHY SHOULD THE SUPERVISOR BE CONCERNED?

Since self-development requires a supervisor's own time and effort, he or she might take a rather selfish approach and ask, Should I be concerned? After all, as a member of management I have it made, haven't I? This, in essence, is what Burt Hall had in the back of his mind, and his thinking was reinforced by Harry Gates. It's also the type of thinking demonstrated by those 65 or so supervisors in the Chicago plant who were the concern of their plant manager. Aside from the high priority of management's expectations, there are three good, selfish reasons why a supervisor should be concerned. Let's look at them.

TO INCREASE OUR PROMOTIONAL POTENTIAL

Reading this book is one evidence of interest in advancement. In the great majority of plants, the supervisor's job is not a dead-end job. In a recent University of Wisconsin survey, for example, plant managers were asked whether supervisors in their plants could advance to higher-level jobs, and 75 percent responded affirmatively. In government, insurance, and banking the percentage responding affirmatively would be even higher.

Evidence of self-improvement activities will always be given consideration by companies when they search their ranks to promote from within. They want to know how well prepared a person is to take on higher responsibility. Common sense tells us that promotions will go to those who demonstrate that they are prepared for them. One sure way of showing interest in a better job is by doing more than is expected—that is, the job plus self-improvement activities.

Supervisors have set themselves apart from the great majority of the working population by accepting the supervisory jobs they now have. Surveys indicate that seven out of ten production-level employees have no interest in supervisory jobs because they don't want the responsibility that goes with them. Many organizations have difficulty finding qualified people to take on the responsibilities of supervision. Supervisors have already demonstrated a willingness to shoulder the extra burden and in all probability have an interest in the promotional ladder. If that is so, the potential for promotion will be enhanced by making self-improvement a way of life.

TO IMPROVE OUR EFFECTIVENESS IN OUR PRESENT JOBS

According to the late Moorhead Wright of the General Electric Company, "Primary emphasis must be on development in the present assignment rather than emphasis on the promotional ladder. . . . The development process should be integrated with the normal conduct of the business so that they work together instead of competing for the manager's time and energy. The manager's work is actually simplified, rather than being made more complex, by the development process."* Supervisors are all interested in how they can do today's job better today, and it stands to reason that the best criterion for promotion is performance on the present job.

Jobs are changing constantly. Approaches to management practices have undergone drastic changes in the past decade. For example, in evaluating management effectiveness the primary emphasis

*From an article entitled "How Do People Grow in a Business Organization?"

used to be on personal traits such as loyalty, judgment, and initiative. Now the emphasis is almost completely on the practice of appraising performance on the basis of results achieved. Those who have had the same job title for the past five years know very well that the job they have today isn't the same job they had five years ago. In a recent University of Wisconsin survey, 87 percent of the plant managers responding said that the supervisor's job carries more responsibility today than it did five years ago. Certainly no one can dispute that conscientiously followed self-improvement activities pay off handsomely in meeting increasing responsibilities.

TO LIVE A FULLER, RICHER LIFE

To some this last reason may not seem valid, but the truth of it became quite apparent in the evaluation of a supervisory training program of a large Wisconsin paper mill. The program had been established for the usual reasons: to improve morale, to lower grievances, to improve productivity, and to lower costs. Over two hundred supervisors participated in the basic program that included discussions of the supervisor's job, human relations, motivation, discipline, job instruction, communication, and self-development over a two-year period. Follow-up interviews were conducted by a university professor with a cross section of about eighty supervisors. When he asked what they had gotten out of the program, he received answers like these: "I'm a better parent than I used to be"; "I don't blow my stack as often or as quickly as I used to"; "I've learned there are two sides to any argument"; "I get along better with my family"; "I enjoy working more than I used to"; "I've learned that my employees are human, too." When their comments were brought together, the great majority were saying that they were enjoying life more. At first glance this information might be totally unexpected. But when we stop to consider that the function of all higher education is to some extent the enrichment of people's lives, such response does not seem so unusual.

If broadening through self-development activities makes a supervisor approach the job with greater confidence and satisfaction, does he or she not have reason enough to begin a self-development program? People's lives are to a large extent what they make of them. We don't, of course, have control over everything that comes to us in life, but we do control what we put into life and especially into our working life. The more we put into life or the job, the more we are likely to get out of it.

CHANGING THINKING | Research done at the General
ABOUT DEVELOPMENT | Electric Company and reported by
the late Moorhead Wright in the article entitled "How Do People Grow in a Business Organization?" contributed greatly to some significant shifts in emphasis in our thinking about management development. Past efforts, for example, to identify the traits of an ideal manager or leader and then to try to develop these traits in all managers were doomed to failure. Wright put it this way,

> The development of people cannot be based upon any set of ideal or specified personality characteristics or traits. . . . The truth is that there just *isn't* any standard pattern of personality traits that make a good manager. . . . So the focus is upon the work rather than the individual personality. . . . Work can be seen—identified—analyzed—measured. . . . This viewpoint provides a more logical, reasonable, and therefore reasonably secure framework upon which to base action, instead of 99 different ideas that somebody might have about what is important in managing.

People spend their whole lives developing their personalities. The chances of changing their personalities are rather remote by the time they are adults. What we should be concerned about is the skills and knowledge required to do our job. Education can contribute greatly to improving our skills or adding to our body of knowledge. Why shouldn't we, then, concentrate our efforts in those areas where we stand a reasonable chance of success and leave personality development to the charm schools?

A second significant change in thinking about development concerns the idea once commonly held that development takes place in the conference room or classroom. It was felt that managers or supervisors were not being developed unless they were attending in-house training programs, outside seminars, institutes, or evening courses, or completing correspondence courses. While these educational experiences can make substantial contributions toward adding to a body of knowledge and broadening viewpoints, we are becoming increasingly aware that most growth occurs on the job. The problem that faces the supervisor in on-the-job development is to see that he or she arranges well-directed growth experiences and does not leave his or her development to chance.

Again the General Electric research touched on this point when

Wright wrote, "A man's development is 90 percent the results of his experience in his day-to-day work. . . . Every man in the Company is having experience in his day-to-day work that tends to develop him or to retard his development. He is daily reacting to the climate in which he works and to his relationship with his immediate manager. And these appear to be more important factors in the developmental process." It's important to recognize from Wright's comments that day-to-day experience may either stimulate or retard development. A supervisor who uses his or her own initiative in cooperating with the boss will move toward positive development.

A third significant change in thinking about growth and development is evident in the shift of primary responsibility for planning and directing developmental activities from the company to the individual manager. The mark of good managership is demonstrated ability to take charge—to make things happen rather than to wait for things to happen. A management-minded supervisor will seize every opportunity he or she can to learn more about how to do the job better. No one learns until he or she wants to learn. Over one hundred years ago, Abraham Lincoln observed, "You cannot help men permanently by doing for them what they could and should be doing for themselves." And even further back in history Galileo said, "You cannot teach a man anything. You can only help him to find it within himself." No matter how much or how little an organization provides in the way of growth experience, supervisors cannot escape their obligation to plan and implement a program of personal development.

THREE ESSENTIALS OF PERSONAL GROWTH

Development, we have observed, does not happen by accident. Well, then, how does it happen? Development is the supervisor's prime responsibility. But where do we go from here? Thousands of management-minded supervisors have found the answers to these two questions. They have found that there are three essential ingredients in cultivating their own growth as managers: an inventory, a plan, and follow-through. The presence of these essentials should assure some growth, but how much growth depends entirely on their quality. Fortunately for us, quality control is in the supervisor's hands. Let's take these points up one at a time.

INVENTORY

What's my status now? What do I need to perform my job the way management expects? How well am I doing my job now? In what areas will improvement activities help me most? A good personal inventory conscientiously conducted should answer these questions for the supervisor. A practical two-phase approach is needed. First, what skills, knowledge, and abilities are required by anyone to do my job today? Second, how well am I performing each of these?

There aren't many people who have a better idea of the requirements of the supervisor's job than that supervisor. Certainly no book could state with any validity what the supervisor's job is. We can recognize some skills and knowledge that are common to many jobs, but the final inventory form is something each supervisor must complete individually according to his or her own conception of the job. Here, then, are some common requirements for the first-level supervisor: job knowledge (for example, knowledge of chemistry, machinery, sanitation, law, building codes, systems programming, products being sold) and the ability to train employees, maintain discipline, improve work methods, plan and organize, delegate responsibility, communicate (in spoken or written form), maintain quality standards, motivate employees, and control costs. Careful consideration will determine which of these and many others have the greatest priority in a supervisor's own job.

Some will find it easier to think of it this way: If the boss were to evaluate my performance, what would I want him or her to consider as a fair list of factors? Many times the form used in an organization's performance appraisal programs will provide a starting point for constructing such an inventory. Certainly, if supervisors are being evaluated for purposes of salary increases or promotion potential, they will want to include the factors on which they will be evaluated in their inventory. They should be able to sift out the six, eight, or ten most important aspects of their job. Let this list comprise the first phase of the inventory.

The second phase of the inventory is obvious. A self-evaluation on how well a supervisor is performing in each of the areas contained in their inventory form is the critical step. A sample analysis form is shown in Figure 2. It shows five levels or grades (ranging from weak to excellent) on which performance can be rated.

Many supervisors ask whether a person can do an accurate job of evaluating his or her own performance. The answer must be an unqualified yes, provided that he or she is fair and honest. No one has a

SELF-ANALYSIS FOR SUPERVISORS

Skills, Knowledge, and Abilities Required on My Job Today	Weak	Below Par	Satis-factory	Above Average	Excellent
Get out production.				X	
Train employees.					X
Communicate w/boss.			X		
Maintain quality.					X
Job knowledge.			X		
Control costs.				X	
Maintain discipline.				X	
Plan & schedule work.			X		
Safety (OSHA).		X			

FIGURE 2

better knowledge about a supervisor's own performance than the supervisor—including the boss. The problem is most frequently one of honestly recognizing strengths and avoiding the tendency to let false modesty downgrade the whole appraisal process. No supervisor would be in a management position unless he or she rated excellent in at least some of the factors that make up a personal inventory. It is just as important for us to recognize strengths as it is to face up to limitations.

THE PLAN FOR SELF-DEVELOPMENT

The first step in planning is a goal to give direction to the planning process. After completing the inventory, supervisors should turn their attention to where they want to go as a result of the self-analysis. Experience teaches that resolutions or vows to do a better job in general don't accomplish very much. The best method is to select one area of the inventory and concentrate improvement efforts on that one knowledge or skill. Since the time available for developmental activities is limited, concentrating efforts on one area yields better results.

For a long time the selection of an area for concentration would have been automatic. Standard procedure specified selecting the weakest area. More recently we have begun to recognize that supervisors might do themselves more good by working on those areas where they are already strong. The theory here is that they are valuable on their jobs because of the strengths they possess and because their interest in the areas of their strengths is likely to be high. Interest and motivation are essential for continued developmental effort. Therefore, it would appear that supervisors are likely to help themselves more and to accomplish more by selecting an area of strength as a target for personal development.

Since development is a personal matter it deserves a more personal approach. What, the supervisor should ask, is likely to do me the most good? If I can help myself most by concentrating on something in which I have already demonstrated strength, then let me do so. On the other hand, if one particular skill is truly lacking, then by all means he or she should take steps to improve in that area. It is important to identify the one ability he or she wants to improve as the basis for planning.

Now whatever has been chosen, what can a supervisor do to help develop a higher degree of proficiency? What resources are available? Figure 3 is simply a form to help think through a variety of activities that would contribute to development. It calls for a general listing of possible activities and resources such as special job assignments, books, staff departments, training available inside or outside the company, analysis of current practices in the area selected, and consultation with the boss.

Figure 4 calls for the specifics of a real plan. Having completed the general list, he or she must now pin down the activities which will be most helpful. The first column requires a definition of specific, realistic activities which would be helpful to his or her growth. The second column allows the supervisor to detail how he or she is going to get started. Such details might include visiting the plant or city library, attending an institute away from the plant, or checking to see what material the training, production planning and control, or industrial engineering departments might have. Essential in the planning of self-development is to establish target dates for each activity. The dates provide a control against procrastination. Dates should be set realistically, keeping in mind the many other demands on our time.

FOLLOW-THROUGH

The best plans for self-development are a complete waste of time until they are put into effect, and that's the hard part. Unless the supervisor has a real desire to improve, not much is likely to happen. Little can be done that hasn't already been done by management to give a person the desire. Assuming that the supervisor has carefully defined the job in terms of the skills and knowledge it requires, that he or she has fairly appraised his or her own performance, that he or she has selected the area in which he or she wants to develop, and that he or she has made a realistic, workable plan, the rest depends on initiative. There are many

PERSONAL DEVELOPMENT PLAN—PHASE 1

To improve my ability to *control costs*

Possible things I can do to develop this ability (for example, consider reference materials, job assignments, consulting those skilled in this area, staff assistance, internal and external training, trade publications and meetings, analysis of current practices):

1. Read a book on costs.
2. Talk to cost accountant.
3. Get breakdown of department costs.
4. Determine areas of waste.
5. Attend U.W. Institute on cost control.
6. Simplify some high-cost jobs.
7. Talk to employees about costs.
8. Set a cost reduction (savings) goal.
9. Talk with other supervisors.
10. Check plan with boss.

FIGURE 3

PERSONAL DEVELOPMENT PLAN—PHASE 2
(Be Specific—Be Realistic)

What I Will Do	How to Get Started: Source of Help	Start Date	Date Completed
1. Read *How Foremen Can Control Costs* by Carroll.	Plant or City Library	Sept. 1	Oct. 15
2. Get department cost breakdown from cost dept.	Gary Smith, cost accountant	Sept. 20	Sept. 25
3. Identify operations with highest costs or waste.	Gary	Oct. 1	Oct. 10
4. Select two operations to improve for cost reduction.	Ray Ford and Gary	Oct. 10	Dec. 1
5. Discuss need for cost reduction with key people.		Oct. 15	Dec. 15
6. Goal: reduce overall costs 3% in next quarter.	Check with Ray	Aug. 25	

FIGURE 4

people in an organization who are ready and willing to help, but they are resources the supervisor must cultivate. Job assignments which provide an opportunity for growth experience will more than likely have to be asked for. Books and periodicals are waiting on the shelves for the chance to make their contributions.

Progress in self-development is measured in terms of the work the supervisor completes toward his or her goal. In terms of performance, did he do what he set out to accomplish? Once everything has been done in the plan, the inventory and appraisal might be repeated. Is further effort in this area indicated, or has the time come to channel efforts into another area? Has the job changed in any way that would require special study? Short-range plans should be frequently evaluated and improved to suit current job requirements. Many supervisors find that they can take the boss into their confidence on self-development plans. The boss has a great interest in what the supervisor is doing and is in a position to give invaluable guidance and assistance. Besides, it never hurts the supervisor to let the boss know that he or she is serious about becoming as effective in the job as possible.

A WAY OF LIFE

Self-improvement is more than developing a plan and following that plan. For the management-minded supervisor self-improvement is a way of life. The supervisor is constantly on the lookout for ways of broadening knowledge and improving his or her value. Opportunities to do this occur almost daily and a supervisor can't afford to adopt the attitude of Burt Hall, who wondered when it would all stop. It never stops. It's part of the job. Let's take a look at some ways a supervisor can become more valuable to the company.

BE ALERT TO THE BOSS'S NEEDS

The supervisor's job is to make the bosses look good and support them in any way possible. If a boss is working on special assignments or projects where the supervisor can make a contribution, the supervisor has a real opportunity to learn and to help. Selfishly, the supervisor can recognize that if he or she helps a superior, the boss is more likely to help when he or she wants assistance or approval to take some special training.

READ TO KEEP ABREAST OF DEVELOPMENTS

Modern-day supervision requires extensive reading. More and more supervisors select periodicals for reading on a regular basis. The trade journals in a supervisor's field do an excellent job of keeping him or her posted on new developments and innovations. Many excellent supervisory publications provide valuable insight into the supervisory job. Reading a book on management techniques every year or every six months isn't too heavy a burden for most of us, and it can pay handsome dividends.

BE AN ALERT LISTENER

Listening is learning. The boss, staff personnel, subordinates, employees—all have ideas and communicate them in conversation. Suggestions for improvement in the department are frequently available just for the listening.

BE AN ALERT OBSERVER

Without exception, supervisors who have participated in any of the variations of the DuPont Observation-Perception program report that they have observed things in their department that they never noticed before. The supervisor need only take a tour of the department for the sole purpose of looking for safety hazards to discover how much goes on right under his or her nose. The supervisor who is constantly observing the department will more than likely find many ways to make improvements.

SET UP TARGETS

Constant improvement of departmental operations is dependent on the supervisor's having standards and meeting or exceeding those standards. Where the supervisor can measure results in such areas as production, quality, costs, and safety, he or she can set realistic improvement targets either monthly or quarterly and keep score. Every target reached is another step to being more valuable to the organization and is something to be regarded with pride as a personal signpost of progress.

Perhaps a supervisor will never achieve everything he or she sets out to do in self-development, but satisfaction will be found in this approach to the job. So the words of Ben Franklin have real meaning, "I never arrived at the perfection I had been so ambitious of attaining, but fell short of it; yet I was by the endeavor a better and happier man than I otherwise would have been."

HIGHLIGHTS

1. Self-development is a growing requirement of the supervisor's job. The supervisor can no longer be satisfied with things as they are but must improve constantly to keep abreast of the changes in the organization.

2. Management expects the supervisor to take the initiative in planning his or her own development instead of the passive attitude "Here I am—develop me."

3. Three reasons why supervisors should be concerned about personal development are:

    a.   To increase promotional potential

    b.   To improve effectiveness in present jobs

    c.   To live a fuller, richer life

4.   Some significant changes in current thinking about supervisory development are:

    a.   A switch from the emphasis on developing "ideal" traits to a concentration on the skill and knowledge required to do the supervisory job

    b.   The recognition that most growth and development occurs on the job and not in the conference room

    c.   The growing acceptance of the idea that primary responsibility for planning and directing development rests with the individual and not the company

5.   Three essentials for the personal growth of the supervisor include:

    a.   A careful inventory of the knowledge and skills required by his or her job coupled with a self-analysis of how well he or she is performing each

    b.   A specific, realistic plan to give direction to his or her efforts

    c.   The follow-through necessary to see that the plan is implemented

6.   People act according to the way they think, and for the management-minded supervisor self-development is a way of life.

DISCUSSION QUESTIONS

1.   Explain in your own words why today's supervisor must be concerned about self-development.

2.   Why is the personal inventory so essential as a first step to self-development?

3.   Is the trend toward putting the responsibility for planning his or her development on the shoulders of the supervisor sound from the company's point of view? From the supervisor's point of view? Explain your answers.

4.   In your own words, evaluate the "traits" approach to self-development. What are its limitations?

5. What kind of on-the-job activities contribute to personal development?

6. Does management have a right to expect a supervisor to engage in self-development activities on his or her own time? Why or why not?

7. What are the advantages and disadvantages of consulting the boss about self-development plans?

CASE PROBLEMS

THE CASE OF HARRY COLLINS

Harry Collins was up the proverbial tree. Last night's annual management night address by Irv Rawlings, president of Mid-States Mutual Insurance, was either a heap of platitudes or a direct message, and Harry wasn't sure which. The "old man" had said that if the company was to grow that people would have to grow. He also said that the future belonged to those who prepared for it and that opportunities to move ahead are awaiting those who demonstrate the capacity to accept greater responsibility. There was more about the company being ready to support self-development activities and the need for managers at all levels to plan their programs for growth.

Harry was in his second year as the North Central District claims supervisor. His law degree and his three years in claims work were invaluable to him as a claims supervisor. He knew he was a good supervisor and he knew the technical aspects of his job as well as anyone. Advancement in this company or any other also was a goal of his. But he hadn't really thought in terms of any specific advancement. If he thought about it at all, he probably assumed his good work would be recognized when the opportunity presented itself.

Rawlings's remarks, then, had a sobering effect. If he really meant what he said, Harry felt he should be working on some kind of improvement plan. But where do you start? After all, claims work doesn't change that much; and if you train your people, supervision isn't that complicated.

1. If a specialist knows his field, what can he do to improve himself?

2. What can Harry do to get started?

3. Outline some possible things Harry might do to implement Mr. Rawlings's challenge.

THE CASE OF CARL YATES

The announcement of the new superintendent of power line construction for Tri-State Electric Company was a bitter pill for Carl Yates to swallow. Ten years as a lineman and another seven as foreman entitled him to a crack at the job of superintendent—especially since the guys on his crews had been kidding him about being number one in line for the job. Carl thought so too. He had even told his wife he thought he would be the company's choice. It wouldn't be much fun telling her that the company had brought in somebody from the outside.

Carl wasn't even sure if it helped knowing that he was considered for the job and why he was passed over. Henry Smith, district manager, told him that he was doing a good job, that they were pleased with his work, and that they considered him very seriously for the promotion. He had also told Carl the company was growing and that there would be other opportunities for jobs bigger than the one he had now.

In the final analysis, Smith had told him, management said that the superintendent's job was going to require more technical knowledge than they felt Carl had. Going underground and nuclear power generation were just a couple of the developments on the horizon that demanded more technical knowledge. In a couple of years, technological advances and increasing demands for power would change the entire organization. "Plenty of good jobs for guys who are on the ball and want to move ahead," Smith said.

Not only did that leave Carl feeling he was at a dead end; he began to wonder if his job was secure until his retirement twenty years away. Is a foreman's job one of being on constant probation?

1. What should Carl's attitude be now?

2. How important is technical knowledge? Isn't the ability to handle people more important?

3. What can Carl do to make up what management regards as his deficiency?

THE CASE OF BOBBIE SANDS

"I'm a woman without a college education, so why should I worry about self-development? In a bank as big as this one, I'm lucky I got to be a supervisor." Bobbie Sands was discussing opportunities in banking with John Forantino, her date for the evening and also a supervisor in the bank's operations division.

John, a graduate of a state university business school, had told her that a college degree wasn't all-important for a career in banking, but that you had to be continually learning and trying to improve. He said that it was more important to management that employees try to grow than that they have degrees or are male. John said that you can learn a hundred times more about banking by working in a bank than by going to college.

"That's easy for you to say. You're a man with the old sheepskin. It's a little different being a woman in a man's world—and without a degree to boot. I want to be around here for quite a while. No getting married and raising a bunch of kids for me. That's no future; but my future here doesn't hold any big promotion either. I'll just do my job, look attractive, and smile at everybody. Maybe I'll get a smile back and a little raise once in a while. That's my future in this bank and the end of my speech," concluded Bobbie.

"I still think you have what it takes. You could easily be a department manager, or even an officer, if you were willing to work for it," John countered.

"You're a dreamer, Sweetie. Take me home. I'm a working girl, you know."

1. Without a college degree can a person advance beyond first-level supervision?

2. Is it as foolish as Bobbie claims for a woman to plan for and work at professional development?

3. In a specialized business such as insurance or banking should a woman's approach to professional development be any different from a man's?

SUGGESTIONS FOR FURTHER STUDY

Bittel, Lester R., *What Every Supervisor Should Know*, 3d ed., Chapter 35, McGraw-Hill Book Company, New York, 1974.

Drucker, Peter F., *The Practice of Management*, Chapter 29, Harper & Row, Publishers, Incorporated, New York, 1959.

Reeves, Elton T., *So You Want to Be A Supervisor*, American Management Association, New York, 1971.

Vernon, Ivan R., *First-Line Management: The Foreman's Role in Manufacturing*, Chapters 2 and 8, Society of Manufacturing Engineers, Dearborn, Michigan, 1972.

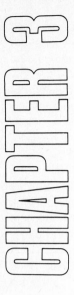

CHAPTER 3

MANAGEMENT COMMUNICATION

THE CASE OF
THE CONFUSED
COMMUNICATOR

Jack Holt, supervisor of final assembly, was sitting looking at the ceiling when Burt Hall stopped in on his way home for the day. Burt and Jack lived in the same neighborhood and shared rides on occasion. The new training sessions on communication prompted Burt to ask Jack if he were going to attend and if they might take turns driving those days.

"Are you kidding?" Jack blurted. "The lousy communication in this outfit has me ready to look for a new job. Life is too short to put up with what I've had to endure this past week. I can think of a hundred guys around here who could make my job easier if they knew how to communicate. Just once, I'd like to find out what they expect of me. How do they think I can do a job if no one tells me what's going on? I haven't got a crystal ball. If old man Palmer wants results, he's got to give me a little cooperation. This is no one-man show. I can't do it all alone."

"Hold on a minute, Jack," Burt kidded. "It can't be as bad as all that."

"You don't know the half of it," said Jack. "Let me tell you what happened just this morning. I was checking over the production reports from Friday and noticed the Acme job didn't go out when it was supposed to. So, I went to see Jake to find out why. He told me that Mr. Palmer had been down Friday morning and ordered him to move the Sampson Company job ahead of everything."

"What did you do?" Burt asked.

"I did what anybody else would do in my place," Jack replied. "I told Jake that from now on he takes orders from nobody but me and that I can't have every Tom, Dick, and Harry coming in here changing production schedules. Then when I calmed down, I went up to Oscar's office to tell him in a nice way that I'd appreciate his making changes through me. Well, I got a quick brush-off. He told me that I wasn't around and that the job had to get out—period. Now, how in blazes can you run a department with cooperation like that?"

Burt didn't try to answer because it was obvious that Jack had more to say.

"Friday afternoon is another good example. Boy, that was a beaut," Jack continued. "The word came down at noon that another job scheduled to be shipped this week would have to go before the weekend. That's not so bad. It happens every once in a while. I figured that if we all pitched in, we could handle it with about two and a half hours overtime. About 2:30 I started to make the rounds to tell everybody we'd have to work late, and you'd think I was asking them to work the whole weekend without pay. Grousing and griping was all I got from nearly everyone. Sure, a couple of meat hounds were happy, but I never heard so many excuses in all my life from the rest. I finally got so fed up with their unreasonable attitudes that I just told them to quit the damned griping and get the stuff out so we could all go home. You'd think that anyone with an ounce of brains would understand that you have to put up with a little inconvenience to take care of a good customer now and then. On top of all that, no one bothered to say anything to Shipping, and the stuff was still sitting down there this morning."

Burt could only ask, "Shouldn't you have followed up with Shipping?"

"Why should I? It's not my job. We got the stuff assembled and sent it down to them. That's where my responsibility ends. If they want to improve communications around here, why don't they start by seeing that everybody does his own job and set up some procedures? Then maybe people wouldn't go behind my back like last week." Jack continued, "When the word got out that Stan Ames was going to be moved up, I got to thinking that Tony Puccia was ready to tackle a supervisory job and planned to talk to Ray about it. Before I even had the chance, Ray was down here saying that Tony had asked him for a crack at the job. Ray told me that he wouldn't make a move without my OK and wanted to know what I thought about trying Tony out. Well, I queered that deal in a hurry. I told Ray that Tony wasn't ready for supervision yet and that I couldn't get along without him while we're so busy. But just as soon as I got rid of Ray, I got Tony in here but quick and let him have it with both barrels.

"I asked him how come he didn't tell me he wanted to be a supervisor and how come he didn't come to me first instead of going over my head to Ray. Well, he looked kind of sheepish and said he thought he had a better chance with Ray, that he wasn't sure of where he stood with me. You know what I said? I said, 'You know now, because you're going to wait a long time before you get another chance.' He's been pouting ever since, but if he gets away with going over my head, pretty soon everybody will be trying it.

"And it's not just my guys that can't communicate. It works two ways, you know. When you're on the receiving end, you have to use your head a little, too. Last Wednesday one of my bellyachers complained that the night clean-up crew wasn't doing its job. It wasn't the first time he complained, so I wrote a memo to the crew leader and told him to get this place cleaned up because I didn't want any more complaints. The next morning you'd hardly recognize the place. It really looked nice. But then things started popping. It turned out that the crew spent the whole night in my department and never got around to the others."

"I know," said Burt, "they sure didn't get over into my area. When I called Barney, he said that you had something special on and had them tied up all that night. I just figured I'd keep quiet as long as it didn't happen again."

"You're probably the only one who did," Jack told Burt. "I had four calls that day from men Barney told the same thing to, so I waited for him to come in Thursday night. I wanted to know why he had the whole crew spend the entire night in my department. The dumb cluck said he assumed from my memo that top brass had been complaining and that I wanted a real spit-and-polish housecleaning. Man, I really told him off. I asked him who in hell gave him the right to assume anything and told him to ask if he didn't understand a simple written instruction. He just put his old tail between his legs and walked off. I'll bet it's the last time he pulls a stunt like that.

"You see what I mean, Burt. If everybody did their job the way

they were supposed to, we wouldn't have any communications problems and we wouldn't be asked to waste our time going to any
communication school. No sir, first I've got to see some evidence that it
helps upstairs, and then we probably wouldn't need it.''

Burt, without much enthusiasm, told Jack that he might be right,
but as long as he had signed up for the program, he would go. Actually
his conversation with Jack stimulated his interest in the program
because he could see in Jack's attitude indications that Jack might be
his own problem. Burt began to wonder whether attitudes would be
discussed in the program, because they certainly seemed to have a lot to
do with Jack's feelings about communication. In fact, the more he
thought about it, the more he became convinced that Jack was in
greater need of communication training than any of the people he had
referred to as his problems.

By the time Burt arrived home, he decided that he wanted to
plunge into the coming program with gusto. The best way to do that, he
felt, was to write down some of the questions he would like answers to, if
not in the first session, then in a later one. Here's what he wrote.

1. What is the supervisor's responsibility for communication?
   Was something wrong with the way Jack was looking at
   communication when he said it stinks in this company?

2. Would more written communications have helped Jack?
   After all, there was that one situation with the instructions to
   Barney on the clean-up crew. What went wrong there?

3. How should Jack have handled the problem of the overtime
   work needed to get that job out Friday night?

4. Nobody likes to be bypassed, and it happened to Jack
   twice—once when Mr. Palmer changed the production
   schedules and again when Tony went to Ray Ford about a
   promotion. Didn't Jack have a right to be peeved? How
   should situations like that be handled?

COMMUNICATION: ATTITUDE OR METHOD?

Burt Hall was beginning to put his finger on one of the most frequently overlooked or misunderstood facets of the complex area of management communication—the tremendous importance that individual attitudes play in the effectiveness of an organization's communications. Without much hesitation most executives, educators, and consultants will acknowledge that communication stands today as management's number one problem. Yet each one of us has the potential to be an expert communicator. We have all the methods and procedures necessary to do an outstanding job. What most of us need is a full appreciation of what communication means, what prevents us from being as effective as we might be, and what we can do to build our communication skills. Once we have developed an understanding of how communication works, we don't need communication commandments.

For years we thought of communication in terms of the media by which we communicate. To the office manager communication meant teletype and letter writing; to the production manager it was blueprints, specifications, production orders, and reports; and to the executive it was policy statements, directives, and meetings. More recently we defined communication as the giving and receiving of the information needed for intelligent action and decisions. Intelligent action and decisions are expected of everyone in an organization from the messenger boy to the chief executive. Yet no one can do his or her job without knowing what is expected and where he or she stands in relation to coworkers. Supervisors must recognize their need for information from their superiors, from other operating departments, from staff personnel, and from employees. Jack Holt's concept of communication was essentially limited to this one-way flow to himself. But supervisors have an equal and often greater obligation to give these same people the information they need to function intelligently. Jack never understood this side of the communication picture.

Today our concept of communication has an added dimension—the dimension of depth. Today we define communication as *the creation of understanding*, recognizing that whenever messages are transmitted from sender to receiver, the whole point and purpose of the communication is to create understanding between the two. What is transmitted may be words, actions, facial expressions, tone of voice, gestures, and even silence, but each contributes in some way to an understanding of what is wanted.

It has been reliably estimated that supervisors spend about 85 percent of their time communicating. Those who question this statement by claiming that they have too much work to do to spend that much time in communication, must ask themselves what they do that doesn't involve communication. Everytime they instruct an employee or give an order, they are communicating. Reading or creating reports, job tickets, specifications, time cards, letters, memos, or any other type of paper work is communication. Attending meetings, listening to employees' problems, complaints and ideas, listening to orders and requests from the boss, talking to customers and suppliers, telephoning maintenance and service personnel, and answering requests for information are all a part of daily communication. It is impossible to function as a supervisor without spending a major portion of the time communicating.

The effectiveness of supervisors and managers is directly proportionate to their skill as communicators. The management-minded supervisor has a keen awareness of the tremendous importance communication has in his or her day-to-day functioning. Each chapter in this book covers a facet of the supervisor's job that is wholly dependent on communication. Whether we're discussing appraising performance, motivating employees, training people, disciplining, giving orders, or initiating change, we're discussing supervisory skills that require the creation of understanding. As supervisors set personal goals in their department, whether they be production, quality, attendance, safety, or cost goals, they realize that effective communication is an absolute necessity in achieving those goals. In Chapter 1 we identified the major responsibilities of a management-minded supervisor. We can easily see that the supervisor's skill in discharging those responsibilities is built on a foundation of effective communication. Management is communication.

Jack Holt personified an extremely shortsighted attitude that seems more and more to prevail in the area of communication. Increasingly, managers are developing a tendency to look outside themselves for the reason for communication failure. According to Jack Holt, Barney, Ray Ford, Oscar Palmer, and his whole department were the fault of the problems he was experiencing. Not once could he see himself as the problem or recognize that he had an opportunity to prevent each of his four problems. Actually any number of people could have eliminated those problems if they had felt it their personal responsibility to create understanding. For example, Barney might have read Jack's memo and questioned Jack about where the complaint had come from and how much extra cleaning was needed. Jack, of course, could have reread his memo and decided that a spoken explanation of what he wanted would have been better. Jack may have been right when he said it wasn't his job to tell Shipping about the rush job coming down Friday night. But suppose he had thought, "This job must be pretty important to keep my whole department on overtime. Just to play it safe, I'd better give Shipping a call to tell them when they can expect it." Not his job? No, but it would have resulted in far better customer and internal relations.

Cooperation and communication in an organization go hand in

hand. When two people have mutual respect for one another, it isn't necessary to spell out rules and procedures for communicating. They'll take care of their communication very nicely and without help. But when two people deal at arm's length out of mutual disrespect, then all the principles and procedures in the world won't help. They'll misunderstand, forget, and accuse each other of poor communication without regard to their own responsibility.

How often have we heard complaints about what a poor job management does of communicating? "If only we had a procedure covering that." "Why didn't they tell me so I'd have it before the union?" "How can I interpret policy when I don't know what policy is?" These are complaints we've all heard from time to time. Management is not "they" but "we," and the supervisor can usually have the information needed if he or she asks for it. When our friends have information useful to us, we ask them for it. We don't complain because they're sitting on it. The same holds true for the supervisor in his or her relations with the boss. The management-minded supervisor recognizes the responsibility to get what he or she needs in order to function effectively and to give what is needed by others to do their jobs.

Supervisors should also recognize the responsibility they have to make the boss look good. Keeping the boss informed of everything he or she needs to know about departmental operations is a vital part of the supervisor's job. What the boss wants to know may include changes in personnel requirements, problems in the department that will affect other departments or that will reach higher levels, changes that the supervisor has had to make, disciplinary actions taken, progress on jobs or projects in which the boss is interested, delays in receiving materials or services, suggestions for improving operations, or anything the boss will need to know in working with his or her superiors. Supervisors should be sure that the boss never has occasion to learn from someone else what should have been learned from them.

Some supervisors have observed that by being precise in communicating with the boss, they have trained the boss to communicate better with them. If setting the example is a good way of training subordinates, why shouldn't it be just as effective in training the boss? As the boss discovers that the supervisor is concerned with keeping him or her posted, that boss begins to appreciate the importance of good communication. Then no one needs to tell him how to communicate. It is done naturally. Improvement in communication between the supervisor and the boss begins when someone becomes aware that improvement is needed and decides to do something about it. Cooperation begets cooperation, and cooperation is born out of good communication relationships.

Effectiveness in communicating is much more the result of attitudes than of methods or procedures. The moment we begin to blame communication failures on particular people, we intensify the misunderstanding. We put people on the defensive and cause them to say things they don't mean which builds greater barriers to understanding. The management-minded supervisor takes an entirely different attitude toward communication. First, he or she recognizes that communication does in fact mean the creation of understanding. Second, he or she constantly looks for ways to create better understanding. For example, when a problem arises, the supervisor asks how to get it straightened out and keep it from happening again; he or she doesn't waste time trying to blame it on someone. Interestingly enough, the helpful, positive attitude in communicating causes others to respond in kind. And since everything depends on communication, a healthy attitude toward communication can be a great asset in meeting management responsibilities.

BARRIERS AND BRIDGES

In any communication there is generally a transmitter and a receiver. A supervisor giving an order, for example, functions as a transmitter, and the employee who is to carry out the order is the receiver. Later, as the employee explains a problem to his or her supervisor, the employee becomes the transmitter, and the supervisor the receiver. Between the transmitter and the receiver we encounter barriers that prevent us from creating the understanding that is the goal of all communication. Countless barriers have been identified by experts in communication, but our purposes will be well served here if we identify five of the more important ones and then examine ways of eliminating them through bridges of understanding.

THE LISTENING BARRIER

Day in and day out most of the supervisor's communicating is done in face-to-face situations calling for explanations, orders, and descriptions. If the receiver is to respond, he or she must not only hear, but must understand. This distinction between hearing and understanding is important because the assumption that listening is the same as hearing is dangerous. We hear with our ears, but we listen with the mind. It is entirely possible to hear every word a person says but to have none of it register. It's like the husband who comes home tired from a day's work and wants nothing more than to kick his shoes off and have some time to himself with the evening newspaper. His wife, who has been alone or with small children all day, wants to talk, and talk she will. Her husband hears her voice, but her words don't take on meaning for him until in exasperation she says, "You're not listening to me."

According to Dr. Ralph Nichols of the University of Minnesota, the average person speaks at a rate of about 125 words per minute.* Yet most of us are able to listen, allowing for individual differences, at rates varying between 400 and 600 words per minute. This spare listening or thinking capacity we have gives us time to get ahead of the speaker or to leave him completely while our minds dwell on other topics.

Most of us have probably experienced this type of mental departure from someone who is speaking to us. Sunday morning church services provide an excellent opportunity to check this phenomenon. We go to church with the very best intention of listening carefully to the twenty-minute sermon. Few of us are able to focus all our attention on that message and resist the temptation to turn our thoughts to the activities of the night before, the plans for Sunday afternoon, or any of the other problems we're facing on the job or at home.

One of the characteristics of the poor listener is that he or she is usually a good bluffer. Seldom willing to admit that he or she hasn't listened, he or she will fake understanding and take a chance—often with disastrous consequences. When confronted with mistakes, the poor listener will counter with, "But I thought you said . . ." Unless a person has truly listened to another, there is little chance of creating real understanding, which is the sole purpose of the communication.

Who, we might ask, has the responsibility for listening—the transmitter or the receiver? The obvious answer is that they both do, but let's make it a little more specific and say that individual supervisors have the responsibility for listening in any communication situation. Communication, we said, will be improved by the person who is aware that improvement is necessary. Certainly we can't afford to adopt the attitude that if our explanation is clear, the responsibility for understanding rests with the receiver, any more than we can say, "If they want me to listen, they will have to find ways of holding my attention." Whether sending or receiving, we must accept our responsibility to see that understanding results. Working to achieve understanding is the job of the supervisor who is aware of his or her communication responsibility.

*From "Listening Is a Ten-Part Skill," *Nation's Business*, July, 1957.

THE FEEDBACK BRIDGE

In any face-to-face communication the receiver is constantly feeding back reactions (either knowingly or subconsciously) to what is being said. For example, we have all observed that glassy, "I don't know what you're talking about" look on the faces of people to whom we are giving directions. They broadcast without saying a word the fact that they aren't listening. Receivers are constantly sending out signals that tell us whether or not they're listening. These signals may be in their posture, in their attitude of attention or inattention, or in the nature of their questions or responses. As we learn to watch for these signs and to interpret them, we develop greater skill in getting our message across. It isn't necessary to accuse people of poor listening when we see their attention wander. We simply say, "Let me see if I can put it another way." Our object is only to ensure that our message is understood. When we blame the failure to listen on receivers, they simply become defensive, and listening becomes even more difficult. As emotions cloud the mental processes, listening with true understanding becomes almost impossible.

Up to this point we've discussed only the reading of natural feedback. When we're not sure how to read the feedback we're getting, it's advisable to build more in. This can be done by asking questions. For example, we might ask a person to repeat key points in an instruction, or to explain what he or she feels might be the logic for following a certain procedure, or to ask for an evaluation of an idea presented. As the listener's responses are fed back, we can determine whether it's safe to proceed or whether we should repeat the explanation. In a lengthy spoken communication the supervisor should build in several deliberate feedback requirements in addition to attempting to read the natural reactions of the listener.

Nichols points out that we can improve our ability to listen by using our extra listening speed to better advantage. He suggests that these four steps be developed into a definite pattern of thought when listening: (1) Try to anticipate what a person is going to talk about or what points he or she is trying to make. (2) Mentally summarize what has been said or what points have been made so far. (3) Weigh the person's evidence by mentally questioning it—Is he or she accurate? What are his or her sources? (4) Listen between the lines to what he or she is really saying with tone of voice, facial expressions, and body movements. Nichols writes, "Not capitalizing on thought speed is our greatest single handicap. The differential between thought speed and speech speed breeds false feelings of security and mental tangents. Yet, through listening training, this same differential can be readily converted into our greatest asset.''

THE SEMANTICS BARRIER

Semantics is the science that deals with the meaning of words. Meanings of words vary according to the people using them. Many communication experts claim that meanings are in people, not in words. We select the words we choose to communicate with because they convey a picture that we have in our minds. Having come from a different environment, the listener may get an entirely different picture because our words have a different meaning for him or her. For example, the word *policy* to an executive is a broad general statement or a guideline. To an employee a policy may mean a very specific rule that prevents him or her from doing something he or she would like to do. The word *profit* has vastly different meanings to the stockholder and the union official. Our past training, our needs, and our interests give meaning to the words we use.

A classic illustration of the semantics problem is the word *fast*. One expert says it has over eighty different meanings. Let's just look at a few more contradictory meanings. By using the word *fast* to describe a horse, we mean that horse is quick—he can run. The same word used to describe the color in a fabric indicates that the color won't run. Or if the horse is tied fast to a stake, it means he can't run. When fast is used as a religious term, it means to abstain, but a fast woman proves to be one who won't abstain from anything. Or as one wag put it, she won't run from anything. What, then, is an employee to think when he or she is told to make something fast?

Every business has a jargon that is peculiar to that business. Consider the difficulties experienced by a new employee who is being trained by an old-timer who is insensitive to the semantics barrier and who subconsciously uses pure jargon to demonstrate how much he knows.

The semantics barrier can create problems even within a company in communication between departments. Specialists in accounting, production, research, sales, and finance are all equally adept at speaking a language all their own. It's not improbable that the head of research would have difficulty in making himself understood when communicating with a production foreman or that a production foreman might have a little difficulty in understanding or making himself understood by the computer programmer. For example, the word *hardware* means something different in different departments.

THE BRIDGE OF GEARING TO THE RECEIVER

Once we are aware of the problem of misunderstanding that can be created by the semantics barrier, we naturally turn our attention to what can be done to remove it. A two-part approach to this problem has proved helpful to many supervisors. First, and most obvious, we need to gear our communications to the vocabulary of the receiver. For example, a person has a great deal more latitude in discussing a production problem with one of the old-timers in the department than in giving directions to a new employee. When we have used words that people don't understand, feedback in the form of facial expression will usually indicate that further explanation is necessary. Special caution is needed when using terms that have obvious common meanings apart from specialized usage. Dr. Berlo of Michigan State University cites the example of the manager who gave his new secretary the only copy of a specification sheet and told her to "burn" it. Burning had come to mean make a copy or burn a copy. Imagine his dismay on learning she had touched a match to that precious piece of paper and tossed the ashes into the wastebasket.

Second, we need to swallow our pride and admit when we're not sure of the meaning of words spoken or written to us. We, too, tend to gamble when we're not sure. The price of pride is frequently too high to pay. We strengthen our standing with people when we seek clarification. Most of us would have far more respect for someone who asks us to be more specific when we request a job "as soon as possible" or "at your earliest convenience." To ask a transmitter exactly what he or she means by a word or term not clear to us is not only evidence of our interest in serving him or her but also alerts that transmitter to the need to clarify his or her language.

THE SELF-INTEREST BARRIER

Personal interests act as filters through which communications are received. We listen to what we want to hear, shutting out what we don't want to hear. Our personal desires can very easily color or exaggerate the meaning of what we hear or read. An excellent example of this barrier was introduced in a recent institute discussion of communication problems. One of the participating supervisors asked the group, "Did you ever hear of a man who got mad when you gave him a raise?" He went on to explain that an employee under his supervision had just finished his probationary period. The supervisor called the man in to tell him that he was extremely pleased with his work, that beginning the following Monday he would go on permanent status, and that beginning the following Monday he would be getting 10 cents an hour more. The employee thanked his supervisor and went back to his job apparently elated. Ten minutes later he was back. He angrily accused his supervisor of trying to pull the wool over his eyes because he found out that the increase was a general one and that everyone in the department was getting that 10-cent raise. The institute group tended to agree with the employee and said, "Well, weren't you trying to pull the wool over his eyes?"

"Look at it from my point of view," the supervisor said. "I was pleased with his work, and I told him so. I was putting him on permanent status, and I told him that. Now, we've just had this general increase, and I told him he'd be getting more money. What's wrong with that?"

Most of us would agree that from the supervisor's point of view there was nothing wrong with what he did. However, from the employee's point of view, there was an obvious connection between his excellent work and the raise. Finding out that everyone else was getting a similar raise was a blow to his ego. From a purely logical point of view, the employee was just praised by his boss for good work, put on permanent status, and given a nice increase. Why should there have been a problem?

If we stand back and take an analytical view, we see that both the supervisor and the employee contributed to the misunderstanding. The supervisor was at fault because he was willing to let the employee think that the raise was a reward for good work which as his boss he had recommended. The employee was at fault because his desire for a feeling of importance colored what his supervisor had in fact told him.

Jealousy and personal interests can play havoc in communication between departments especially where rivalry for the boss's favor exists. If management puts more emphasis on results without emphasizing a real understanding of the total approach at the department level, employees will often put department or personal goals ahead of the welfare of the whole organization. When personal interests become all important and communication takes place on an emotional level, real understanding is nearly impossible. An empire builder in a firm is not likely to add much, if any, substance to the realm of another.

THE EMPATHY BRIDGE

The importance of empathy for proper supervision will be mentioned several times in this book. By "empathy" I mean simply the ability to put yourself in another person's shoes and see things from his or her point of view. To develop empathy is to develop a sensitivity to the feelings and needs of those with whom we deal. In the chapter on self-development we recognized that the "ideal" manager cannot be defined in terms of personal qualities and that supervisors will be better off if they concentrate their developmental efforts on skills and knowledge. The most prominent exception to that principle is the need to improve our ability to empathize in working with and in communicating with people at all levels.

Building the empathy bridge over the self-interest barrier requires us to analyze our communications from the standpoint of the other party. When we listen, for example, can we ask ourselves, Why is he or she saying that? Why does the other person feel that way? What would make him or her ask that? In responding negatively to employees' requests, can we couch our response in terms that will help them understand why the answer must be no and perhaps suggest alternatives that will demonstrate that we have given serious consideration to their needs? When personal interests have clouded the true meaning of a communication, the person capable of empathy stands a much better chance of contributing to real understanding. When we *try* to understand a person or a situation, we usually succeed. We reap the additional benefit of encouraging others by our example to try to understand our viewpoint.

THE PLANNING BARRIER

We might more appropriately label this the *lack of planning* barrier. Spending so much time in communicating, would it not be logical for the supervisor to devote considerable effort in planning his or her major communications? When scheduled to discuss a change in job assignments with an employee, does he or she stop and ask how to explain it in such a way as to be sure the employee will understand? When a complex project must be assigned to a subordinate, does the supervisor sit down beforehand and outline the points he or she must cover to give a complete picture? If an employee asks for an opportunity to discuss a personal problem, what does the supervisor do to ensure providing full and undivided attention? If the supervisor must make a report either spoken or in writing, does he or she outline it with the objectives, needs, and interests of the receiver in mind?

Examples of poor planning of communications are endless. Consider what Bill Powers might have achieved in building morale when he called Orv Lane in to discuss a change in jobs. Bill had singled Orv out because he had a talent for the type of work involved. Bill regarded it as a promotion for Orv, but he was so anxious to have Orv accept that he made it sound too easy. Orv got the impression that he was being asked to do kid's work and turned Bill down, insulted by the request.

A paper mill supervisor confessed, while attending an institute, that he had muffed a real chance to help an employee. The wife of one of his back-tenders in the mill was going to return home from a mental institution. The employee wanted to discuss the problems of bringing her back into normal family and social life in addition to asking for time off to make the adjustments. Obviously nervous in discussing so personal a matter, the employee became increasingly annoyed with one interruption after another—first by phone, then by other workers' questions about production matters, then by the phone again, and so on. Finally, in exasperation the employee walked out and put his request for time off in writing. A little planning in these situations could contribute greatly to building a bridge of understanding between supervisor and employee.

THE PLANNING BRIDGE

Planning more important communications is usually not very complicated or time-consuming. It comes almost naturally to the supervisor who is aware of his or her responsibility to create understanding. Most communication planning can be achieved by mentally answering the six planning questions that follow. *What* am I trying to get across—understanding of a transfer, action on a grievance, praise for good work, a suggestion for improvement, a report of progress on a project, or acceptance of an idea? *Who* am I communicating with—a stubborn employee, a worried person, a boss in a hurry, an aggressive union steward, a loudmouth, a shy individual, an impatient customer, a delinquent supplier, or an unconcerned maintenance man? *When* is the best time to communicate—now, after I've cooled off, at the end of the shift, during the lunch break, when the project is completed, or the next time he or she has a similar problem? *Where* is the place to communicate—in my office, at the machine, in the cafeteria, in the conference room, or away from the plant? *How* should I communicate—face to face, in a meeting, with a memo, over the phone, in a letter, by telegram, over the P.A. system, on the bulletin board, or through the suggestion system? *Why* am I communicating—to inform, to persuade, to sell, to publicize, to listen, to solve a problem, to discuss, to instruct, to give an order, or to report?

In any given communication situation, we can see how quickly the answers to these planning questions can be pinpointed. And yet it becomes obvious even to the most inexperienced how these questions lead naturally to planning a communication which is likely to lead to understanding. It's not a major job, but rather common sense applied to management's number one problem.

THE BARRIER OF FAILURE TO SEE THE NEED

All too often communication problems are the result of sins of omission rather than sins of commission. To many authorities the failure to see the need to communicate is the greatest barrier of all. It isn't that we communicate so poorly, but that we don't communicate at all. How often have we said or have we heard others say, "I didn't think it was necessary to tell him"; or, "I assumed she would know that"; or, "Can't they draw their own conclusions?" Almost daily we are made aware of our dependence on good communication in order to do our jobs well, but for many supervisors that's where the awareness ends. Like Jack Holt, many supervisors are keenly sensitive to the responsibility of others to keep them informed and will look anywhere outside themselves for the cause of failures.

For example, a farm-implement dealer in the Middle West telephoned a rush order for a tractor to his branch office. He was quite specific in identifying the attachments and options he wanted. But when the tractor arrived in his yard, he was on the phone protesting that he couldn't deliver it to the farmer because it didn't have a hydraulic transmission. "You didn't order it," said the branch manager. "You know damn well that I *always* want the automatic transmission in my area," retorted the dealer. And where does it go from there? Both are right. Both are wrong. Either could have avoided the misunderstanding if he had been a little more aware of his communication responsibility. It's easy to see now that when ordering a special tractor, the dealer should have specified the automatic transmission along with the other options or that the branch manager, in taking the order, should have clarified this vital feature rather than assume a standard transmission when the automatic was not mentioned.

The "failure to see the need" barrier provides fertile ground for the grapevine. In the absence of accurate information, rumors start and spread like wildfire. Contrary to what many writers say, the grapevine is not a good means of communication. Feeding the grapevine accurate information does not ensure clear communication. Everyone can without much effort think of several examples of rumors spread through the grapevine that grew out of all proportion simply because someone didn't see the need to give the correct information through official channels.

THE AWARENESS BRIDGE

Most of the problems created by poor communication can be quickly solved by a person with average intelligence. As we have already mentioned, we all have the potential to be expert communicators. The moment we become aware that the possibility of misunderstanding exists, our common sense will dictate what steps are necessary to prevent that misunderstanding.

One example of developing that all-important awareness comes in the realization that putting everything in writing is not the answer to most of our communication difficulties. We have seen over the years an outcropping of memo pads suggesting that we avoid spoken orders. All too often this approach is the result of defensive communication attitudes designed to establish the blame for communication failures. The whole approach fails to recognize the superiority of face-to-face communication over the written. We have already recognized that we communicate with facial expression, tone of voice, pauses, gestures, and posture. These supplement oral communication and are completely lost in written communication.

By and large it is much more difficult to create understanding in writing because all we have to convey meaning are words recorded on paper. The opportunity for instantaneous feedback is lost. Every opportunity for creating misunderstanding is present. Jack Holt's memo to Barney on the clean-up crew is a case in point. Or consider the reactions caused by the office manager who used a memo to announce the creation of a central stenographic pool. He wrote, "All men in the office who do not have private secretaries can now take advantage of the girls in the stenographic pool." Enough said?

Truly management-minded supervisors are aware of their responsibility to communicate completely. They know that the methods and procedures by which we communicate are only aids to help them create understanding and that their own attitude is the real key to communication effectiveness. How do we develop that vital awareness? Here are three suggestions.

Strive Continually for Understanding

As we consider the hundreds of communication situations we face, the ultimate goal of creating understanding should be a part of our thinking. How often, when we have written a memo, do we check it for the possibility that the receiver might misunderstand what we have intended? Do we recognize the responsibility we have to be sure our subordinates have all the information they need to perform their jobs? Are we aware of what the boss needs from us in order to make the decisions he or she faces? Do we work at listening to others, knowing that unless we do, we are short-circuiting communication and preventing understanding? When uncertainty clouds our communication, do we build in the feedback necessary to clear the atmosphere? The way we think determines the way we act. We can be the instrument by which communication improvement is achieved, or we can be a Jack Holt, condemning everyone and everything for the communication failures around us.

Put Communication on a Positive Basis

Here's a real test for the person who would be a management-minded supervisor. When problems arise, as they inevitably will, are we big enough to concern ourselves with how to prevent their happening again rather than finding someone to crucify for the failure? Jack Holt was primarily interested in finding scapegoats for the situations he himself helped create. Certainly the most unsophisticated observer could see how Jack could have put every one of his complaints on a positive basis and contributed to harmony and cooperation in his department rather than sowing the seeds of dissension. Burt Hall, as inexperienced as he is, sensed immediately that Jack's negative attitude was largely responsible for his difficulties.

Accept the Personal Challenge of Communication

If communication is management's number one problem, we might very well ask, "What can I do about it? If it's a worldwide problem, I'm only one man. It's too big for me." Many supervisors have recognized that their world is the people around them with whom they have day-to-day contact. Certainly it's not hard to see that Jack Holt's world is made up of people like Ray Ford, Burt Hall, Barney, Tony Puccia, and those people in his department who pitched in to get that rush job out on Friday night. With this perception of our world, the critical question is, Are we creating the communication problems in our world, or are we devoting our energy to their solution? The management-minded supervisor is determined to be a part of the solution rather than a part of the problem.

Communication, whether intra- or interdepartmental, is a matter of creating understanding between people. Improvements will be made, not by programs and techniques, but by supervisors who sense that they alone can do something about better communications in their world.

Improvement doesn't begin somewhere up or down the line; it starts with our own awareness and our willingness to take a look at our own communication attitudes.

HIGHLIGHTS

1. Communication is the creation of understanding, and effectiveness in communicating is dependent on the supervisor's attitude much more than on the methods and procedures used to communicate.

2. Management is communication, and a manager's effectiveness is directly proportionate to his or her skill in communicating.

3. There is a disturbing tendency, when communication problems arise, to look outside ourselves for the cause rather than to concern ourselves with what we might do to help create the necessary understanding.

4. Harmony and cooperation in an organization are totally dependent on good communication.

5. The management-minded supervisor has a very clear-cut responsibility to keep his or her boss informed, to make the boss look good, and to see that the boss is never surprised by learning from others what should have been learned from the subordinate.

6. When we communicate we are likely to encounter barriers to the creation of understanding. These barriers can and must be bridged. The following barriers and bridges are recognized.

	Barrier	*Bridge*
a.	Poor listening	Feedback
b.	Semantics	Gear to the receiver
c.	Self-interest	Empathy
d.	Poor planning	Answer planning questions
e.	Failure to see the need	Develop awareness

7. The key to improving communication is the development of an awareness of the importance of communication in performing our jobs. Suggestions for developing that individual awareness are:

   a. Strive continually for understanding.
   b. Put communication on a positive basis.
   c. Accept the personal challenge of communication.

DISCUSSION QUESTIONS

1. How many ways does a supervisor communicate in a day? List as many as you can.

2. Cite three examples of problems you have experienced because of poor communication—at home or on the job.

3. Explain in your own words why the supervisor's effectiveness as a manager is directly proportionate to his or her skill as a communicator.

4. Why are harmony and cooperation in an organization totally dependent on good communication?

5. How can you explain the tendency of people to blame someone else when communication problems develop?

6. Five common barriers to communication were identified in this chapter. How many others can you list?

7. Discuss what should have been done to avoid the problems you described in Question 2.

8. The responsibility for listening is defined as our own whether we are sending or receiving. Do you agree or disagree? Why?

9. Identify five words or phrases from your own work situation that would likely be misunderstood by an outsider.

10. It is more difficult to communicate in writing. What situations call for written communication?

CASE PROBLEMS

THE CASE OF JOSH SAMUELS

Civil Service sure as hell isn't the cradle-to-grave security everybody wants to think it is. And the stereotypes of lazy, incompetent civil service employees are about as inaccurate as anything can be. At least that's the way Josh Samuels's supervisor saw it. In fact, the reverse of both beliefs was creating his problem right now.

For weeks now rumors of a substantial reduction in force (R.I.F.) in the agency had been circulating. No one in a supervisory or management position, least of all Josh, could learn anything for sure. The rumors, all claiming to be from reliable sources, ranged from minor reductions to a total wipeout.

Every day someone claimed to have the inside story on a new version. Josh, who had a reputation for leveling with his people, successfully discounted the rumors for a while. But when they persisted, work output began to be affected. His employees were now spending time listening to, relating, or trying to verify the latest rumor. Speculation increased to the point that his more senior and best-qualified employees were starting to shop around.

It didn't make sense, unless there was to be a very large-scale R.I.F., that his people would be affected. On the other hand, they're the kind of people who are smart enough to get out while jobs at comparable classifications are possible.

Josh was convinced that a minor R.I.F. was the worst that would happen and it was mighty discouraging to see things starting to fall apart for no good reason.

1.   What can a supervisor do in a situation like this?

2.   Is it advisable to use the grapevine to start counterrumors?

3.   Can the agency director do anything to alleviate the situation?

THE CASE OF KATY KAMMERER

The office had settled down again after a good week to ten days of tension. Most of the disturbance centered around some gossip that was unfounded, but upsetting nevertheless. Jim Braun, office supervisor, traced a part of the gossip to Katy Kammerer but not enough to prove that she started the whole thing. That was the whole trouble with Katy, you were never sure when she was stretching the truth and when she was completely factual.

Jim had worried for some time about what to do about Katy. She had developed the habit of stopping at his office several times a week at the end of the day to "chat." Katy told Jim everything that was going on among the women in the department. She seemed to enjoy their confidence. In Katy, Jim had a direct line into the office grapevine. Accuracy was not Katy's primary concern when it came to communicating the office goings-on. Still she was reliable most of the time, and she really did enjoy keeping Jim posted.

Jim realized that he depended increasingly on Katy to help him keep his finger on the pulse of the office. Katy alerted him several times to little differences that were developing, allowing Jim to stop them before they became real problems. As "useful" as she had been to him, Jim began to question whether or not he should discourage Katy's end-of-the-day visits.

On occasion he suspected that she was enjoying her "communicator" role so much that she might even be making things up or stretching things to make them seem important. He knew that to cut her off meant losing a valuable source of information. There was even the remote possibility that instead of being a friend and supplier of information she would turn some of her gossip against him.

1. What are the advantages and disadvantages of having a "Katy-type" communicator?

2. Can you maintain the information source and improve on its accuracy?

3. How might employees "use" Katy to communicate with Jim? Is this good or bad?

THE CASE OF FRAN BILLINGS

Dr. Grimes was a nice enough guy and an excellent doctor, but like many other doctors he was just too busy to be anything but a poor communicator. Fran Billings, nursing supervisor, was trying to console one of her young nurses, Jan Orms, who was in tears.

Jan had just gotten a lecture from Dr. Grimes about "practicing medicine" with his patients. Jan explained to Fran that the patient was upset because he couldn't get anything from Dr. Grimes. "I just tried to reassure him," Jan wept, "and old Grimes said I raised his expectations to an unrealistic level. If he'd only talk with his patients, then we wouldn't get pinned down."

This wasn't the first such instance. Many times her nurses complained to her about Dr. Grimes, and Fran sympathized but felt helpless. She did her best to support Dr. Grimes because she knew how busy he was, but she also knew that she was reaching the end of her rope in seeing her subordinates taking a beating because of his shortcomings.

1. What, if anything, can Fran do to get Dr. Grimes to understand what problems he's causing?

2. How should she handle her nurses' complaints about Dr. Grimes's poor communication?

3. What advice should she give her nurses?

THE CASE OF DALE O'BRIAN

Dale O'Brian, department head in Social Security Administration, was the subject of a discussion between two of his subordinates. Adam and Irene were both supervisors who found reporting to Dale a bit trying at times.

A conscientious, dedicated civil servant, Dale had a couple of irritating habits that made communicating with him difficult. With over thirty years in the service, Dale had experienced and could handle everything that ever happened.

"Every time I want to discuss a problem with him he tells me how it's been handled in the past. Half the time I don't even finish and he's got the answer. He never seems to want to hear my ideas. Just do this or that. It's like getting the brush-off, and I don't think he means to be that way," Adam explained. "But a guy gets discouraged from even discussing things with him."

"I know," Irene countered. "I used to think he didn't realize I had a brain in my head. Now I find he's that way with everybody. He just acts like he knows it all. He doesn't listen and he's always jumping to conclusions. Sometimes I think it's the only exercise he gets. Yesterday he finished four of my sentences in a five-minute discussion. I hate getting cut off in the middle of a thought."

"One thing is certain," Adam declared. "Old Dale stopped learning years ago. For the rest of his days, he's just going to be 'big daddy' to anyone who works for him. In an agency this big, there must be more challenging places to work. I'm going to start shopping around."

1. Just how does one go about communicating with a person who knows it all and is constantly jumping to conclusions?

2. What happens to growth and progress under such an administrator?

3. Is the problem sufficiently large to cause a subordinate to "shop around"?

SUGGESTIONS FOR FURTHER STUDY

Bittel, Lester R., *What Every Supervisor Should Know*, 3d ed., Chapter 5, McGraw-Hill Book Company, New York, 1974.

Haimann, Theo, and Raymond L. Hilgert, *Supervision: Concepts and Practices of Management*, Chapter 5, South-Western Publishing Company, Incorporated, Cincinnati, 1972.

McLarney, William J., and William M. Berlimer, *Management Training—Cases and Principles*, Chapter 5, Richard D. Irwin, Inc., Homewood, Illinois, 1970.

Reeves, Elton T., *How to Get Along with Almost Everybody*, Chapters 7 and 8, Amacom, New York, 1973.

Steinmetz, Lawrence L., and H. Ralph Todd, Jr., *First-Line Management*, Chapter 11, Business Publications, Inc., Dallas, Texas, 1975.

Wiksel, Wesley, *Do They Understand You*? The Macmillan Company, New York, 1960.

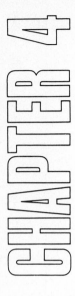

CHAPTER 4

MANAGEMENT OF CHANGE

Demands for more production had been increasing almost weekly. Burt Hall was diligently staying on top of the situation but looking forward to leveling off so he could relax the pressure he was putting on his people. They were cooperating beautifully. Burt was proud of the results they had achieved but knew full well that he was now getting the maximum he could expect from them. Both Oscar Palmer and Ray Ford had indicated their pleasure with the response of Burt's department. Recently they had promised Burt some relief if pressure for more production continued.

During the past week Burt noticed a couple of methods engineers looking around the department, but he was too busy to bother much with them. He was satisfied with their explanation that they were just making a few observations. He didn't particularly care much for the methods boys, and since he didn't know these two, he let them go their own way. As long as they didn't get in anyone's way, Burt ignored them.

Burt was visibly upset, then, when Ray told him that two new contracts would mean another 15 percent increase in production requirements and that some changes would have to be made in his department. The change would involve breaking up the jobs done now by two five-man groups and introducing two new people to each group. By reducing the number of operations each assembler or adjuster performed and rebalancing the sequence over seven stations rather than five, the necessary production volume could be achieved—at least that's what the methods engineers using predetermined time standards had predicted. They had it all worked out into a neatly packaged system: layout, instructions, standards—the works.

Some new testing equipment would have to be installed at the end of the line to handle the added volume, four new people brought in and trained, and ten present employees trained to do jobs requiring fewer operations on many more assemblies. Burt, to put it mildly, didn't like it. He saw two smoothly operating groups disrupted, changeover delays, resistance from the crews and the union, and a lot of extra work for himself. "It looks fine on paper," he mumbled, "but wait until you try to fit people who have been busting their guts for us into those new jobs."

Burt suggested handling the increase, which he felt was only temporary, with overtime. And if it continued, a second shift could be added. He was assured by Ray that all forecasts pointed to further increased requirements. The contracts which prompted the change were only the beginning of a potential long-range arrangement. Ray explained that overtime was too costly except for very short-range emergency situations. The added costs of second-shift operation could not be justified until such time as more departments would also have to add second shifts. Ray said that Personnel was already interviewing people to find the four new assemblers they would need.

After giving every possible reason to keep the present system and still being told by Ray that the change would be put into effect, Burt grudgingly started to prepare for the initiation of the new system. First he called in Greg Archer, the union steward. Greg listened to Burt's almost apologetic description of the proposed changes. In conclusion, Burt mentioned to Greg that he assumed they would get a lot of objections from the union. Greg said he didn't see why they should. There would be four new members and a couple of the present jobs would be upgraded. Greg said that looked pretty good to him. Burt asked if they weren't concerned about the overtime they would lose out on. "Overtime is fine," replied Greg, "but the union is interested in more steady jobs.

Give us reasonable allowances for adjusting to the new setup, and you won't hear any squawks from us.''

So far so good. He still didn't like the change, but not having to fight the union helped. Burt took the same apologetic approach in explaining the plan to the employees in his department. He stressed the fact that it wasn't his idea, that he didn't like it, but it would have to be done. As might be expected, Burt started to get the resistance he was looking for. Several didn't like the idea of changing the makeup of the crews by adding new people. They were working like a team, they said. The new ones might not fit in. Burt just shrugged his shoulders and said that they would have to hope for the best. There were complaints that the new jobs would be more monotonous, with fewer operations to perform. Burt said, ''I know it, but what can I do?''

Somebody said he ought to go to bat for them. That hurt Burt. He told them they. didn't have any idea how hard he fought the new setup.

Later on that day Norm Wiley, his best assembler, and Dave Bangs, his best adjuster, asked Burt for a chance to talk with him. They all agreed to get together at the end of the shift. Both Norm and Dave were loaded with questions, many of which had never occurred to Burt. Would the present members be given any preference on the jobs they wanted? Would seniority govern? How many more units were they expected to assemble? Who was going to train the new people? Would the five people on the present crew have to stay together, or would two experienced people go to one of the crews? That would put four new people on one crew, but give you one crew of experienced people to set the pace. What kind of wage adjustments would be made, since a couple of jobs would be upgraded? Would all the jobs be restudied, since both new methods and new testing equipment would be installed? Had arrangements been made to move the completed units away from the end of the line? Would quality standards be just as high? New people and more people working on a unit would make it more difficult to maintain quality. Was there any possibility of a special crew to rework rejects instead of sending them back through? Could something be done to improve the finish on the parts they were getting? There would be less time to stop and deburr or polish parts during assembly.

An impartial observer listening to their conversation would have said that Norm and Dave were simply seeking straightforward answers to previously unanswered questions. He might also have observed that some of their questions were actually well-intended suggestions on how the change might be implemented more smoothly. Burt didn't see it that way. He regarded their questions as more of the resistance he had been anticipating. In the beginning he answered to the best of his ability, without any show of emotion. As time went on, however, he became more and more defensive. He began to show annoyance. When they seemed not to agree with him, he said they were resisting change. He lectured them briefly on the fact that their security was wrapped up in the company's being able to satisfy its customers.

While no arguments developed, the usual friendly relationship between Burt and these two men was missing. Burt concluded by telling Norm and Dave that he had given them all the information he could. He said that if they had any more objections, they had his permission to take them to Ray Ford. "I just don't like being the middleman, taking a beating from both sides," he told them.

The next day Burt related to Ray Ford as accurately as his bias would let him the reactions he had from those involved in the change. He gave Ray an almost word-for-word playback of his conversation with Norm and Dave. He commented that resistance to change was going to make it a lot tougher than he had thought to get things rolling smoothly again. It was a real surprise, he told Ray, that two of his best men objected the most. "You'd expect it from some people," Burt said, "but not from Norm and Dave. I figured they would provide me with my biggest support."

Ray replied, "They still might, although it sounds as if you gave them a rough time. I'll back you all the way, Burt, but if they do give you trouble, come to me. At the moment, though, I'm more concerned with your analysis of Norm and Dave. It doesn't sound to me as if they were resisting. If anything, they were trying to be helpful. They had a couple of ideas there that we should check into."

"For instance?" asked Burt.

"Well, clearing up that bottleneck at the end of the line, for one. I didn't know you were having a problem there. Why, neither one of us was aware that the assemblers were having to deburr and polish some of the stuff they were getting. I'll check with Fred Jones on that right away and see that what you get is top quality.

"Look, Burt," Ray counseled. "Step back and take another look at this whole thing. We've got to expect some resistance to any change as big as this. A lot of people are involved. But is it possible you're seeing resistance where there really isn't any? Questions about a change don't necessarily mean resistance. It's so easy to see resistance in other people, but so hard to see it in ourselves. Think about it, Burt. I've got to go down and see Fred."

He left Burt sitting there wondering:

1. Can a person be guilty of resistance to change without ever realizing it?

2. What should a supervisor's role be when confronted by a change like this?

3. If resistance to change is inevitable, what can be done to minimize or to overcome it?

4. What was Ray's real opinion about how I handled things? What made him ask me to think about it again?

THE NEED FOR CHANGE

American business is in a period of change that dwarfs anything we have known in all history. It is so inescapable that it is most unwise for any person in business to ignore it. So pervasive is the change affecting so many aspects of business operations that many top executives are suggesting that the only permanent element in the business environment is change.

Competition, of course, stimulates much change. Everyday businesses fail because their management does not know how to keep pace in our dynamic economy. It is no longer uncommon to read of well-known, once successful companies being absorbed by more progressive firms. Occasionally we witness a once-flourishing industry dwindling to nothing because the need for its products ceased to exist.

Competition on a price and quality basis from companies producing similar products and services is now a commonplace. New materials have made serious inroads into markets that once were exclusive. Consider, for example, how paper has moved into areas which were once the exclusive domains of lumber, glass, and textiles. Paper pallets have replaced wood pallets. Paper boxes have made wooden fruit boxes a thing of the past. Paper containers have almost eliminated the glass milk bottle. Paper clothing, household draperies, and toweling have had an impact on textiles.

Change stimulated by domestic competition is easily recognized. Often overlooked is the fact that worldwide trading will intensify that need. Europe, Asia, and South America are increasing their impact on our domestic economy. In time Africa, too, will have to be reckoned with as a serious competitor. World trade, of course, offers unlimited opportunity to expand the markets for our products. To compete we must constantly be improving our methods, technology, and productivity.

Let's identify the major change agents. Automation, science, and electronic data processing have become almost a way of life. There is a progressive substitution of machines for human labor. Competition among companies that have automated machinery and those that have not has become severe. Remarkable advances in the area of science have influenced the productive techniques of business. These include the discovery and growth of atomic fission as a source of power, the development of artificial substances, and progress in the fields of electronics and miniaturization of circuits. The development of electronic data processing equipment, called "computers," has dramatically increased the amount of quantitative data that can be assimilated and made available for analysis and decision making. The use of computers has resulted in significant savings of clerical labor costs, savings of time in preparing reports, greater accuracy, and the development of new information.

Additional factors related to change are the shift in emphasis from production to distribution, the growth of interest in space research and the exploration of space, the shift from an industrial to a service economy, and consumerism. It has become possible to produce more goods than can be sold profitably in spite of the fact that segments of our population have substandard incomes and the rate of unemployment is too high. Obviously, this calls for a shift in emphasis from production to distribution and the use of idle productive capacity to take care of these needs and wants. The large volume of contracts for research, development, and manufacturing of weaponry and propulsion awarded by the federal government has brought about rapid growth in the productive facilities of many companies. Because of the growth of automation and other technological developments, it has become possible to turn out more and more goods with fewer workers. As a result, the growth of the number of workers employed in the service fields has been more rapid than that in the production of goods. This trend appears to trigger an increase in the employment of women and a weakening of the influence of labor unions. Perhaps the greatest phenomenon influencing change is best described as the consumer protection movement which has as its basic motive the bringing of safer and more satisfactory products to the consumer market.

In coping with change, management is under continual pressure to adjust the conditions of employment. Supervisors are challenged to find new approaches to handling workers and ways to upgrade worker performance.

THE SUPERVISOR'S
ROLE IN CHANGE

Burt Hall is in most respects a good supervisor. All too often supervisors feel, like Burt, that they're in the middle—presented by higher management with the job of initiating their changes and at the same time resisted by the employees under them and the unions who use them as the target for their objections. It's a feeling management-minded supervisors can't afford to harbor. They aren't management's changes; they are the supervisor's changes.

The plant manager of a large printing company in the Middle West was recently reviewing a proposed supervisory training program developed by his training director and an outside consultant. The program was very comprehensive. It was the result of much study and analysis of the needs of the firm's supervisory force. After carefully considering the course outline, the plant manager put it on his desk, looked up and said, "Not bad! But unless you build in something I don't see here, it will never get off the ground—not with my approval. Somewhere, you have got to teach our foremen that they can't stand in the way of the changes we have to make to stay in business."

He went on to explain that when new presses and new equipment were introduced, it was their foremen who resisted most strongly—not the employees, not their unions. He said that he wanted something in that training program that would open their minds, something that would help them see how change was a part of staying alive in their highly competitive industry and that would convince them that their job was to implement change, not block it. "Now," he said, "you bring me a program that will do that in addition to all these other things, and I'll give it my blessing."

Essentially what he was saying was, "Get these foremen to act like managers." Supervisors are not the middlemen in the matter of implementing change. They are clearly and unmistakably on the side of management. Upon accepting supervisory positions, workers become part of management's philosophy and practices. The progress, the growth, and the changes are theirs to support with enthusiasm if they are to consider themselves as members of management. In spite of an outstanding production record, it was his attitude toward change that caused Oscar Palmer and Ray Ford to question Burt Hall's management potential—and with good reason. He was reluctant to make the change from the very beginning. Much of the resistance he encountered was of his own creation. The employees under him were in many cases reflecting Burt's attitude. They simply took his lead.

Many new supervisors are slow to realize that they have an

unquestioned obligation to support management's changes. Perhaps this is because so few new supervisors are told in so many words what is expected of them. It is assumed that having become members of management, they are sympathetic to all changes proposed. Unless the responsibility to implement change is made absolutely clear, the new supervisor striving to stay on top of production is likely to regard changes as a deterrent rather than a help or a necessity.

Half the battle in initiating changes in a department is developing the proper attitude toward change. So often those who have the most difficulty in introducing change are the ones who subconsciously resist it themselves. As an example of the importance of attitude let us consider the case of a young professor at the University of Wisconsin. Working in adult education with foremen and supervisors several years ago, he had become quite proficient as an instructor in the techniques of work simplification. He was quick to recognize the importance of the human element in improving methods, and devoted much of his study and teaching to ways of overcoming resistance to change. Within a relatively short period of time he was asked to talk at many management meetings on overcoming resistance. He became an expert on eliminating resistance to change. Imagine the shock, then, when the director of his department told him that he was the first to throw cold water on new ideas in their weekly staff meetings. The director cited five or six specific instances where the "expert" had reacted to new ideas with, "It won't work"; "It will cost too much"; "Our customers won't buy it"; "We've been doing it this way for ten years; why change now?" and "Let's sleep on it for a couple of months." Was it possible for him to tell others how to overcome resistance to change and not realize that he was the world's worst example? It was.

Of course, the most important thing to the professor and the director was the question of how to remedy the situation. After much discussion, one simple step was agreed upon. Our young professor agreed that before he reacted negatively to any ideas in the future, he would first ask himself, "What's good about it?" The result was almost a transformation. Negative thinking was replaced with suggestions for improvement. He became an idea man rather than a "no-man." Nothing had really changed but his attitude. At last he saw himself as the personification of the very thing he was working against, and he was determined that good ideas were not going to die at his hands.

How many supervisors could benefit by the same approach? As they look at the changes that they are charged with implementing, can they ask themselves what's good about them? It's really the first step toward developing the personal enthusiasm that higher management expects supervisors to have. it's the attitude that stimulates enthusiasm for change rather than the typical resistance.

RESISTANCE TO CHANGE

People do resist change. To claim that they don't would be to close our eyes to the facts of life. However, it would be equally unrealistic to state that resistance to change is either automatic or universal. It is encouraging that employees' reactions to change so often depend upon how the change is presented to them. And how that change is presented to them is completely under the supervisor's control.

One of the first steps in overcoming resistance to change is to understand what the reasons for its existence are. As so many supervisors who have stopped to analyze the problem have observed, we can't overcome it until we know what it is and why it is there. Let's look, then, at some reasons for resisting change—some of them very real and some imaginary.

Personal economic loss is certainly a good reason for resisting change. Potential loss of job, downgrading, transfer to other departments requiring lower skill, loss of overtime—all pose threats to a feeling of economic security. Where these threats do in fact exist, we can naturally expect a marked lack of cooperation and even concentrated resistance to any change that would bring them about. Our experience shows, however, that management has done an outstanding job of minimizing and eliminating such an economic loss. For example, when seeking ideas for methods improvement, a company usually tries to ensure that people will not lose their jobs as a result of any improvements actually installed. Pay rates are frequently guaranteed until the employees affected can be placed in positions requiring commensurate skill. Much concern over economic loss, then, is imagined by anxiety-ridden employees. This concern generally occurs when changes are not fully explained and sold to the employee.

Implied in many changes is a criticism of the way things have been done in the past, and it's fairly safe to assume that no one likes criticism. Burt Hall, for example, was strongly oriented to production and rightfully proud of his department's achievements. We can easily see how he might mistakenly interpret the changes he was asked to make as a criticism of his ability to meet the new demands. His resistance took the form of suggesting the alternative of overtime to increase output.

Most of us have at one time or another asked for criticism because we know that it's good for us and that it helps us grow. Yet we hope that nothing in our behavior justifies criticism—we're only human.

That's why, in implementing change, we need to be especially careful to assure people that the change is not a criticism of them or of the methods they have been using.

Unfortunately experiences with changes of a similar nature in the past have a tendency to make some employees distrustful, suspicious, and even angry. Frequently this is a condition over which a supervisor has no control because the bad experiences happened before he or she came onto the scene. An alert supervisor, however, will quickly recognize when his or her people have been so conditioned. The supervisor must then make an effort to prepare his or her people for the change by helping them understand how it will affect them individually and by showing them both the short- and long-range benefits of the change. The supervisor will want to stress that he or she is anxious and willing to help make any adjustments to facilitate the change. By doing this, awareness of their needs and feelings is demonstrated and the supervisor's own job made infinitely easier.

The human ego sometimes creates an almost impenetrable barrier to the implementation of change. Many people are afraid of losing status because a new job doesn't seem as demanding as the old one. The concern that once-valuable skills are no longer needed disturbs those who felt pride in those skills. Others dislike seeing younger people move ahead of them. Countless other emotional reactions make the initiation of change difficult. We all have a need to feel important. That need is frustrated when people are not consulted on changes concerning their jobs. Much of Burt Hall's resistance might be traced to this cause. His pride in his ability to get out production was dealt a blow when the methods engineers and higher management worked out a new method and handed it to Burt without consulting him. Subconsciously he fought back by dragging his feet.

But the human ego can also be important in facilitating change. People are far less likely to resist change if they are given the chance to participate in it. Burt would have liked to be in on the formulating of the change. Denied this chance, he radiated his own lack of enthusiasm. He thus missed the golden opportunity to involve his people in the implementation of the change. Norm and Dave opened the door for a constructive approach, but Burt was too much on the defensive to recognize the opportunity.

Age is another commonly cited reason for resistance. We acknowledge that the older people get, the more they resist change, and the more set in their ways they become. Even Burt Hall said he expected the greatest resistance to come from his older people. Yet age, by itself, has little to do with how well we learn or how much we resist change. If age is a factor at all, it tends to be a positive rather than a negative influence. There is much evidence to show interest in improvement, inventiveness, and creativity at very advanced ages.

Ben Miller, writing in the American Management Association's Research Study Number 44 (1960), "Gaining Acceptance for Major Methods Changes," contradicts the commonly accepted preconceptions we have about age and change. He states that, in the six companies studied, there was evidence that older people are more willing to accept change than others. Here are two of the reasons he gives for this unexpected finding. First, older people tend to have a stronger identification with the company or the department they've known for years. This identification develops an interest in seeing the company grow and prosper. It's natural that they should want to associate themselves with changes that will cause that growth. Secure in their jobs, they can perhaps see their own security enhanced rather than threatened by change. Second, a long background of experience enables older employees to understand the change—a key factor in cooperation. Cooperation results when people have a clear understanding of why cooperation is needed.

Many supervisors wouldn't be in the job they hold unless they were very much open-minded. Most of them will admit that they are more open-minded today than they were ten years ago. To remain effective, they can't afford to resist change. Yet they assume that the older other people get, the more they resist change. Either they do not see themselves in the same light as they see others, or they do not give other older employees their due. Mr. Miller is suggesting that we take another look at age and resistance to change.

Burt Hall's reaction to his conversation with Norm and Dave prompts us to recognize one last cause of resistance to change. He interpreted their questions as resistance. Ray Ford cautioned him to take a more objective look at their questions. Ray might have followed his comment with an explanation pointing out that questions might very well be evidence of interest in the job and of a very healthy, positive attitude. Actually Norm and Dave were indirectly making some very sound suggestions. As members of management, supervisors should interpret questions concerning changes as a desire for information and not as resistance to change.

Having to deal as often as they do with the implementation of change in their departments, it's especially important for management-minded supervisors to take a healthy, positive, supportive attitude toward change. They start by recognizing that it's just as natural for people to want to improve as it is for them to resist change. The problem is both to stimulate the desire to improve and to suppress the tendency to resist change. Resistance is easy to detect or suspect in others, but seldom do we recognize ourselves as the boss who never wants to listen to a new idea or as the subordinate who stands in the way of progress.

CREATING A CLIMATE FOR CHANGE

How people react to proposed changes is greatly influenced by the kind of climate for change that the supervisor has created in the department. Burt Hall is a perfect example of what should not be done. Now, how is the right kind of climate created?

It begins, of course, by having the enthusiasm for progress and change which builds a healthy climate. Supervisors are first, last, and always members of management. A dynamic organization will be constantly seeking and introducing new methods, new equipment, new people, new standards, and new internal organizational structure. The enthusiastic support of these changes is the obligation of management-minded supervisors. Employees are quick to sense that a supervisor is dragging his or her feet, and they will play it safe. Why should they stick their necks out until they know where the boss stands? Management expects and assumes that its front line is in complete harmony with its decisions. It has every right to make such assumptions.

Creating the right climate is more than just passing changes on. It involves encouraging employees to seek ways of improving their jobs. Seeking suggestions and ideas from employees requires that a supervisor listen and seriously consider suggestions. It's easy to see that there's a great deal of ego involvement in coming forth with an idea for improvement. Employees can quickly develop a sour attitude when their ideas are ignored or ridiculed. Change can become a way of life— exciting and dynamic. The leadership supervisors provide determines the climate in which they initiate change.

HOW TO INITIATE CHANGE

Often it is easier to carry out a job if there is a specific plan to follow. When major changes are to be installed, careful planning and preparation are necessary for success. Here, then, are six steps that many supervisors have found helpful in initiating major changes.

Get Ready to Sell

Much of the difficulty a supervisor encounters in getting cooperation stems from the employees' lack of understanding of how the change will affect them. With a little effort he or she can find most of the answers to employees' questions before they are even asked. Burt Hall, with a little empathy, could have anticipated most of the questions Norm and Dave asked him. What is the reason for the change? Whom will it benefit and how? Will it inconvenience anyone and for how long? Will training or retraining be necessary? How will the training be carried out? Will earnings be affected? When does it go into effect? Will there be a transition period when adjustments can be made? Armed with the answers to these questions, a supervisor can head off many objections and can develop a plan to present the change.

Identify Sources of Help

Why should a supervisor shoulder the burden alone? Staff people can frequently be a great help in preparing to sell a change by explaining technical aspects and demonstrating new techniques. Instead of fighting them, as Burt Hall was unconsciously doing, wouldn't it be smarter to recognize the potential staff specialists have for helping initiate a change? After all, the long-range responsibility of staff specialists is also to promote a progressive, productive, profitable company.

One of the most overlooked sources of help in introducing changes are the informal leaders in the work group. With their help the job becomes easier. Giving recognition to informal leaders puts them in a cooperative frame of mind and on management's side. They maintain and strengthen their leadership. Norm and Dave were demonstrating their leadership in coming to Burt. Instead of welcoming their help, he showed annoyance and sent them to Ray Ford. Bypassing the informal leaders causes them to demonstrate their leadership by organizing the resistance. Since the union steward in a department is often the informal leader, his or her cooperation ought to be solicited. The backing of union stewards makes the job easier. This is not to say, however, that management's position on the change can or should be compromised.

Older employees should also be seriously considered as a potential source of help in selling changes. Frequently younger employees will take their cue from the response of the old-timers. Whenever a supervisor can identify opinion leaders, his or her first approach should be through them.

Anticipate Objections

Changes that upset routine, require new knowledge or skills, or inconvenience people are bound to meet with some objection or resistance. Looking at a change from the employees' point of view will usually be enough to help determine what their objections are likely to be. Knowing the objections, we can, with a little creative thought, turn these objections into advantages. For example, when Norm and Dave raised questions about the extra work involved in adjusting to the change, Burt had a perfect opportunity to tell his leaders how much he was counting on them to sell the necessary adjustments to others. He could have at that moment turned two potential objectors into real allies. It really doesn't matter how much authority supervisors have or think they have; they should recognize that they can't force people to their way of thinking. If they want cooperation, not just grudging compliance, they have to win it. Snowing a person with reasons or logic won't do the job. People are going to have to be made to feel that the change is really best for them, and that won't happen until their objections are seriously dealt with.

Sell Benefits

Everyone is concerned with, "What's in it for me?" "Will the change mean more satisfying work, greater security, opportunity to show what I can do, more responsibility, more pay, less fatigue, less confusion, greater independence?" The benefits used to try to motivate people to cooperate should be put on as personal a level as possible. It would be dishonest, however, not to recognize any disadvantages that a change may bring. These can usually be countered with long-range benefits.

Listen in Depth

Employees have a right to be heard. Their questions may be their way of demonstrating interest in their jobs, or as in the case of Norm and Dave, a means of making suggestions which would facilitate the change. Burt was hearing their questions, but a little in-depth listening would have helped him tremendously. If employees are treated with respect, like equals they probably will respond in kind. They will feel better, too, if they know their concerns have been considered. What they say doesn't always echo what they feel. It's possible, we know, to resist change without verbalizing objections. In the same vein, it is possible to challenge without being uncooperative.

Follow Up

It is easy to resent the salesperson who loses complete interest in us just as soon as the sale is finalized. After having conscientiously sold the benefits of a change, isn't it of tremendous long-range importance for a supervisor to see that his or her promises have materialized? Did any difficulties develop that weren't anticipated? Are adjustments necessary to realize the full potential benefit of the change? A sincere interest in how the change has affected the employee and a willingness to make adjustments help build the climate in which future changes will be initiated.

Now, and in the years to come, a supervisor's effectiveness as a member of management will be measured in large part by his or her skill in initiating change. In an era when change is the only constant, a supervisor demonstrates management-mindedness by answering the challenge that change presents with enthusiastic support.

HIGHLIGHTS

1. We are in an era of unprecedented change in business and industry. The foreseeable future will bring more and more change, and the supervisor is the key person in initiating change at the employee level.

2. Supervisors' own attitudes are the key to how effective they are at initiating change. As members of management they have an obligation to support change with enthusiasm. Management-mindedness is measured by willingness to accept change and by skill in initiating it.

3. People do resist change, but not automatically or universally. It is just as natural to want to improve as it is to resist change. Many times the difference between the two depends on whether or not the employee is involved in the implementation of the change.

4. The reasons why people resist change include the following:

    a. They fear economic loss.
    b. They fear the unknown.
    c. They fear loss of status.
    d. They feel that criticism is implied.
    e. They have had unfortunate experiences with change.
    f. Damage to the ego may be brought by the process of change.

5. Older employees are more likely to accept changes than to resist changes.

6. Setting the example with an enthusiastic attitude toward change is important in creating a climate for change. Also important is the ability to develop mental flexibility—"the ability to meet new problems with new solutions."

7. There are six steps for initiating change. The supervisor must

    a. Get ready to sell
    b. Identify sources of help
    c. Anticipate objections
    d. Sell benefits
    e. Listen in depth
    f. Follow up

DISCUSSION QUESTIONS

1. Identify and discuss three changes that have taken place in your work situation in recent years.

2. Do you agree or disagree with the proposition that the supervisor is the key man in initiating change at the employee or production level? Discuss the reasons for your position.

3. Describe a time when someone you know resisted a change. Why did he resist?

4. In this chapter a claim was made that older employees are more likely to accept change than resist it. Do you agree or disagree? Discuss your answer.

5. Can you cite an example of an instance when an employee over fifty years of age accepted a change more readily than younger co-workers?

6. Discuss the statement that it is just as natural for people to want to improve as it is for them to resist change.

CASE PROBLEMS

THE CASE OF HANK EVERS

The company has always had rules about gambling. But for years everyone turned their backs on the football pool cards, world series pools, and "big game pools." After all, it was a lot of fun, some people won a few bucks, and most important, nobody got hurt.

Top management had indicated it is going to start enforcing the no-gambling rule and expects supervisors in both shop and office to be the watchdogs.

Hank Evers, data processing supervisor, has been a leader in setting up the office pools. Figuring odds has been a special interest of his. Now his responsibility will be to police the no-gambling policy.

His employees have indicated they expect him to find ways of "getting around" the policy. He has heard many employees inside and outside his department say there is no way to stop people from making an occasional wager.

Because of his interest, Hank in a sophisticated way is regarded as the "resident bookie." Even the plant people call Hank to find out if their "penny ante" card games at lunch time are included. His own assistant wanted to bet Hank ten to one that the company couldn't stamp out gambling completely.

1. How far should Hank go in stamping out all forms of gambling in his department?

2. What can Hank do to get his employees to accept the change?

3. What are some of the reasons people would resist such a commonsense change?

THE CASE OF FREDA HARMON

Affirmative action was one of those social action movements that might affect the shop but not the office. At least that's the way Freda Harmon, supervisor of the steno pool, felt about it. Suddenly, very suddenly, she was brought to the realization that affirmative action was to be more than just window dressing.

Freda had two requisitions for stenographers waiting in personnel for over two weeks. At last some action came in a call from Earl Hersey, personnel director. He would be sending four applicants for interview tomorrow. They were all well qualified; two were white and two were minority workers. Mr. Hersey said that he expected Freda to approve two of the applicants to fill the vacancies in her department. He reminded her that the equal employment opportunity and affirmative action policy called for a percentage of minority and female (or male, in some cases) personnel in each department and in every job classification throughout the company.

Freda had no minority workers in her steno pool. She thought she would have no problem accepting minority employees, but felt sure that the others in the department would. The stenos had never talked about whether they would object to working with any employees from minority groups. Freda just assumed they would react negatively.

1. What should Freda look for in interviewing the four applicants?

2. What steps should Freda take in preparing her department for the change?

3. What should be done in orienting the new employees in the department when they arrive for work?

THE CASE OF HARRY BOSTROM

Business was exceedingly good in the Horning Insurance Agency, which had just moved into its own new office building downtown. Most of the procedures were transferred from the old building, and things were functioning smoothly in a very short time.

Mr. Horning, agency manager, told Harry Bostrom, office manager, that he wanted the office open during the noon hour. The new convenient location with its excellent parking would mean that many of their customers would want to transact business during their lunch hours. New business might also develop if the office was open through the noon hour.

There are twelve women on the office staff. Reactions to moving had been mixed. One of the big selling points in gaining acceptance of the move had been that they could lunch together and shop together during the noon hour. Now it will be necessary to have two employees in the office during each noon hour—one to act as receptionist and the other for general work.

Harry knows the women won't like this move. Their excitement at spending lunch hour downtown has been obvious. He is sure they will regard it as an encroachment on their freedom. Some of the "liberated" ones particularly will resist the change. And if they resist, a majority will likely go along with them.

1. What steps should Harry take in preparing to sell his staff on the change?

2. Why would they resist the change?

3. What strategies might he use in carrying out Mr. Horning's orders to stay open during lunch?

SUGGESTIONS FOR FURTHER STUDY

Evans, C. George, *Supervising R & D Personnel*, Chapter 9, American Management Association, New York, 1969.

Haimann, Theo, and Raymond L. Hilgert, *Supervision: Concepts and Practices of Management*, Chapter 15, South-Western Publishing Company, Incorporated, Cincinnati, 1972.

McLarney, William J., and William M. Berlimer, *Management Training—Cases and Principles*, Chapter 15, Richard D. Irwin, Inc., Homewood, Illinois, 1970.

Toffler, Alvin, *Future Shock*, Random House, New York, 1970.

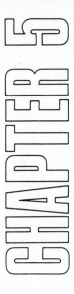

CHAPTER 5

GETTING ALONG WITH THE BOSS

THE CASE OF THE IMPERFECT BOSS

"Just when I think I've got him figured out, he ups and throws me off balance." Burt was describing his most recent meeting with Ray Ford, assembly superintendent. Jack Holt, supervisor of final assembly, listened attentively while he drove along.

Burt had described how Ray had just paid him a visit at the end of the shift. Apparently it was to express his pleasure with the way the two new expanded assembly groups were working out. He was especially pleased with the way quality was being maintained while they were beating production requirements. Performance on those new contracts had made the customers happy and their future business was practically assured. Ray had some nice words for Burt and his effectiveness as a supervisor. His parting comment as he left Burt's office was, "You see now what I meant about most of your fears concerning that change being ungrounded. Too bad our foresight isn't as sharp as our hindsight. Anyhow, it was a nice piece of work, Burt, and I wanted you to know I appreciate what your people are doing."

"Do you know what I mean, Jack? One minute he builds me up with high praise, then he knocks me down with that dig about the way I resisted the changes. I know I didn't look too good on the way I handled that one, but we pitched in and did the job. I just can never figure out where I stand with him."

"Ah, Ray's not so bad," Jack responded. "All in all, he's a pretty good egg. He sure could do a lot to improve his communications, though. I've said it before and I'll say it again, he could make my job a lot easier if he'd just communicate so I know what he's thinking—what he wants. You've got no complaints about the big pat on the back, though."

"I'm not complaining about the praise. I like it as well as the next guy. But he put me in a box with that change. Like you say, if he had let me know what was going on before they sprung it on me, I might have handled it differently. As far as I'm concerned, Ray and Oscar both could have given me some support before ramming that change down my throat and criticizing me for resisting it."

"Like I say, Burt," Jack laughed, "what management in this company needs is a good course in how to communicate."

"That's not the answer, Jack. Ray had had the course and talked me into taking it," Burt countered.

"Then why in hell isn't he applying some of it?" exploded Jack.

Burt suddenly found himself in that odd position of wanting to defend Ray when he had been the one who started complaining about him in the first place. A guy could do a lot worse for a boss than Ray Ford, Burt thought to himself. It sure would help, though, to know what he was really thinking instead of trying to outguess him. What it comes down to is that Ray doesn't really do things badly as much as it is that he doesn't do a lot of things at all. Sins of omission rather than sins of commission.

It would be nice, he continued thinking to himself, if Ray would give me some real feedback about how I'm doing and what really is expected of me. If a supervisor is going to support his boss, he has to know what his boss wants. I could have handled that change with a lot more enthusiasm if only they had let me in on it from the beginning. Ray made me feel kind of sheepish complimenting me for something I was actually blocking. A guy's got a right to be peeved, he thought.

Sinking deeper into contemplative thought, Burt wondered how it would feel to know exactly what the limits of your authority and responsibility are, to know whether or not you could count on the boss's support if you took strong but appropriate disciplinary action, to know whether the boss really considers you a part of management, to know if he would go to bat for you and your employees, to know if he means it when he says he wants suggestions and ideas, to know before the union steward when a change is made in company policy, to know when you've done something he doesn't like. In short, what it would be like to have a pipeline to what he's thinking about at all times. He could make my job so much easier. If only I didn't have to second-guess him.

If I were boss, I'd sure let my subordinates know what's going on. Embarrassment accompanied the thought as it flashed through his mind because Burt realized at the same time that he was a boss. Could it be that what he saw as Ray's shortcomings, his own people might say were his weaknesses too?

"Hey, Burt, you're home," Jack called out. "For a guy who just got a pat on the back from the boss, you're sure moody. I'll have to tell Ray to go easy on that stuff 'cause it goes to your head. See you tomorrow."

"Yeah, see you tomorrow," Burt responded as he got out of the car and headed toward the house. As he walked he pondered, "How does a guy go about improving boss-to-boss relations? Ray isn't perfect, but then I guess I'm not either."

Let's review some of Burt's concerns.

1. Identify and evaluate Burt's complaints about Ray Ford.

2. Both Jack and Burt thought their jobs would be easier if Ray Ford did a better job at his. How so?

3. What does a boss expect from a supervisor-subordinate?

4. If the boss doesn't communicate, what can the subordinate do about it?

UNDERSTANDING THE BOSS

"I have a suggestion," said the vice president of a small company evaluating a supervisory development institute at the University of Wisconsin. "You're doing a fine job of teaching supervisors how to get along with their employees, but you're not even touching their biggest problem—getting along with their bosses. That's what they worry about most."

Don't most supervisors experience the same concerns and frustration that Burt Hall expressed about his relationship with Ray Ford? No doubt there are many many supervisors in all kinds of organizations who are unable to reach even Burt's level of understanding and compassion when he said, "Ray is really a pretty good guy, but he doesn't make my job any easier when he doesn't communicate."

When our own needs to accomplish, to look good, to support the organization are frustrated by a boss who doesn't seem to care, it's exceedingly difficult to recognize that the boss has those same needs. Impatience and unhappiness with the shortcomings of a superior can easily block our ability to look at the boss as an individual. Whether that boss is a man or woman, works for government, industry, institution, or a retail business, he or she is a human being who has attained a very responsible position in the organization.

Having reached that level of understanding, we know that bosses have the very same intense need to succeed that every supervisor has. Success is associated with the attaining of objectives. To meet a deadline, reach a quota, maintain a standard, exceed an objective gives any person a feeling of satisfaction. When those things happen, it's easy to be a good supervisor. Ray Ford's taking the time to seek Burt out and express his appreciation is a good example. Unfortunately we sometimes lose sight of who had helped us reach success. On the other hand, a manager at any level who fails to reach an objective experiences the same frustration that sometimes causes antisocial, antiorganization, or antisubordinate behavior. Why? Because bosses are human too.

It's reasonable to assume that any manager wants a positive, fruitful relationship with his or her subordinates. To have a subordinate's respect and cooperation is a universal managerial need. The same is true, of course, in any human relationship—husband and wife, parent and child, within a circle of friends. We see and feel our need to be accepted constantly. Why should we have difficulty in recognizing that same need in a boss—a social individual who needs to achieve and be accepted?

While it may not always be true, generally the higher people go in an organization the greater the responsibility they bear. The boss, then, in all probability has the weight of a heavier burden than the subordinate, even though we feel our own most. The president of a very large Minneapolis-based firm told a gathering of first-line supervisors from around the country, "The problems you have to solve, the decisions you have to make are every bit as tough as mine. The difference is the number of people affected when I make a decision. It's a tremendous responsibility." He went on to explain that a supervisor was responsible for a department and the decisions made by the supervisor affected that many people. A superintendent is responsible for several departments; a division manager for more, a vice president for still more, and so it goes.

If we review the seven major responsibilities of a supervisor outlined in Chapter 1, it becomes apparent that the boss carries those same responsibilities to a greater degree than we do. They need to see that production gets out, that resources of people, money, and materials are most efficiently used, and that quality of product or service is maintained constantly.

Complaints about the boss not communicating are the most common in the boss-subordinate relationship. We hear Burt Hall and Jack Holt both complaining about Ray Ford's poor communication. So often it isn't because the boss doesn't want to communicate or doesn't care; it's a case of the boss not being informed. In a large Milwaukee concern a communication training program for top manufacturing managers was established. A common complaint of the group members was the lack of communication from the executive level. All in all, the program was well received, and it was decided to offer it to the plant superintendents. Then, in turn, the general foremen had their innings, and finally the first-line supervisors participated. At each level, the same complaint. At the lower supervisory level the complaint was expressed most frequently, "This training is fine for me but the person that really needs it is my boss." When told the boss had had the program, the response was always, "Well, why isn't he using it?" The only conclusion—the boss is human or the boss can't communicate what he or she doesn't have.

The boss has another need, and that's for communication or support from below. What an embarrassing feeling to be in the position of not knowing something that happens in his or her own department! Every supervisor ought to be able to recognize that the boss has a boss too, and doesn't like to have to explain a situation or a condition that he or she knows nothing about. At the top of the organization, management's biggest communication problem is, How can we find what's really going on when everybody filters out what they don't want us to hear and passes on only the good news? Isn't it fair to assume the boss needs an accurate picture of what's going on in the departments under his or her direction?

Because the boss does carry more responsibility, his or her time is even more limited than the supervisor's. You'll almost never find a supervisor who doesn't have enough work to keep busy. Time is precious. And again each step up the ladder increases the demands on time. Most supervisors are sensitive to this fact, but many forget it and become irritated when the boss is not available for consultation.

If one can accept the fact that bosses are human, then perhaps we can also understand that a boss has no wish to be high-pressured by a subordinate. Just as we all resist being pushed by a child, a spouse, or a salesperson, so also does the boss hate to be nagged unreasonably to take an action before being certain it's the right thing to do. The "nagger" can be found in an office, in the plant, in government service, in a bank. The reaction to this type of person is always the same—it's negative. Anyone seeking a way to alienate bosses needn't do much more than needle them constantly about implementing an idea they're not quite sold on.

It's been said several times in this chapter and probably will be said many more because it is so important: Bosses are human. They want to do their best. They want to look good. They want to be respected and accepted by their subordinates, and, being human, they perceive themselves as doing the things to earn that respect. They are also capable of wrong judgments, of losing their tempers, of forgetting to communicate, of making the same mistakes we all make. Burt Hall was making the first giant step in improving his relations with Ray Ford when he came to the realization that he himself was a "boss." Perhaps he was beginning to realize that most of us don't play half as good a game as we know how to play and want to play.

HELPING THE BOSS UNDERSTAND YOU

Each of us will work best with those we know and understand. Again bosses are no exception. The better bosses understand that supervisors share a common concern for achieving mutual objectives the more likely they will work cooperatively with supervisors and see them as allies. The boss needs to understand that the supervisor can operate most effectively when the relationship is defined and limits of authority are clarified. If, for example, a manager sees the supervisor overstep the limits of authority, the perception is likely to be of a pushy, power-hungry person who needs to be sat on. On the other hand, if the supervisor doesn't use the authority the position carries, the boss may see an individual lacking the aggressiveness and drive necessary in a young subordinate. In either case the relationship is strained because they didn't reach a mutual understanding of the subordinate's authority. How, then, can a supervisor help the boss understand?

SHARING

We all get so wrapped up in our own concerns that it's sometimes difficult to really share. Yet it's in the sharing that boss and subordinate move forward together.

Helping the organization reach a goal is taken for granted as a job of every manager. But a supervisor can help the boss by letting the boss know that the supervisor is in sympathy with those goals, that his or her solutions to problems are aimed at attaining those goals, that he or she is concerned with any conditions which might block the attainment of these goals.

To ask for feedback on progress, to show an interest in how other departments under the boss's supervision are faring are means by which we share the boss's concerns. Telling that boss of our concern to do well in our job is another form of sharing that's needed. We assume he knows of our concern and interest, but the boss will enjoy hearing that his subordinate is trying.

SELLING

Nothing is wrong with some subtle selling of ourselves. Why shouldn't the boss learn when we've succeeded so he can share the pleasure? It can't hurt for him to know our pleasure in resolving a problem, in satisfying a need of one of his other departments, in supporting a policy or a change with our employees.

Any boss will give lip service to the idea that new ideas from subordinates are welcome and needed. Yet most will lack enthusiasm for an idea that is popped at them without any supporting data or arguments. Instead of popping an idea at the boss and pouting when it isn't accepted, why not accompany the idea with some insight into how well it's been thought through. We give the boss a far better understanding of our respect for his position when we sell ideas in a logical presentation oriented to costs and benefits.

SHOWING

Actions speak so much louder than words that any supervisor concerned with improving relations with the boss can start by demonstrating that he or she is anxious to contribute to achieving the goals of the department. There is probably no better way of gaining boss support than by making him or her look good through the performance of our department. To share with the boss our interest in getting the best possible results from our department is likely to put him or her in the position of wanting to help.

A supervisor can demonstrate management-mindedness by determining the objectives or goals that are to be attained. Some logical areas for goal setting would include quantity of production, quality of production, reduction of customer complaints, improving on-time deliveries, reduction of down-time, acquisition of new accounts, improvement of clerical accuracy. If we establish objectives in three or four key areas, develop some ideas in the form of a plan to accomplish them, and share them with the boss, we demonstrate our interest in the organization. This puts the boss in the role most would prefer—that of a coach or helper. In this way, we have made it possible for the boss to respond in terms of giving support to one who cares, who shares his or her objectives.

The majority of managers at all levels dislike and would like to avoid performance appraisals. Yet they universally acknowledge that subordinates have a right to know where they stand with the boss. The reason most want to avoid performance appraisal is that they feel uncomfortable "sitting in judgment" and they fear a subordinate's resentment of criticism. Here is where the supervisor can help the boss. What's wrong with asking for a chance to review performance and sharing some thoughts about the future?

Much of the reluctance of the boss to share can be overcome by the supervisor taking the initiative. Not many managers will hesitate to set aside time for a subordinate who asks for the opportunity to review performance and to discuss future plans. This supervisor-initiated sharing can really clear the air for a positive boss-subordinate relationship. If, for example, Burt Hall were to ask Ray Ford for a chance to discuss how he was doing, he would undoubtedly get it. Then, instead of wondering where he stood with Ray, he would know. Instead of bemoaning a lack of direction from above, he would have it. Both Burt and Ray are conscientious and dedicated and possess a great deal of common sense. How sad that Burt should feel that he's in the doghouse after getting a nice pat on the back. Unfortunately in the absence of sharing, each can become suspicious of the other and head into a relationship neither wants.

We work best with those whom we like, with whom we agree, whom we respect, whom we understand, whom we perceive as helping us. So does the boss. If a supervisor can find any way to create those feelings in the boss, he or she is likely to find the feeling reciprocated. It's a matter of helping the boss understand us and our desire to help the boss look good.

**VIEWING
THE RELATIONSHIP**

Loyalty is sometimes regarded as an old-fashioned concept, but it is one of the greatest needs today in the boss-subordinate relationship. Across the land in every conceivable kind of organization, managers are expressing the need for the loyalty of their subordinates. They also hope for evidence of loyalty to the enterprise. Any manager wants to feel that the policies, decisions, rules, and action plans that are handed down to the supervisor for implementation are supported by that supervisor. Bosses don't want to be referred to as the "they" who take all those unreasonable stands.

The need for the personal loyalty of the boss is just as great among subordinates. Supervisors naturally want to feel that they have the support of their bosses. This two-way need for loyalty is most likely to be satisfied in a climate of openness and honesty. We can see the first indication of a lack of that openness in the Burt Hall–Ray Ford relationship, where each begins to suspect the motives of the other. A void in communication then feeds the suspicions.

A healthy boss-subordinate relationship demands good communication. The tendency of subordinates to filter out the bad news and pass on only what makes them look good cheats the boss of the opportunity to make intelligent decisions and recommendations. It denies him the opportunity to come to the aid of a subordinate in trouble. And in time it robs him of the desire to support. A supervisor has little excuse when the boss learns bad news from another source. All too frequently when that happens the bad news has been exaggerated to the detriment of the supervisor.

A close look at the boss-subordinate relationship will quickly reveal that the boss has a vested interest in the success of his or her supervisors. When the subordinate performs well, the boss looks good. Much is to be gained in recognizing this fact by both boss and subordinate. Bosses should understand that by helping the subordinate perform they are helping themselves. When the subordinates understand the boss's vested interest in them, they will tend to be less suspicious of what the boss really wants. Bosses want their subordinates to succeed.

In viewing the boss-subordinate relationship, another important factor appears. There is a great deal of misunderstanding over the perception each has of the supervisor's authority. In a recent study at the University of Wisconsin, it was discovered that boss and first-line supervisors disagreed over 50 percent of the time on almost all of forty incidents relating to supervisory responsibility. With that level of disagreement, what happens to the relationship? If a supervisor is convinced he or she has less authority than the boss feels was given, the boss is likely to regard the subordinate as lacking initiative, unable to make decisions, hesitant, and short on management potential. On the other hand, if a supervisor feels he or she has more authority than the boss is willing to delegate, he or she will be seen as overaggressive, pushy, eager, or power-hungry. Two supervisors working for the same boss but having different ideas about their authority will naturally wonder about consistency in administration. The potential for confusion and disharmony is great in such a situation. Misunderstandings about the use of authority provide a ready base for uncooperative attitudes, mistrust, and impatience. When such feelings exist, each lacks confidence in the other, and support of the other supervisor becomes unimportant.

One of the most talked-about facets of the boss-subordinate relationship is the matter of delegation. Through delegation a manager develops subordinates, accomplishes more, and effectively utilizes time. On the receiving end of delegation, the supervisor develops competence to handle ever-increasing areas of responsibility, sharpens decision-making skills, and increases promotion potential. Because it calls for real trust in an intimate personal relationship, the benefits of delegation are frequently lost. A boss who regards delegation as a means of dumping undesirable or idiot work on a subordinate reaps the harvest of resentment. Inability to see the difference between the precision of good order-giving and the freedom allowed in good delegation generally results in the creation of supervisors who are immobilized by fear of making decisions.

Supervisors, on the other hand, harassed by the pressure of insufficient time, can resist delegation designed for developing their decision-making muscle. After a few futile attempts to delegate activities or functions to a reluctant subordinate, who can blame a boss for claiming the supervisor lacks drive or job interest?

How satisfying it is for both when boss says ''I approve'' after a subordinate brings him a decision or solution to a problem! Naturally the boss thinks well of the supervisor who presents solutions to problems because such initiative is evidence that the supervisor knows his or her job and that responsibility is being taken seriously. How much easier it is for the boss to respond positively to an individual who is thoughtful and actively concerned.

Having said that, it's important that we recognize a potential trap. One might read into the paragraphs above that a supervisor should never take problems to the boss because it's a sign of weakness. Fiddlesticks! One of the boss's functions is to assist in the resolution of problems. The boss's satisfaction many times will come in helping a subordinate find the way out of the problem-solution wilderness. Before sharing problems and their solution with the boss, however, it is important for the supervisor to first define the problem and to think out probable solutions. Although a manager does not want to do the supervisor's thinking, his or her greater experience should come into play and can be triggered when a subordinate says, "I need help," and really means it.

The chain of command is a closely guarded concept. Subordinate reports to boss who reports to boss who reports to boss and so on up and down the line. At no time should a person bypass his or her immediate boss nor should a manager bypass an immediate subordinate to deal with a person another level down. Bypassing is identified as undermining, as deception, or as lack of support. The principle is sound, but as with most principles, situations do develop where a bypass is appropriate. For example, a real disagreement might develop over an order the boss has given. The supervisor, in effect, has a grievance. If all reasonable avenues of possible agreement have been explored, the supervisor should have the opportunity to take his disagreement upstairs, but only if all avenues of possible agreement have been explored.

The bypass should be known by the boss. In fact, in most cases, it will have his blessing. The subordinate must also have the integrity to take upstairs only facts and arguments already discussed with the boss. An obligation exists to present both sides of the disagreement as objectively as possible.

Bypassing can be tolerated if it isn't frequent and if communication at all levels is complete, open, and accurate. To do less is a disservice to the boss, which can only lead to nonproductive, uncooperative relationships.

In examining their own relationships with the boss, supervisors will ultimately have to recognize as Burt Hall did that bosses are not perfect. When a supervisor asks, "Why should I communicate when my boss doesn't?" there is only one logical answer. Because it is good management. If the boss is really a poor manager, does it mean the supervisor must also be poor? If a supervisor has the ability to recognize a weakness in the boss, should he or she have the strength to compensate for the deficiency and to support the boss before other employees?

**IMPROVING RELATIONS
WITH THE BOSS**

The vice president mentioned in the beginning of this chapter told the university professor, ''Give the supervisor and foreman who come to you some solid tips they can use in relating to their bosses. It would help them more than anything else I can think of.'' With that advice in mind, here are some suggestions for getting along better with the boss.

BE AN ASSISTANT

When you are a supervisor, then you are an assistant to someone, no matter what your official title. Why not do what an assistant does—*assist!* You are there to help and to support. If a management decision or change is resisted by employees, back up the manager, but also help him or her understand the extent and degree of the resistance. Let your boss see you as a source of assistance. It will pay dividends.

SET THE EXAMPLE AS A COMMUNICATOR

You can train the boss to be a better communicator by setting the example. Find out what the boss wants and needs to know. A few minutes' thought will produce a fairly good list. Bosses need to know the status of work in the department, any deviations from standards of cost, quality, and quantity, precedent-setting personnel problems, customer reactions to service, mistakes you might have made (rely on your own explanation rather than an exaggerated version from someone else), progress on a pet or critical project, and so on. Bear in mind that the boss's time is valuable. Learn to keep your reporting orally or in writing as brief as possible, consistent with satisfying the boss's need to know.

When you've been inconvenienced because the boss didn't pass something on, let it be known (but nicely). For example, ''I might have handled the Jones account more tactfully if I had only known,'' or ''We could have met their deadline if we had known exactly what they wanted.'' If the boss has been sitting on information, the fact that it was not shared with you will be recognized. By taking the initiative tactfully, it is more likely the boss will think to communicate helpful information.

BE CONSIDERATE OF TIME PRESSURES

You probably will never meet a manager who doesn't have more than enough work to fill a workday. Sooner or later everyone learns that there never are enough hours in a day to carry out every job responsibility as thoroughly and capably as he or she should. And with greater responsibilities, it's no wonder bosses are not always available when they are wanted.

Even though your relationship with the boss is a very friendly one, courtesy and consideration strongly suggest the wisdom of an appointment. If the boss has a secretary or assistant, schedule an appointment. The big advantage here is that the secretary can suggest a time when you will probably get the boss's undivided attention. When the boss operates without secretarial assistance, it's still a good idea to phone or poke your head into his or her office and ask, "Can we get together at two o'clock to discuss employee reaction to the new rules on absenteeism and tardiness?" or "Would 2:30 be a good time to clear up some of the wrinkles on the new inventory system?" This way you give the boss an opportunity to adjust afternoon plans and to get ready, mentally and in terms of information he may wish to have on hand, for the discussion you want to have.

If experience teaches that the boss's availability is extremely limited, it's a good idea to make a list of questions to be covered. It's quite disconcerting to finish one of those rare talks with the boss and then remember two or three items you forgot to bring up. In consideration of the boss's time constraints, it is important that you avoid side excursions to discuss the weekend football game, your analysis of the energy crises, or your most recent accomplishment on the tennis court. Unless the boss initiates such discussion, you can safely assume the appropriate moment is not at hand.

When problems are to be discussed or presented, be sure you have your analysis completed and your recommendations clearly in mind. If the boss likes your solution and says, "I approve," your performance rating will be high. If you don't feel qualified or capable of making a recommendation, at least have a list of alternatives ready for consideration. Alternative lines of action or options will help to speed up the choice of a preferred solution.

Perhaps a face-to-face meeting with the boss isn't at all necessary. Much information can easily be passed on with a short simple memo. For example, "You'll be pleased to hear that Marilyn Gardner checked out of the hospital yesterday." Or, "We're completing work on the Acme order this morning." Or, "Sales in Region Four topped last month by $125,000." Any of these routine events could be reported to the boss by memo, especially if he or she is pressed for time. Generally it's best to limit each memo to one subject. That way the reader has more flexibility in discarding some and setting others up in a tickler or subject file.

ACCEPT DELEGATED FUNCTIONS WILLINGLY

When your boss delegates a responsibility to you, it is a demonstration of trust in your ability to perform that for which he or she is ultimately responsible. You are being given an opportunity to grow and show what you can do. If your boss is human (and we've been assuming right along that he is), there will be some misgivings about delegating. Most bosses are reluctant to overload an already busy subordinate. They also frequently conclude that they may be giving away part of their job, and it's not easy for most managers to let go of their private preserve of operations. Other bosses feel insecure about repercussions if a delegated job isn't handled as well as it might have been had they done it. A few bosses even fear that a subordinate supervisor's performance in carrying out a delegated function will cause an unfavorable reflection on their own capabilities when viewed by higher management.

A boss can be encouraged by experiencing willing acceptance of a delegated activity or he can be turned away from a practice he wasn't enthusiastic about in the first place by a reluctant subordinate. In the latter instance, the rationale he then gives is, ''It's easier to do it myself.''

TAKE THE INITIATIVE WHEN THE BOSS DOESN'T

Look for a moment at the complaints and concerns of Burt Hall. He said he didn't know where he stood with Ray. He wanted a little direction. His real complaint was that he didn't know how Ray felt about the way he had handled a major change in his department.

You needn't suffer such uncertainties if you tactfully take the initiative. In most cases the boss is not deliberately withholding information. There are just too many demands being made on the boss's available time. If a subordinate asks him a question, he's happy to answer. If the subordinate doesn't, it winds up under the heading of things the boss meant to get around to but didn't.

If you want some direction from the boss, why not start by charting that direction yourself and getting his reaction to it? This can be accomplished by setting objectives in three or four areas of departmental operation, asking the boss to review them and react to them. Most bosses would be highly pleased to see such initiative on the part of their subordinates. They'll also be happy to share their thinking on what the major objectives for the department should be.

If you want a performance review, why not ask for it? It's far better than suffering the uncertainty that Burt Hall is experiencing. If it takes a while to get it, it is still worth going after, particularly if it clears the air on where you're going and how you're going to get there.

If you are in doubt about the limits of your authority, list the areas in which you have doubts, such as purchasing materials, granting time off, ordering maintenance on equipment, taking disciplinary action, changing a price, skipping a step in a procedure, or terminating an employee, and ask for a chance to clarify them. A common method of grading the levels of authority is as follows: (1) do nothing; (2) notify boss, let him act; (3) recommend action but wait for boss's approval; (4) act, then notify boss; (5) complete authority to act without reporting. You can take areas in which you are uncertain about your authority, assign the highest level you feel you have, ask your boss to do the same, and compare. If you agree, fine. But if you don't it's a splendid opportunity to discuss your differences. Obviously, there is a high correlation between the level of authority and the boss's confidence in your performance.

CONSULT HIM ON MAJOR DECISIONS—ESPECIALLY THOSE AFFECTING OTHER DEPARTMENTS

You can avoid the complaint of many supervisors that they are not supported in their decisions or that they are overruled by higher authority. Instead of making impulsive decisions (we might prefer to call them decisive actions) in sensitive areas, it would be well to inform the boss of your intentions so he can react to them. This is especially important when the action affects other departments or functions. The boss has a broader perspective of the organization and can protect you from making mistakes. The boss also is in a better position to go to bat for you if informed ahead of time of poor actions. For example, you might find the decision to terminate an employee is premature in view of precedents that have been set, or that a method improvement in your department would cause another department more work.

BE A FRIEND—WITHOUT GOING OVERBOARD

You can be a friend to the boss. They need and want friends. Unfortunately there is an unwanted barrier to warm relationships between boss and subordinate. Inviting the boss to join occasionally in coffee breaks and lunch will be appreciated by many. If he or she exhibits a preference for nonfraternization, that should be respected.

To share the same concern in the boss's outside interests that you would in a subordinate employee's is common courtesy. If the boss has a hobby, show an interest. We all like an interested listener to what we do, think, or accomplish away from the job.

Cooperative boss-subordinate, husband-wife, supervisor-to-supervisor relationships are found where the two individuals like and respect one another. As Will Rogers, old-time sage and comedian commented, "It's awfully hard to dislike someone who likes you."

DISAGREE IN PRIVATE

Your boss is a representative of management just as you are. He or she is an extension of management philosophy and policies just as you are. It's inevitable, however, that the time will come when you question the wisdom of a management directive. That's when a healthy boss-subordinate relationship is tested. How tempting it is at that time to express our dissatisfaction with what "they" upstairs want to do.

The place to question a management directive is in private without emotional displays. Here is where it becomes especially important to look at that directive from management's viewpoint. With genuine consideration of the boss's position, you'll find you're less likely to use emotionally charged words like asinine, stupid, or unreasonable. Such attacks only serve to widen the area of disagreement. Logical arguments coupled with a demonstrated ability to see both sides of the disagreement might change the boss's mind or convince the boss to take the case upstairs for reconsideration.

After disagreement has been aired and not resolved, it's also important to know when to stop disagreeing and start supporting. In airing your disagreement, you'll learn management's reasons or the boss's reasons for taking a particular action. It's those reasons that must be understood by your employees. Look back to Burt Hall's reaction to the major change in his department in Chapter 4. He voiced his concern about the change and suggested some alternative approaches to Ray Ford. Ray countered with reasons why the change was necessary and why Burt's suggestions weren't practical. That is precisely the point at which Burt should have gotten behind the change, supported it with his employees, and stop referring to the change as "their" idea. Probably there was some "I told you so" feeling on Ray's part when he told Burt, "It's too bad our foresight isn't as good as our hindsight."

RECOGNIZE YOUR BOSS'S HELP AND ACCOMPLISHMENTS

Much will be said in later chapters about the need to give recognition to an employee's contribution to his or her job and the department.

Generally we think of praise and recognition as something that flows down each level of the hierarchy from boss to subordinate. There is absolutely no reason why the flow shouldn't go both up and down the line if positive working relationships with the boss are desired.

When the boss has given you support or assistance, a simple "Thank you" or "I appreciate your help" is common courtesy. If the boss's unit has accomplished some goal such as a high sales record, improvement in output, or a tough project accomplished, why shouldn't you recognize that fact with a "nice going" or "congratulations—good job"? The boss's need for recognition is the same as yours. Bosses appreciate praise just as much from subordinates as from superiors—maybe more. Just be sure it's sincere and not overdone. Insincere praise or overabundant praise becomes apple-polishing.

In summary, the relationship we want to have with the boss is in large part of our own making as subordinates. A supervisor need only look at what he or she wants from the boss—support, communication, assistance, recognition—to recognize that the boss wants these same things from the subordinate. Isn't it logical that in order to get more of what we want from the boss we have only to give the same to him? Control over who starts improving the relationship starts with us as supervisors because we have no control over the boss. Our relationship with the boss will be more fruitful and satisfying if that boss perceives us as a means of reaching objectives.

HIGHLIGHTS

1. A supervisor is as much, if not more, concerned with getting along with the boss as getting along with his or her employees.

2. The boss is human and has the same needs and concerns as anyone else up and down. The boss's responsibilities are greater and the demands on available time are more severe.

3. Communication is a two-way street. Both boss and subordinate must recognize the other's need to know. The boss can be trained to be a better communicator.

4. It's important that supervisors help their bosses understand them as individuals by:

   a. *Sharing* concerns for seeing the organization accomplish its objectives and asking for feedback on progress to that end.

    b. *Selling* the boss on ideas for improving the function rather than popping them at him or her and pouting when they aren't accepted.

    c. *Showing* the boss exactly what the supervisor wants to accomplish in the department.

5. In viewing the boss-subordinate relationship we see that:

    a. The need exists for good old-fashioned loyalty.

    b. The boss has a vested interest in the success of his or her subordinates.

    c. Each needs a clear understanding of the supervisor's limits of authority.

    d. Delegation is means of building up both boss and subordinate if it is well done.

    e. The boss expects a supervisor to solve his or her own problems and bring to him (with recommendations) only those that can't be resolved at the supervisory level.

    f. The chain of command needs to be respected, but under certain conditions bypassing can be condoned.

6. In trying to improve relations with the boss, these suggestions are offered:

    a. Be an assistant.

    b. Set the example as a communicator.

    c. Be considerate of the pressure on available time.

    d. Accept delegated functions willingly.

    e. Take the initiative when the boss doesn't.

    f. Consult the boss on major decisions.

    g. Be a friend.

    h. Disagree in private.

    i. Recognize the boss's help and accomplishments.

7. Supervisors have just about as much influence and control when it comes to improving the relationship as the boss does.

DISCUSSION QUESTIONS

1. Do you agree or disagree with the statement that the supervisor has as much control as the boss in improving the relationship? Explain.

2. What are specific things you can do to lessen the time pressure your boss experiences?

3. What specific things can a supervisor do to help his or her boss understand the supervisor as an individual?

4. Expand on the statement that the boss has a vested interest in his or her subordinates and wants to see them succeed.

5. Outline the steps you might take in selling the boss an idea you have for purchasing a piece of equipment costing $1,000. You are sold on it.

6. Think of a time when you disagreed with your boss and wished you could have gone over his or her head. Describe what might be done to get permission to go "upstairs" with your idea or difference.

7. How is it possible to be a friend to the boss without others thinking you're "apple-polishing"?

8. Explain what is meant by the statement that both the boss and subordinate grow when delegation is well done.

CASE PROBLEMS

THE CASE OF SID HARTWELL

Sid was discouraged. He had supervised sales in his four-state territory for only one year and he had just finished "sort of" an appraisal with his district manager. His district manager said he was pleased with Sid's work, but Sid felt there were some things left unsaid and he couldn't bring himself to ask the boss to open up.

Sales had increased about 8 percent in his territory and business was good. It could be better if deliveries from the plant were better. His men were claiming selling would be easier if shipments were on time and they didn't have to use shortages as an excuse all the time.

While the district manager was complimentary about Sid's accomplishments, he made several references to the "potential" in the territory. He also seemed to suggest, without saying it, that he wasn't satisfied to find that the increase in sales had come from the same accounts. His questions about whether Sid's territory was getting its share of the market and about what the competition was doing were embarrassing. Sid didn't know except for a couple of isolated instances. He didn't really have an answer, either, for why they lost two accounts to their competition. The boss wasn't exactly pleased with Sid's inability to answer the questions, but he let him off the hook without saying anything.

"Trouble with the boss is he never levels with a guy, but I guess I'm getting by," Sid thought.

1.   How might Sid get the direction he says he wants?

2.   Is Sid getting by? Where is he headed?

3.   As the district sales manager, plan to review Sid's performance.

4.   If you were Sid, what would you do now?

THE CASE OF CHRIS CARTER

Chris Carter was seething. As office supervisor in the file department of Jackson City's health department she had been doing her job as well as anybody in City Hall. Why, she wondered, does Dr. Froman have to single me out for all this extra responsibility? Ever since the director got back from that conference he's been dumping all his work on the rest of us. "He calls it delegation, but it's just ducking his responsibility as far as I'm concerned," she mumbled.

Dr. Froman, director of the city health department, had told Chris he would like her to do an analysis of current filing systems and develop some recommendations for a new records retention program. Together, then, he said that they would propose an overhaul of the present setup to the mayor's administrative assistant.

"I don't know where to start. Why doesn't he bring in a specialist or consultant? What's wrong with the present system? If he doesn't like it, why doesn't he tell me what's wrong? How far can I go in spending money and time? What's he trying to do to me? He's just taking advantage of me because I'm a woman, and then he'll turn around and take all the credit. If I didn't have so much time in on this job, I'd quit!" Chris said.

1.   What should Chris do now?

2.   How should she be reacting to Dr. Froman's delegation?

3.   What should Dr. Froman have done to get a more enthusiastic reaction from Chris?

THE CASE OF LOWELL EASTMAN

"I've got just about the most impossible boss in the world to work for," Lowell Eastman, line supervisor of Independence Telephone Company, declared. "I haven't heard a kind word from him in the six years I've worked for him. If he ever smiled, his face would crack. He gets his kicks out of giving people hell. He expects you to know everything, but he tells you nothing.

"If I want to find out what's going on, I have to ask the union steward. The clerks back in the office know more about operations than I do. Every time I need him for something he's too busy, but I better not be busy when he wants something.

"We get all this stuff from topside about giving employees recognition. Why should I when he never does? It sure would be nice to get a compliment once in a while from the old buzzard. I don't mind him raising hell with me once in a while; but when he bypasses me and lowers the boom on some of my crew, I really burn. But what can you say? I guess he's the cross I have to bear."

1. What might account for the boss's treatment of Lowell?

2. What are some possible consequences of a manager operating on the basis of "You're doing all right as long as you don't hear from me"?

3. What could Lowell do to improve relations with his boss?

SUGGESTIONS FOR FURTHER STUDY

Bittel, Lester R., *What Every Supervisor Should Know*, 3d ed., Chapter 42, McGraw-Hill Book Company, New York, 1974.

Black, James M., and Guy B. Ford, *Front-Line Management*, Chapter 22, McGraw-Hill Book Company, New York, 1963.

Famularo, Joseph J., *Supervisors in Action*, Chapter 14, McGraw-Hill Book Company, New York, 1961.

Ficker, Victor B., *Effective Supervision*, Chapter 7, Charles E. Merrill Books, Inc., Columbus, Ohio, 1975.

Reeves, Elton T., *How to Get Along with Almost Everybody*, Chapter 1, Amacom, New York, 1973.

PART TWO
LEADERSHIP SKILLS

The true genius that conducts a state is he, who doing nothing himself, causes everything to be done; he contrives, he invents, he foresees the future; he reflects on what is past; he distributes and proportions things; he makes early preparations; he incessantly arms himself to struggle against fortune, as a swimmer against a rapid stream of water; he is attentive day and night, that he may leave nothing to chance.

FRANCIS DE S. FENELON (1651–1715)

PERFORMANCE OBJECTIVES

A supervisor will be able to measure his or her ability to lead the people in his or her own department against the following criteria:

1. To recognize each employee in the department as an individual unique and different from all others.

2. To know three or four key pieces of personal information about each employee, such as job goals and ambitions.

3. To be able to identify an employee's reasons for behavior the supervisor deems unacceptable before taking or recommending action.

4. To be able to persuade an employee that a job means a lot more than money and security.

5. To recognize and use nonfinancial incentives in the day-to-day operation of the department.

6. To recognize that insincere forms of recognition amount to manipulation and to recognize when they produce a reverse or negative response.

7. To have made a job training plan before each job taught a new or transferred employee.

8. To have used step-by-step the six-step system for training with every new employee brought into the department.

9. To have trained every person in the department who is expected to train others in the use of a job training plan and the six-step system for training.

10. To have accepted the fact that training of employees is a personal responsibility, whether delegated or not.

11. To be able to leave the department at any and all times, confident that things will go on normally.

12. To have created a climate where adherence to rules by all employees is regular and uniform.

13. To be able to take corrective action without creating resentment of authority.

14. To be able to recognize when decisions on complaints or disciplinary action can develop into formal grievances.

15. To consistently recognize that the boss and personnel department must be advised of action taken if their support is expected.

16. To be able to control one's temper when challenged by a grieving employee or union official.

CHAPTER 6

UNDERSTANDING THE INDIVIDUAL EMPLOYEE

THE CASE OF FEARLESS FRANK CONNORS

"Just give him a little more time. He'll have you tearing your hair out too," Frank Connors, supervisor of the toolroom, was saying to Burt Hall. "He's just a stubborn kraut. Thinks he's smart, but he hasn't got enough sense to come in out of the rain. They're all alike. The only muscles he uses are in his mouth."

The object of Frank's tirade was Eric Mader, who had worked in the toolroom until about a month ago, when he had requested and secured a transfer to Burt's assembly department. Frank said he had been impressed with Eric when he first hired him as a helper in the toolroom. Eric dispensed tools, stored them, and kept records. There was plenty of activity to keep him busy. What caused Eric and Frank to be at odds with one another was that Eric constantly looked for shortcuts and tried to improve on systems that had been serving the toolroom well for many years. Frank had caught Eric a couple of times making small changes on his own—changes that Frank had previously vetoed when Eric first suggested them.

"When I clamped down on him, he got sullen. But people can't keep going behind your back and disobeying orders," Frank told Burt. "He's there to do a job—to do what he's told. What difference does it make to him how the work is done as long as he's well paid for the time he puts in?" Frank went on to explain that he didn't talk to Eric any more than he had to and that Eric didn't do any more work than was absolutely necessary to keep Frank off his back. When Frank did criticize, Eric was always ready with alibis. "I honestly don't know how a guy so dumb could come up with some of the stories he did. It didn't even sink into his thick skull when I refused his merit increase. Instead of straightening out, he got worse. That guy is a professional goldbricker," Frank said shaking his head. "You're welcome to him, Burt, and don't say I didn't give you fair warning."

Burt had found Eric to be a hard worker with an unusual interest in doing his job well. Eric's dedication had attracted Burt to him very soon after he had OK'd the transfer. Eric had been born in Germany but had come over at the age of five with his parents just before the Second World War. The war years and early postwar years were difficult for him because he was never sure that people trusted him. Close friendships were a luxury he never enjoyed. His father taught him respect for work and set an example for him in finding satisfaction in producing more than was expected of him. Eric found that satisfaction in the jobs he held until he came to work for Frank. He felt that Frank just wasn't interested in seeing him do a good job. Bitter feelings developed after Frank called him a "crazy kraut." Eric wanted to work for the company but confided in Burt that he would have quit if the transfer hadn't been approved. He said he couldn't work for a boss he couldn't respect.

Burt reflected, after Frank had left, that he had almost muffed the ball with Eric himself. After about a week on the job, Eric came to Burt with an idea for a bench fixture that he said he could knock out himself after hours. The fixture would save several motions and enable Eric to get more work out. Almost automatically, Burt started to reject the idea by telling Eric to get a little more experience before starting to change methods that were doing the job. By the time Eric finished his explanation, however, Burt could see the possibilities and gave him the green light.

A significant increase in Eric's output excited Burt and two other assemblers doing similar work. With Eric's proud permission, Burt had two more fixtures made and installed for the other two assemblers. Eric not only got his pat on the back from Burt but was recognized by several fellow employees who admired his idea. Ray Ford stopped by to observe the fixture. Burt had asked Ray to do this. Ray was so impressed that he sent Eric a commendatory letter the next day. Eric was beaming when he showed his letter to Burt. Watching Eric work, Burt wondered how Frank Connors could be so wrong about Eric. He was everything you could ask for in a production employee if you treated him right.

Maybe that last thought was what got Burt to thinking about Larry James again. Larry and Burt certainly weren't tuned in on the same wavelength this past week. Something had happened to Larry's attitude, but Burt couldn't put his finger on it. He had just about decided he'd call Larry in next week to get things out in the open.

Larry James was very quiet and serious, and a steady young black worker. His steadiness, general reliability, and quiet manner made it easy to overlook him or take him for granted. Burt, for this reason, hardly knew Larry. For example, he didn't know that Larry was very sensitive about never having finished high school. As a matter of fact, Burt didn't even know that Larry didn't have his high school diploma. He didn't know either that Larry was anxious to advance and worried a great deal about the handicap his lack of education and his race posed. Burt did know that Larry was inclined to be slow because everything had to be just right. Burt couldn't remember a single instance of any rejects or mistakes in Larry's work. Burt couldn't have known, then, that Larry had just made a personal decision to start going to night school to get his high school diploma. He couldn't have known because Larry didn't want to broadcast his deficiency by letting people know he was going back to school.

It was the very morning after he made the decision that getting ahead required his going back to school that Burt stopped by his workplace. Larry had just finished a job, and the inspector had OK'd it as Burt walked up. "That's the way, Larry, slow but sure," Burt said to him, intending the remark as a compliment to Larry's consistently high-quality work.

Larry, however, flushed and said, "Well, I do the best I can."

Burt responded with a smile and the comment, "That's what I mean. You're OK—keep it up." Burt didn't see the disappointment register on Larry's face as he walked away. He felt that Larry had the recognition coming and that he really should show more of his appreciation of Larry's work on an informal basis.

To Larry the props had just been cut out from under him. He interpreted Burt's comments as a double-barreled criticism of his work and wondered how much his limited education had to do with it. He knew how concerned Burt had been about production. It hurt, then, to have Burt tell him that he was slow. When anyone tried as hard as he had, Larry felt, just being told "You're OK" was a big letdown. Since he had been giving his best to the job, Larry began to think maybe he should look for a job where he could show up a little better. This concern, this worry, was reflected in Larry's attitude in the days that followed Burt's brief conversation with Larry.

There weren't any problems, any arguments, any changes in his output, but Burt could see and feel that something was bothering Larry. It was especially puzzling to Burt since the change came about right after he had taken the trouble to give Larry a pat on the back. Burt thought his comment had been a compliment. He was telling Larry that quality was just as important to him as quantity. To Burt, telling a man that he was OK was about as personal as you could get without getting sloppy. At least that was the way Burt felt. Burt never dreamed that their conversation had anything to do with whatever was bothering Larry. But he thought he still had better have a talk with Larry. "Funny," he said to himself, "how different two people can be. Paul Botts is almost the complete opposite of Larry."

Paul was a good employee, a worrier, and a talker. Paul's wife had for some time been having minor internal problems. Just this past week the decision had been made that surgery was the only course left. Naturally Paul was concerned about his wife even though their doctor assured them there was nothing to worry about. Another problem Paul had was how to take care of their three elementary school children during his wife's hospitalization. He told Burt that he had found a woman who could come when the kids got home for lunch and stay through the supper hour. He didn't think he could find or afford another woman to come in during the morning to help them dress and get their breakfast. The kids usually weren't up yet when Paul left for work at 6:30 A.M.

Burt had suggested that they work out a schedule for Paul whereby he would come at 8:30 A.M. and work the extra hour and a half at the end of the shift. Then the woman who was helping out would be there when the kids got home, and Paul wouldn't lose any money when he needed it most. Paul said that he appreciated Burt's thoughtfulness but didn't think Burt should make so much of an exception.

"If you do it for me, you'd have to do it for everybody, and I don't want to make problems for you," he told Burt.

"Look, Paul," Burt replied, "right now it's important to both of us that your family is taken care of and that your wife goes to the hospital without any worries about the kids or your job. If adjusting your schedule for a couple of weeks will do that, I'm glad I can help. Everyone in the department knows we have to keep regular working hours, so I don't think we're going to get any wholesale requests to change working hours. You're going to have your hands full with the job, keeping things going at home, and visiting your wife, so don't worry about my justifying an exception in your working hours. If there's any worry on that score let me do it. You just take care of mamma and the kids.''

Tears came to Paul's eyes as he thanked Burt and told him a guy couldn't have a better boss. It made Burt feel good. He hoped that he wouldn't get any objections from Ray Ford and the personnel department when he told them what he had done. He knew that if he had been in Paul's shoes, he would have appreciated the same consideration.

As he thought about how Frank Connors had handled Eric Mader, how he himself had nearly muffed the chance he had to let Eric show his stuff, how Larry was behaving since he complimented him, and how Paul Botts thought he couldn't have a better boss, Burt mentally conceded that understanding people was certainly a challenge for a supervisor. There just didn't seem to be any rules for handling people. But a man sure did have to think about his responsibilities for directing the people who worked for him.

1. How should supervisors develop a personal philosophy for handling the people in their departments?

2. Should supervisors have to get involved in the personal lives and problems of their people?

3. Obviously all people can't be treated alike, but what guidelines can members of management use in working with people?

4. What put Frank Connors, an experienced supervisor, so completely at odds with Eric Mader, who turned out to be a top-notch worker in Burt's department?

5. How should a good supervisor handle the problem Burt will face in calling Larry James in to clear the air?

6. How should we evaluate Burt's handling of Paul Botts?

7. What happens if we ignore our responsibility to treat people as individuals?

THE MANAGEMENT ATTITUDE TOWARD HUMAN RELATIONS

Many new supervisors are puzzled today at what their attitude toward human relations should be. We are confronted with a range of conflicting philosophies. At one extreme is the idea that people are our greatest asset and are to be treated with the utmost kindness and respect. At the other extreme is the idea that people are paid well to do a job and therefore should simply do what they are told. The situation is further confused because some managers give lip service to one philosophy and practice another.

Historically we have seen marked changes in management's approaches to human relations. Only a few decades ago, in the 1930s, the bull-of-the-woods philosophy prevailed. A foreman was usually the toughest man available. He was able to handle anyone who got out of line, and he gave orders with a "do it or else." An employee who questioned his approach was quickly informed that if he didn't like the way things were being run, there was always someone waiting to take his place. The labor market was a buyer's market, and employees couldn't afford to question anything. The foreman of that era certainly didn't have to worry about human relations. The words weren't even in his vocabulary.

In the late thirties and in the forties a number of things happened to shape a new way of thinking about the role of the individual in industry. The impact of the first significant social research at Western Electric's Hawthorne plant was making itself felt. The discovery, for example, that such changes as breaks in the workday could contribute to increased production opened many eyes. Further it was found that recognizing people as individuals and that separating groups for special study also contributed to healthier attitudes toward work.

The growth of unions put a few dents in the armor of the bull of the woods. The enabling legislation of the Wagner Act meant that employees' organizations became more and more a force to be reckoned with. Autocratic foremen saw their authority diluted and found that unfair treatment of employees resulted in costly grievances. The pressure of unions forced a reevaluation of our human relations practices.

The Second World War added still another dimension to our thinking and our management practices. With most able-bodied men in military service, we found our plants populated by housewives, young people of high school age, retired people, and men with physical limitations who were moved into more essential occupations. These people needed and usually received consideration of their individual problems in adjusting to the war effort. When "Johnny came marching home," more adjustments were needed—both on his part and on the part of those who were directing his work life.

Adding all these factors together, with the psychologists and human relations experts leading the way, the pendulum had swung completely away from the bull-of-the-woods philosophy to the other extreme. By 1950 the best label we could give to our thinking about human relations was "the era of sweetness and light." This was the period in which an employee could do no wrong. The objective of a supervisor was to keep people happy. Seldom was an employee's request refused. This attitude permeated top-management thinking as well. It wasn't uncommon for an executive to state that the primary objective of the company was to be a good corporate citizen, to provide employment, to provide a fair day's pay for a fair day's work, and to provide the best possible working conditions. These are admirable goals, but hardly the objective for being in business; the primary objective that we generally and honestly recognize today is to make a reasonable profit. In the long run all the goals mentioned above are possible only when the enterprise is making a profit and can support the best in personnel programs.

Today we are experiencing the return swing of the pendulum to a philosophy somewhere between the two extremes. We now openly recognize the profit motive for being in business. Managers clearly see their profit responsibilities not only to the stockholder but to the employee and community as well. The long-range welfare of the employee requires a growing profitable organization. The job of a supervisor is to contribute to profits and to help employees understand that they, too, have a responsibility to contribute to the profit picture.

This healthy concern for profit or budget control does not mean a return to the bull-of-the-woods philosophy. We haven't come all this way with our knowledge of what makes people work only to chuck it out the window in a program of cracking down on them. Truly management-minded supervisors will recognize the tremendous investment the company has in its work force and will treat subordinates with respect and dignity. They will also expect adherence to rules and established standards of performance. Personal popularity cannot be given priority over all other considerations.

An example of how easily the middle-of-the-road approach to human relations can be misunderstood occurred in a plant in New York. An outside consultant was conducting a series of training sessions for supervisors in a small plant. The leader had spelled out essentially the same points made in the introduction to this chapter. He concluded the first session by stressing the supervisor's responsibility to enforce plant rules and to see that standards of quality production were met. The next morning the plant manager was waiting for his training specialist with the question, "What in heaven's name did you say to George yesterday? He's turned into a tiger. Before the day ended I had two of his people in my office complaining about the unmerciful chewing-out he had given them without checking the facts or listening to explanations." George had interpreted the consultant's remark as the beginning of a new "get tough" policy and went at the job with gusto. He was determined that no one would brand him a wishy-washy supervisor. His impulsive behavior and lack of judgment had already been noticed. This most recent incident simply made it clear that George should not have been a supervisor, and he was eased out of his job within a month.

A part of the confusion about how to approach the human relations aspect of the supervisor's job stems from the fact that there is so much inconsistency in practice all around us. There are those who give lip service to considering individual problems and feelings while practicing the bull-of-the-woods approach. Others advocate the get-tough theory but never take a firm stand on anything. Almost any organization has its tyrants as well as those who just let things run themselves hoping it will all work out in the end. Most supervisors who are serious about wanting to do the best possible job as members of management eventually come to the realization that they must develop a personal philosophy about handling their people. When supervisors stop to think about their job and their people, they can generally agree on a number of approaches—approaches which should help fashion a philosophy.

1.   The job of managers is to get things done through people. No longer producers, their effectiveness is measured in terms of what subordinates produce.

2.   People are a very tangible asset in any organization and should be treated with consideration.

3.   Most employees expect to work, want to work, and are most satisfied in a department where they are producing. High production and high morale usually go hand in hand.

4.   To settle for less than employees are capable of giving is a failure to respect them as individuals.

5.   Employees look to a supervisor for direction, knowing full well that they must live as good citizens—adhering to rules and performing up to standards. Failure to get such direction can only result in a lack of respect for supervision.

6.   Employees by and large would rather please their bosses than displease them.

7.   For most people work is one of the most meaningful aspects

of their lives. They can find in work both dignity and personal
satisfaction, depending upon how the supervisor presents it
to them.

8. Individuals can control how hard they will work—indeed
    whether they will work at all. This raises the question of who
    really is the boss. The challenge facing supervisors is to
    create a climate in which people will want to continue to give
    their best.

Now the logic of the middle-of-the-road approach emerges more
clearly. To spite the individual needs of people, to treat them as tools,
and to follow a drivership policy makes employees resist proper
standards of performance through lack of interest, uncooperative
attitudes, tardiness, and absenteeism. To ignore the human side of
supervision, to pay no attention to human feelings, and to fail to provide
direction and leadership will frustrate employees as well as negate the
responsibilities accepted by managers.

UNDERSTANDING OTHERS STARTS
WITH UNDERSTANDING YOURSELF

Not long ago a supervisor who was highly regarded by her employees
confided to a friend, "Every time I'm tempted to criticize the work of
someone else, I ask myself if I have done anything to help create the
situation that needs correcting. More often than not, it changes my
whole approach to a more considerate one than I would otherwise have
used. Even when I have done nothing wrong, I have started to see the
situation from the viewpoint of the other person, and I force myself to
treat that person as a human being with feelings like my own." The
thought expressed here brings to mind something many psychologists
have stressed in trying to help managers understand people: To
understand others we must first try to understand ourselves. Perhaps
what tempered this supervisor's criticisms most was giving thought to
how she might receive such criticism herself. By identifying her own
feelings she forced herself to consider the feelings of others.

Gaining insight into our own behavior is commonly cited as a
primary objective of any seminar or institute on understanding people.
We acknowledge the value that comes in taking a good hard look at
ourselves. How, for example, are we as supervisors regarded by the
employees working under us? If they think highly of us, what have we
done to earn their respect? If we seem only to be tolerated, what in our

behavior has created such indifference? If they are outright antagonistic, can we find in our own attitudes and actions any cause for such feelings? Perhaps all three conditions exist with different individuals in the department. Can we then find reasons for the varying reactions to our supervision? Such questions are not meant to suggest that the fault for every problem lies within ourselves. Common sense dictates, however, that if it does, we are better equipped to deal intelligently with problems when we understand our own role in relation to them.

To recognize that we have definite attitudes about work, about supervision, about responsibility, and about praise and criticism is the first step in recognizing that all members of the organization have definite attitudes about the same things, although certainly not the same attitudes. We work toward the realization of our goals and ambitions just as everyone else does. The vigor with which we pursue our goals and the methods we use to pursue them will differ.

We should know our strengths and where we contribute most to the organization. Equally important is the need we have to take stock of our shortcomings and any limitations that might handicap our ability to supervise people. Are we particularly quick to lash out at one violation of rules and turn our back on another? Are we keenly sensitive to feelings of others, or are we inclined to expect people to do their work and leave their feelings at home? Do we have any bias or prejudice against nationality or racial groups, female employees, some political persuasions, religious sects, union activities, boisterous behavior, or gossip? Before any such limiting bias can be removed, it must first be recognized.

Most of us will acknowledge that a mark of a mature supervisor is the ability to adjust to difficult or unexpected situations—to make decisions without displays of irritation or temper. How well are we able to roll with the punches? What kind of leadership do we provide when the going gets rough? A part of understanding ourselves is gaining the insight which allows us to put our finger on the things that prevent us from using our better judgment. Again, if we can recognize these weaknesses in ourselves, we can better understand how others can be victims of similar emotional reactions. It's not hard to see, then, that a supervisor who controls his or her temper is better equipped to control problem situations. Most of us can think of a situation in which one party to a disagreement lost his or her temper while the other party maintained control. We know immediately that the person who kept temper under control also controlled the situation. At all times we have need as managers to be in control of ourselves whether we are dealing with people above or below us in the organizational hierarchy.

The late Dr. John Schindler of Monroe, Wisconsin, spent much of the later years of his life speaking to a wide variety of groups and individuals on how to live a fuller, richer life. Contained in his talks was some homely advice on how to achieve emotional maturity—advice that any of us who accept the responsibility for directing the work lives of others can benefit from. One of the things Dr. Schindler always started with was the suggestion that a necessary part of growing up emotionally was the development of an ability to assume responsibility independently of those around us. Our great need to develop a management-mindedness rests in part with this ability to develop a sense of independent responsibility—to view our jobs in terms of what we control.

Dr. Schindler also stressed that hostility, anger, belligerence, and aggressiveness are signs of weakness. How often have we seen people deluding themselves by shouting and displaying their temper as a means of showing who's boss? Dr. Schindler counseled that gentleness and kindness are our real strengths.

He frequently pointed out that maturity is in part the ability to distinguish fact from fancy. Every day we are challenged to exercise this ability—by rumors spread by the grapevine, by the feeling that persons are out to get us, by the temptation to worry about things that may never happen. He said that another quality of the mature person is flexibility and adaptability—finding and using the best solution in a problem situation. A simple system for doing this, he advised, was not to look back after a catastrophe, but to look ahead in order to decide how much good can be introduced into the future.

Many supervisors who have either heard Dr. Schindler speak or read his book say that what has helped them most in handling people was his statement that a mature person had a *giving* rather than a *receiving* attitude in relations with people. We have all read of people's needs to be loved, accepted, recognized, and respected. The immature person is constantly concerned with how to find satisfaction for these needs. The mature person, on the other hand, recognizes these needs in others and is concerned with what can be done to satisfy them. The beauty of this philosophy is that it frees us from much of the worry about how we're treated. We find that our needs are automatically satisfied by those who regard us as good people to work for. A supervisor interested in improving his or her ability to understand others and in deepening self-understanding would find Dr. Schindler's book *How to Live 365 Days a Year** well worth reading.

*Published by Prentice-Hall, Inc., Englewood Cliffs, N.J., 1954.

INDIVIDUAL DIFFERENCES

"Treat them all alike"—impossible, ridiculous, we say. No two people are ever exactly alike. They differ in thousands of ways. Twenty people working under us will have twenty different personalities—each requiring a different approach. Most of us will quickly acknowledge the truth of that statement, but how easy it is to forget it in the search for some quick and easy formula that will guide us through every situation. People are basically and irrevocably individualists at heart. Management-minded supervisors accept the idea that the better they know their people as individuals, the better equipped they are to deal with them.

One of the real pitfalls we face is to engage in "either-or" thinking about our people—the tendency to classify them in one of two extremes. For example, we might say that Bill is either smart or stupid; if he's not fast, he's slow; if he's not lazy, he's a hard worker; if he's not pleasant, he's a grouch. Frank Connors operated this way. He saw his people in terms of such extremes. Eric Mader was at various times in Frank's eyes lazy, stupid, stubborn, and a loudmouth. In some respects it's the easy way. People are automatically classified and pigeonholed. There's no problem trying to understand them—just one quick judgment and they're either for us or against us.

Burt, on the other hand, was showing some early signs of developing the awareness of people as individuals which will mark him as an understanding boss. He wondered why Eric Mader was so different from Frank's picture of him; he was puzzled by Larry's behavior; and he recognized that Paul Botts deserved special consideration. Recognizing that people are not all alike, that each has strengths and abilities, is the first step in understanding people. Burt's wondering why his people behaved the way they did put him on the threshold of seeing that personality is a reflection of all that a person has been, is, ever will be. Personality simply means the total person. How people react today is the result of everything that has ever happened to them. Our own personalities, for example, have been shaped over a lifetime by our parents, our teachers, clergymen, friends, groups we've been a part of, our bosses—a combination of experiences that has been uniquely our own.

Our particular concern is to recognize that an individual's set of values is the result of situations, training, and associations in which we have had no part. Why should Paul Botts have worried because Burt stuck his neck out to change his work schedule? It was no skin off his nose. What made Larry put a reverse interpretation on Burt's compliment? What made Eric a top producer for Burt and a goof-off for Frank

Connors? To be effective in dealing with these three, Burt needed to know something about them as individuals. Paul Botts made this easy. He was a talker. Larry, on the other hand, was quiet. Burt was the first to admit that he didn't know what made Larry tick. He really hadn't given him much thought at all. Larry was a stranger to Burt. Unless Burt gets to know Larry better—his hopes, his worries, his special problems—he will probably continue to misunderstand him.

Failure to know the people under us as individuals forces us into the position of having to base work assignments and personnel decisions on generalizations about people which are rarely valid. When we hire, we hire the person. That person's dreams, their family, interests, problems, values, abilities, and goals are all a part of the individual we place on the job. It is obvious that the better we are able to match a person's abilities and interests to the requirements of the job, the more productive he or she is likely to be. But too often that's where we stop. What do we know of where anyone wants to be in five years, of what hopes he or she has for his or her children, of what values have been shaped by parents, the church, and other supervisors? Until we know and understand some of these, we don't really know the person.

PERCEPTION AND SUPERVISION

By perception we mean the meaning or interpretations we attach to the people and situations we face. We look at others in terms of our own values. We see the world in the light of our own needs and interests—our likes and dislikes. No two people see things exactly the same way. Again, for example, we have seen Eric Mader through the eyes of Frank Connors as a loud, lazy troublemaker. From Burt's point of view, Eric was eager, hard-working, enthusiastic, and pleasant. The same man was perceived in entirely different ways by different supervisors. Larry and Paul certainly didn't see Burt in the same light.

Before we can understand the interpretations others place on our actions, we must first understand how we arrive at our own interpretations. As managers we have a reasonably clear understanding of the need for quality production and profit. We have accepted these management objectives as our own. If anything interferes with the realization of those goals, how are we to interpret it? How, for example, do we view a methods engineer who wants to disrupt a production sequence to try out a new idea? How about a key employee who stays home with a cold? How about a grievance which gets everybody talking? Certainly our own needs will color our evaluation of such incidents. We can be just as certain, however, that the other party in each situation will have perceptions similarly influenced by personal needs. Unless we recognize how such attitudes are developed in others, dealing with the dynamics of human relations can be extremely frustrating. A lack of sensitivity to the feelings of others results in snap judgments and inconsiderate treatment.

We have all known people who bragged about their ability to size up a person in a hurry. "Just give me a minute with him, and I'll have him pegged," they'll say. Anyone with an ounce of common sense will know that this is impossible, but we are frequently confused when these people say they have an almost perfect batting average. The fact we overlook is that people who make such boasts usually have the means to make them come true. Once a job candidate is sized up as just what we've been looking for, it's easy to overlook his or her mistakes to substantiate our judgment. On the other hand, when we have pegged people as no good from the start, they have an uphill battle because we can so easily find fault. One of the real dangers in making snap judgments is that those same judgments tend to make us inflexible in handling people. We can so easily see in the behavior of others what we want to see.

Out of this tendency to look for what we want to see grows the temptation to look for our own image in people. Managers have frequently been accused of promoting those who operate the way they do. A biographical article on a major college's football coach illustrated the point. In the article his days as a high school and college player were described in terms of personal hardship—his father died at an early age; he was partly responsible for supporting his mother and family; he had a tough time making ends meet, etc. Because a prime responsibility of a big-time coach is recruiting, the interviewer asked his subject what he looked for in boys when he was considering them. The coach responded, "I look for a boy who's had a tough time, who hasn't had things handed to him all his life. I look for a kid who's hungry." He might just as well have said that he wanted boys who grew up the way he did because they make better players.

Above all we should be aware of the need for caution in judging people and their actions. It's important that we recognize the dreams, ideals, values, and feelings of others in directing their work lives and interpreting their behavior. We should not automatically ascribe to employees—or to superiors—the motivations, needs, and desire that we have. The best route we can follow in exercising this caution is to develop what many successful and management-minded supervisors regard as the single most important trait of a manager—empathy.

EMPATHY IN SUPERVISION

In previous chapters we accepted as a definition of empathy the ability to put ourselves in the other person's shoes and see things from his or her point of view. We should recognize that empathy does not mean giving in to people or using a wishy-washy approach to management. To understand the reason why a person takes a stand does not necessarily mean that we agree with that stand, but it does equip us to deal more effectively with a person even though we may disagree with him or her. Empathy enables us to consider viewpoints other than our own.

In working with people who are bothered by personal problems, the ability to empathize is of special value to the supervisor. I am using "empathy" to mean an ability to appreciate the feelings and the needs of others without becoming emotionally involved yourself. It is not exactly a sharing of the feelings of a troubled person; for sharing feelings may color our judgment. I am thinking of a somewhat more detached attitude—an attitude that says, "I know how you feel; I know why you feel. I understand."

The ability to empathize can be particularly helpful to the supervisor in areas of discipline, labor relations, and grievance handling. All too often emotion-laden charges and countercharges fly back and forth. If we can see the reason behind the charges, understand the feelings, and proceed along a reasonable course which keeps us in command, we are in a stronger position. Most of us would agree that this approach is better than trying to shout an adversary down with the arbitrary use of authority. When one party can empathize, more often than not an effective compromise can be reached without injury to the feelings of either.

A supervisor attending a human relations institute related an incident which demonstrated how her boss was able to empathize without ever knowing the meaning of the word. The supervisor had only been in the position for five or six months. She was uncertain of how much she could open up with the boss. So she stewed and fretted a couple of weeks about a problem she had until she got up enough nerve to have it out with "the old man." Then one morning, with knees knocking, she stood in the doorway to the boss's office and asked for a few minutes to discuss a problem. The boss looked up, invited the young supervisor in, and got out of his chair to meet her. As they met in front of the desk, the boss pointed to his own chair and motioned the supervisor to sit down saying, "Tell me about it, but I want you to see it from that side of the desk." While the new supervisor was trying to recover and collect her thoughts, the boss plunked down in his visitor's chair, saying,

"And I'll try to see it from your point of view." Relating the incident to the institute group, the supervisor said that the action completely took the wind out of her sails, that the problem totally resolved itself, and that the boss was a man she highly respected from that point on. "It's one thing" she said, "to have your head screwed around 180 degrees, but the real thing was to know he was willing to try to see my side of the problem. You can't help respecting a person like that."

During a plant supervisory training series that met once a week, the subject of empathy was introduced and discussed. The conference leader sensed that the concept had been taken to heart, but he didn't realize how much with one supervisor until the following week. Ten minutes before the meeting was to start, she sauntered into the conference room and said to the instructor, "Hey, Jim, you remember talking about empathy last week? Well, I went home and tried it on my husband. It works!" Of course it works. It works anywhere, anytime. It's simply a matter of giving consideration to others. Who among us doesn't respond positively to having our feelings and viewpoints being given consideration? That's why we find this ability to empathize important not only to supervisors, but to husbands, wives, salespeople, executives, teachers, and clergymen. Whenever we find ourselves in contact with others, the need for empathy exists.

Psychologists tell us there is a reason for all behavior—not always a rational, recognizable reason, but a reason. The challenge facing us as supervisors is to try to understand the reason why our people behave the way they do instead of labeling their actions as unreasonable. Actually, when we stop to think about it, anytime we say people are unreasonable, we are confessing our inability to see the reason for their acts or statements. Have any of us ever done anything unreasonable in our lives? Of course not. We have done things we have been sorry for. We have made mistakes. But seldom, if ever, have we done anything without reason. Unreasonableness is always from the standpoint of the observer. Other people are unreasonable—not me! Empathy challenges us to look for the reasons why people do and say the things they do. Had Frank Connors been able to empathize with Eric Mader, he might have gotten some insight into Eric's wish to improve the work methods he was using and thus have found himself with a crackerjack employee.

As supervisors, we can empathize, or we wouldn't hold the positions we do. We can't be managers and be completely insensitive to the feelings of others. We practice empathy as naturally as we smile or shake the hand of a new acquaintance. The real test is to practice empathy deliberately, knowingly. When we get upset with a person's behavior, can we ask ourselves what's the reason for such behavior? If someone makes an unreasonable demand of us, can we find their reason? Doing so may help us sell our reasons for having to refuse. It's amazing what we can discover about people if we make ourselves sensitive to their feelings, their attitudes, their needs.

Empathy can make our lives fuller and richer by showing us where we can make contributions to those around us. To be able to settle an argument rather than prolong it, to be able to shed light on a perplexing problem, to be able to prevent a grievance, to be able to recognize special effort—these are the rewards of conscientiously doing our best to empathize. As Burt Hall did when he adjusted Paul Botts's work schedule, empathizing is managing with a heart.

WHAT SHOULD SUPERVISORS KNOW ABOUT EMPLOYEES?

We can see that it is easier to practice empathy with those we know best. Or as we have observed before, the better we know people as individuals, the better equipped we are to deal with them. But what, we might ask, is it important for me to know about my employees? Leaving out all the sentimental details and getting down to practical everyday worthwhile information, what should we know? This question is asked of about fifteen supervisory institute groups a year at the University of Wisconsin. The response of hundreds of successful supervisors who have given very serious thought to this question makes up the following list of things we would do well to know about each of our people.

Family

An individual is his or her family. Geographical separation of that person at work does not remove him or her in thought from that family. With most people one of the easiest ways to hit a responsive chord in opening up a conversation is talk about their family. Let's think for a moment about some of the people who work for us. How many of them would show greater pride in the accomplishments of their children than in their own performance? To know something about a person's family is to know a great deal about the individual. Is he or she married? How many children does he or she have? What are their names and ages? What schools do they attend? What things does the family enjoy doing together? The number of employees working under each of us would naturally limit how much information we could profitably gather and keep, but just raising the questions suggests to us how much better we could get to know our people.

Education

With the increasing emphasis being placed on education today, we find it more and more important to know something about a person's educational accomplishments. This emphasis is certain to increase in the years to come. Matching people's training to their work is only one reason for our concern. If a person is taking night school or vocational courses while on the job, that may well indicate an interest in a better job and a willingness to work at improving his or her worth. Most companies now require at least a high school diploma before they will consider a person for a supervisory position. In many cases a college degree is a necessity for promotion. In guiding and counseling employees on their careers with the company it is necessary to know their educational backgrounds. What a mistake it would be, for example, to encourage a person's supervisory aspirations without detailing the company's educational requirements. To overlook the technical education of people in our department when better jobs open up is shortsighted. Many of us consider it an obligation to encourage additional training for those who seem in other ways to have the potential for higher-rated, more responsible jobs.

Work Experience

Where have our people worked previously? What skills and abilities do we have in our work group that might be more profitably utilized? Are job training plans geared to the previous experience of the trainee? What does the pattern of previous employment tell us? Has performance been good? Is there a pattern of job-hopping or making trouble?

Outside Interests

We often find a clue to understanding a person better in knowing the things that interest him or her off the job. If nothing else, knowing an employee's interests may help us establish a communication bridge with that employee. Is he or she an avid baseball, football, hockey, or golf fan? Is the employee a spectator, a participator, or both? Undoubtedly there are a number of do-it-yourself handymen just looking for the opportunity to discuss their latest project with us. The person who takes the family camping during vacations and weekends wants to talk about it. Often these conversations give us insight into what kind of people are working for us. In addition to letting us learn more about individuals, our willingness to listen shows that we have an interest in them as more than just a means to get out production.

Goals and Ambitions

How much do we really know about what our people want out of life? Do they want just steady jobs with no worries? Do they want to move into more highly skilled work? Do they want supervisory or higher-management positions? We really don't know people until we know what they want to do with their lives. One of the most satisfying aspects of our job can be the encouragement, the stimulation, and the coaching we give to a person who wants to carve out a career in our firm.

Other Information

Individual supervisors may disagree at this point about how much more we should be expected to know about individuals in order to understand them. Each of us in the long run will have to determine what we think we must know about those who work for us. But we might consider what other supervisors have indicated they want to know. Here are some of them: birthdays; anniversary dates of employment or promotions; financial status; religious beliefs and affiliations; community activities; personal problems; politics; hobbies; union loyalties; personal habits; attitudes toward company, work, and supervision; nationality; and countless other things that make a person an individual. Many of us will recognize that we're beginning to touch on some extremely sensitive areas. In fact, some state laws forbid asking about such things as religious affiliation. On the other hand, knowing that a person's religious affiliation affects an attitude toward profanity in the shop or office is helpful. Occasional profanity may be a part of our vocabulary, but few of us would use it in talking to a person who might take offense. It isn't the possession of such information that can create problems, but the unwise or prejudicial use of it or reaction to it.

An example of how seemingly unimportant facts about a person can help a supervisor appeared in an evaluation of a supervisory training program in a Wisconsin paper mill. One supervisor was relating applications he had made of material discussed in the meetings, and he said that he had made good use of the idea of recognizing the birthdays of his employees. His department was the wood yard. Whenever one of the men had a birthday, the supervisor walked out to see him and wished him well. His approach was tuned to the personalities of the men working for him. He might walk up to one man and say, "Hey, Jughead, how does it feel to be another year older?" He might say to another, "You know, Smokey, I'd like to give you the day off, but I can't, so happy birthday anyhow." The point is, he wasn't corny about it, and he did get a positive response from even the toughest of the gang.

DEPARTMENT ROSTER

Name	Birth-day	Family and Dependents	Education	Work Experience	Outside Interests and Goals	Miscel-laneous

FIGURE 5

Another supervisor attending the same meetings reported that he had nearly stopped attending when it was suggested that supervisors recognize employees individually on their birthdays. "How stupid can you get?" he asked. "I'll be damned if I'm going to go out and wish my guys a happy birthday."

In order to empathize deliberately and knowingly, we need to know as much about employees as we can. Their attitudes, their needs, their feelings, their behavior are the dynamic expressions of personality, and personality is the product of everything that has ever happened to an individual. We can never begin to know everything there is to know about a person, but the more we know, the better we are able to empathize.

Many supervisors have found it helpful and revealing to take inventory of what they really do know about their people. Taking inventory is quite simple and not very time-consuming. The first step is to make a list of those things we feel it's important to know about the people working for us. Then we might use a roster of names of those who work for us, and fill in as many "must know" items as possible. Some of us may find that we know our people better than we realize. Others may find that we have strangers working for us; but in this situation we have already given ourselves some direction in getting to know our people better.

USING A SYSTEM

It helps to have some kind of system to keep the desirable information about employees where we can get at it quickly. The form of the system isn't really as important as having some organized way of recording pertinent information about people. Some supervisors have used an index card for each person, keeping on it the vital statistics for quick handy reference. Some use a loose-leaf notebook for the same purpose. The blank departmental roster shown in Figure 5 is another example of how important personal details can be recorded. Whenever a useful bit of information is picked up in conversation, the supervisor makes a note of it as soon as he can.

The information kept in such a record is not "black book" information that we might not want anyone to see. It is, rather, facts which will be helpful to us in future contacts with employees. Some of us may be inclined to think of such a record as a lot of unnecessary paper work, but consider the value it would have at a time when discussions of a personal nature with an employee are necessary—as in reviewing performance, discussing transfers or promotion, counseling on a personal problem, assigning special projects, or disciplining. If reviewing the record just before such a discussion did no more than start us thinking of that employee as an individual with feelings, dreams, and desires, the record would have served its purpose.

We should consider how to gather information for such a record. Obviously it's not a good idea to take a blank departmental roster out on the floor and start interviewing employees, explaining to them that you read in a book that it was a good idea to get such information. What we need can be gathered from a number of sources over a long period of time.

Listening to employees is probably the best single source of information about their family, their interests, their ambitions. Just a few minutes of listening to a person talk about the family can be tremendously revealing. Provide the opportunity for listening, then. In addition to providing information, listening to a person shows respect for him or her as an individual.

Personnel department records provide another valuable source of such information as dependents' names and ages, home ownership, educational background, previous work experience, wage adjustments, hobbies, and memberships in lodges. The personnel department has proved to many supervisors to be an ideal place for starting such a system because it has so much information immediately available.

Performance reviews with employees are another excellent means of learning more about them, especially if they are encouraged to speak out. Many of us know supervisors who feel that the performance review is their show and that they must do all the talking. Yet we can't learn while we're doing all the talking. Finding out how an employee feels about his or her supervisor, job, and future with the company might very well be an added objective of a periodic performance review. This should be a time when employees can get things off their chest and plan with the supervisor how to perform in the months to come.

Company-sponsored social and recreational activities provide an opportunity to see the employee outside the work setting. Bowling, golf, softball, and dartball leagues are examples. Picnics and Christmas parties give us the chance to meet the families of our employees and—perhaps more important—gives them the chance to meet us.

Supervisors living in small and medium-sized communities have yet another valuable source of information—the daily newspaper. One burly foreman volunteered in a seminar discussion that he regularly read the society page in the paper first. To look at him, most of us would have guessed the society page to be the last thing he would ever read. Coming from a community with a population of 15,000, he said that hardly a week went by that he didn't read that an employee's wife or child had gotten some honor, served on a committee, or taken part in a community or social event. He said he always made it a point to see that person the next day and talk to him briefly. He found the sport page similarly helpful.

In summary, the management-minded supervisor should recognize his or her responsibility to represent the company to its employees. The employees certainly know how they want the company to treat them. Each employee has the right to expect the same from the supervisor. Employee relations, after all, are just another way of finding out how employees feel toward management. Members of management have an obligation to understand and treat their people as individuals, according them the respect which is their due. Certainly, higher management expects no less of the management-minded supervisor.

HIGHLIGHTS

1.   Management attitudes and philosophies on human relations have changed from the bull-of-the-woods approach to the era of sweetness and light, and then to a middle-of-the-road approach which recognizes the employee as a valuable asset who is to be treated

with respect but who is expected to contribute to a profitable enterprise.

2. Understanding people in the organization begins with self-understanding. When we begin to recognize our own feelings and attitudes and how we got them, we can move to an awareness of the impact of feelings on the behavior of others.

3. Emotional maturity or stability, according to Dr. John Schindler, is a matter of:

   a. Developing a sense of independent responsibility
   b. Recognizing that anger and hostility are signs of personal weakness
   c. Being able to distinguish fact from fancy
   d. Developing a giving rather than a receiving attitude toward life and toward others

4. Failure to know employees as individuals forces us into the position of having to base work assignments and personnel decisions on generalizations about people which are rarely valid.

5. Empathy, the ability to put ourselves in another's place and see things from his or her point of view, is regarded by many as the single most important trait of a management-minded supervisor. Most of us empathize without thinking about it. It's tougher, but more important, to empathize knowingly and deliberately when faced with difficult situations.

6. To understand employees better as individuals, we should know something about:

   a. Their family life
   b. Their education
   c. Their past work experience
   d. Their outside interests
   e. Their goals and ambitions

7. It's a good idea to use some kind of system, such as a departmental roster, to record information which will be helpful in getting to know employees better. Information for such records can be gleaned from:

   a. Listening to people
   b. Personnel records
   c. Personal observation
   d. Performance reviews
   e. Local newspapers

DISCUSSION QUESTIONS

1. Is there a bull of the woods in your organization today? Without naming him or her, describe some of the attitudes that make that person a bull of the woods.

2. Which demands more knowledge of human relations—the bull-of-the-woods approach, sweetness-and-light approach, or middle-of-the-road approach? Explain your answer.

3. Explain this statement in your own words: "To settle for less than an employee is capable of giving is a failure to respect him or her as an individual."

4. Describe a supervisor you know or have known who practiced empathy. Cite some examples.

5. Discuss why a supervisor should know something about the department's employees' families, children, hobbies, goals, ambitions, and outside interests in order to work more effectively with them.

6. List what you feel a supervisor should know about people. Then take the names of six employees you know (your own, if you're supervising now) and take inventory. How many of the things you said it is important to know do you actually know about those six? How about your whole department?

7. Set up a departmental roster similar to the one shown in Figure 5. List five employees, and compile the desired information either by talking with each employee or by consulting records, or do both. Next, list your whole department, and do the same thing.

CASE PROBLEMS

THE CASE OF ART BELLMAN

"I just can't figure her out," Art Bellman, supervisor of First National Bank's operations department, was telling his wife. "She says she wants responsibility so she can be promoted, but every time I ask her to do something a little out of the ordinary she squawks. She says I'm taking advantage of her because she's a woman. I think she's in her change.

"All I'm trying to do is give her a chance to show what she's capable of. For ten years she's been content to do clerical work, now suddenly she wants to move up. I don't think she's capable of any more than she's doing, but suddenly she's determined she's not going to be held down in this 'man's world' anymore. If Grace Conway wants any help from me she had better get off my back and stop shouting feminist accusations at me. I can't understand what gets into a woman like her—almost forty years old, no husband, no kids, no responsibility, and she wants to be an executive. Could be what she needs is a man!''

1. What kind of help should Art be giving Grace?

2. Evaluate Art's attitude toward Grace.

THE CASE OF ELLEN GRANER

Reviewing her first full week as a supervisor, Ellen Graner, pharmacy supervisor in the Metro-Medical Center and Hospital, thought it could be worse; but she knew she had a lot further to go than she thought at first. Ellen expected the men to resent taking orders from a woman, but they seemed to respect her knowledge and accept her as boss. Perhaps it was because she had been very cautious in how she gave orders to them.

Her women employees were another matter. Ellen had assumed no problem with them—after all she was the most qualified and the logical one for the job. They should be happy a woman had been recognized and promoted. Yet they seemed to resent her—nothing overt—just a coolness that suggested they were less than enthusiastic about having her as their supervisor.

Where Ellen had felt a closeness with several of the young women in the past, there was now an invisible barrier that kept her at a distance. She guessed that she really didn't know them as well as she thought she did. The friendliness that she was so sure would assure her success as a supervisor was strained now, and she wondered if she could ever really be one of them again.

Ellen had never been aware that the whole department, including herself, had been so lax in adhering to rules. Late starting, personal phone calls, overstaying coffee and lunch breaks, and frequent extended chatting she now realized were going to have to be attended to.

"If they don't like me now, what will happen when I start to enforce the rules? Where do I go from here?''

1. What might explain Ellen's being accepted by the men in the department and not the women?

2. How should Ellen go about winning the trust and confidence of her women employees?

3. How should Ellen approach the problem of tightening up on the rules?

THE CASE OF ALICE CENTER

"How unreasonable can she be?" Alice Center, office manager of the State Building Contractors Association, asked herself after Dorothy Rammer outright refused to work overtime. It was just a few days before the annual convention and there were still a million details to be arranged.

"She knows convention time is the busiest time of the year. She was told when we hired her two years ago that the two weeks leading up to the convention are hectic and that everybody has to work long hours," Alice lamented. Dorothy had also been told that personal considerations had to be set aside to assure a smooth-running convention.

"Why does she pull this stuff when we need her most? She's our best worker when she's here and if she won't work everybody else will resent working even longer hours to pick up her share of the load. I just can't accept 'personal reasons' to justify her not accepting her responsibilities. You wouldn't think a forty-year-old widow with teenage children would find a date so important. Or is it a date? She surely needs the money. She's told me that often enough. Why does she have to be so unreasonable? I'd hate to fire her, but what choice do I have?"

1. What choices does Alice have?

2. What would you do with Dorothy if you were Alice?

3. Prepare to handle the situation.

SUGGESTIONS FOR FURTHER STUDY

Bittel, Lester R., *What Every Supervisor Should Know*, 3d ed., Chapter 2, McGraw-Hill Book Company, New York, 1974.

Schindler, John A., *How to Live 365 Days a Year*, Prentice-Hall, Inc., Englewood Cliffs, N.J., 1954.

Shout, Howard F., *Start Supervising*, Chapter 4, Bureau of National Affairs, Inc., Washington, D.C., 1972.

Steinmetz, Lawrence L., and H. Ralph Todd, Jr., *First-Line Management*, Chapter 5, Business Publications, Inc., Dallas, Texas, 1975.

Vernon, Ivan R., *First-Line Management*, Chapter 5, Society of Manufacturing Engineers, Dearborn, Michigan, 1972.

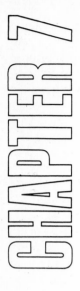

CHAPTER 7

MOTIVATING IMPROVED PERFORMANCE

THE CASE OF
MOTIVATING
MIKE MORAN

Young Mike Moran had Burt Hall baffled. How can you accuse one of your better producers of loafing on the job? Yet that's what Burt had to do. Ever since taking over Assembly Department B Burt had had his eye on Mike. In fact, long before he became a supervisor, Burt had noticed the way Mike worked—and didn't work.

An exceptionally friendly and talkative young man, Mike bothered Burt by his frequent practice of stopping his whole crew to tell them a joke or a story. It didn't bother Mike that it was during working hours or that anybody might be watching. He just seemed to enjoy telling stories and being the center of attention. The trouble was that the rest of his gang enjoyed him, too. That's what made it tough to clamp down—there was no chance of using group pressure on him, for Burt had tried that with a marked lack of success.

Soon after he took over the department, Burt was determined to straighten that crew out, but he waited a couple of months before moving in. Because Mike was such a friendly guy, Burt was sure that he'd have no problem motivating him to get on the ball. The crew was on a group incentive. It shouldn't be hard, Burt thought at the time, to get them to see how much they were losing by standing around and talking. He waited for an opportune time to launch his campaign. One afternoon Burt heard the whole crew burst out laughing while he was standing nearby checking a job. As Burt walked over, Mike was holding the floor, telling of one of his escapades. Mike held the complete attention of the crew—all were enjoying his performance. No one seemed to mind that Burt had joined the group. Mike acknowledged Burt's arrival with a smile and a nod, but continued with his story. Burt interrupted by asking if anything was wrong.

Mike caught the inference in Burt's question. Speaking for the crew, he assured Burt nothing was wrong and explained that he was telling them about his last date. Sensing that Burt was annoyed, he also added that it could wait and that they would get busy. Mike, without question, was the informal leader of the crew. He had no official designation as leader, but the crew followed him just as surely as if he carried the plant manager's title.

Mike's crew produced extremely well. When they worked—and that certainly was most of the time—they couldn't be equaled in their output. Burt had no quarrel with their total production: they were comfortably ahead of the other crews doing the same work. But the frequent nonscheduled breaks for storytelling did bother Burt. He reasoned that their production could be even better if they would stick to business. Their nonproductive time could be converted into badly needed production. Further, if they kept busy, they wouldn't be setting a poor example for the other crews and the rest of the department. Mike was the pacesetter for the crew, so Burt decided to start on him. The next morning he asked Mike to stop by the office during the break.

Burt started out by explaining that he wanted to talk about idle time. No sooner were the words out of his mouth than Mike asked if their production record was slipping. Burt had to acknowledge that it wasn't, but he said, "Mike, think of the money you could be making if you'd cut out the storytelling and keep that crew busy."

"What good is money if you can't enjoy it?" Mike asked. "I've seen too many people, my old man included, sweat their whole life away to rake in money. When they finish, what have they got?—A lot of miserable years and no way of knowing how to enjoy what's left. No sir, Burt, life is too short to spend every minute of it trying to make more dough. I want to enjoy myself. Now—while I can. Tomorrow will take care of itself. We'll keep up our end of production, but don't ask me to go around with a long face trying to squeeze out that last drop of blood.

We've got a good producing crew. We'll see you get a fair day's output.''

''I didn't mean for you to drive them,'' Burt apologized. ''I just meant that the time you spend horsing around could be put to better use. You could be making more money without working any harder—just steadier. You can still enjoy working, but you'll never get ahead if you don't take things more seriously. We're all here to produce. It looks like hell to have your crew sitting around gabbing when they should be working.''

''OK, Burt,'' Mike said. ''We'll quiet down. If we aren't keeping up our end of production, you let us know.''

The conversation hadn't gone exactly the way Burt wanted it to. He didn't anticipate that Mike would react the way he did to the chance of making more money. Things did improve for a while, but in a week or so the old pattern was right back where it had been. Burt decided that if he couldn't get to Mike, he would work around him. One at a time, he arranged to talk to Dave Braun, Gladys Reed, and Manny Hill. The fifth member of the crew, Jane Shands, was relatively new, and Burt didn't think he should involve her.

The reactions of Dave, Gladys, and Manny were the same. They all felt that it would be nice to be making more money. On the other hand, their incentive earnings were pretty good—better than those of the other crews. Besides, it was a lot of fun working with Mike. Each said they would try to buckle down and cut down on the talking. But the pattern of response repeated itself—first some improvement would be made, and then they gradually went back to their old habits. Burt was convinced that it wasn't malicious. They were doing a fine job on production. It was frustrating, though, to keep knocking your head against a wall without getting any results.

As much as anything, Burt was worried about the appearance of things. He often wondered how he would explain how the crew could sit around laughing and talking if Oscar Palmer should happen to walk through while Mike was spinning one of his yarns. Even if they were producing well, it would be hard to justify a party on the job. It might be even worse if some other high-ranking executive walked through at the wrong time.

Burt was puzzled by his failure to motivate any of the crew. Why didn't they respond to the carrot he held out for them? Isn't everybody interested in more money? He remembered how he worked to make out and how it paid off. He remembered, too, how pleased his wife was with the increase he got when he was made supervisor. Yet Mike showed no interest at all, and the rest of them were interested but apparently not enough to put any pressure on Mike to stop horsing around. If a supervisor couldn't motivate his people with money, what in heaven's name was left?

Since it was obvious to Burt that he couldn't solve his problem by holding out the financial incentive to Mike and that his chance of forcing the issue with disciplinary action was not good, he searched his brains for alternatives. The only thing he could come up with was the possibility of using Mike as a utility man—transferring him to other crews. Maybe he could use Mike to spark higher productivity on other crews. There was no denying that Mike was a leader and that when he worked, he took everyone with him. The trouble with that approach was the risk of having Mike spread his practice of playing around. At least the way it was now, Mike infected only one crew. Perhaps containment was a wiser policy. But if Mike could stimulate higher production, it would really help. "With Mike's seniority, he couldn't be forced into a utility position," Burt thought. "You'd have to motivate him, and I'm right back where I started. It's a puzzlement."

Mike Moran had Burt Hall baffled!

1. How can we justify Burt's concern about Mike Moran—did he really have a problem?

2. What might be some of the reasons Burt failed to motivate Mike to buckle down?

3. If the rest of the crew really wanted more money, why didn't they keep things going when Mike stopped to tell his stories?

4. Burt felt that if a supervisor couldn't motivate his people with money, there wasn't much left. What else does a supervisor have to motivate his employees?

THE MANAGEMENT-MINDED SUPERVISOR AND MOTIVATION

Several of the conclusions reached in previous chapters point up the need for skill in motivating employees to improve their performance. First, supervisors have accepted the responsibility for high-quality production at the lowest possible cost. We have agreed also that their effectiveness as supervisors is measured not in terms of what they produce but in terms of what others produce. We know that the management process requires skill in planning, organizing, motivating, controlling, and innovating. Thus we can see that the ability to motivate is a key skill for a supervisor. In fact, that's really what this whole book is about. In succeeding chapters we'll consider such areas as training employees, using discipline, handling grievances, giving orders, and innovating. Behind each of these subjects is the challenge of getting people to do what we want them to do, and that's what we mean by motivation.

Having been placed in the management position that is in direct contact with the production employee, the supervisor is strategically situated to use motivational practices which will have the greatest payoff. No one is in a better position to creat a climate conducive to high worker production. Without fear of exaggeration we can say that the supervisor has greater control over the factors that motivate employees than any single management group. This control is both a promise and a demanding challenge. Certainly, we can recognize that a supervisor who can motivate effectively will not only advance in the organization, but will advance the organization itself.

The supervisor's responsibility for motivating employees is shared with higher management. Supervisors have no control over policies in the areas of wages, labor relations, expenditures for physical working conditions, and long-range planning. It cannot be denied that these policies do influence the motivational climate in which the supervisor works. But, as we shall see, their effect on employees is limited when it comes to stimulating an attitude of dedication to the job. The factors that supervisors alone control through day-to-day contact have much more far-reaching effects on the striving of an individual to give his or her best to the job. Higher management has the obligation to provide a base of fair wages and working conditions, stable employment, and competitive fringe-benefit programs. Above that base, supervisors continue to fashion the environment in which people work. They carry their management's desire to provide a healthy climate in which to work to the place where the work is done. To be truly management-minded, supervisors need to understand the motivational factors that they control. This we shall try to do through an examination of commonsense experiences and recent research on employee motivation.

Let's begin with a definition of motivation. We might say that to motivate means to move. Management, however, is concerned with the direction of that movement. We can motivate negative as well as positive behavior. The dictionary says that to motivate is to provide with a motive. That definition, too, is lacking for our purposes, since we might say that salary does that. Dwight Eisenhower was credited with saying that, "Leadership is the ability to get a person to do what you want him to do, when you want it done, in a way you want it done, because he wants to do it." Here, it seems, we come much closer to defining the challenge that motivation poses for us.

First we should pay attention to the words "what you want him to do." There is no suggestion here of our abandoning responsibilities to management. A supervisor's responsibilities are to direct the work of the department and to insist on adherence to standards of performance. To be able to do this in such a way that individual employees want to achieve the same results is the really tough part of the job. The supervisor needs to know the wants of employees in the work situation, the skill of communicating the objectives or goals of the organization to them, and the ability to make them accept those goals as their own. Making employees want to do the job the way we want it done will serve as a definition for what we mean by motivation.

If we accept that definition of motivation, we establish a need to know what employees want from their job. Or, to put it another way, we need to know what will make them want to do their best work with a minimum of supervision. For every generalization we make about people, any of us can cite a number of exceptions. But we will have to make some general statements, and each of us will have to determine individually to whom they do not apply and why.

By and large, people want to work. Working gives meaning to their lives and satisfies their need to accomplish something of worth. It is unfortunate when people can't find this satisfaction in their work, because they will then seek it in other areas of their lives. People want to be respected for what they know and for what they feel as well as for what they do. The bull of the woods usually fails to recognize this. Most people who accept the goals and objectives of the organization will control their own performance with very little supervision. Part of the skill of motivating employees, then, is skill in selling departmental goals to the individual. Many employees who fully understand their roles in the success of an enterprise will seek responsibility rather than run from it. The supervisor's job becomes, essentially, one of trying to mesh the individual's needs with the goals of the department and the overall organization. To the extent that supervisors can demonstrate to employees (notice we said *demonstrate*, not *tell*) that what is wanted most from the job will be realized through excellent performance, they will be successful in motivating them.

We took note in the previous chapter of the fact that most employees would rather please their boss than displease him or her. Most of us have had occasion to doubt that statement, but a few moments of careful reflection convinces us of its truth. For example, Burt Hall may have felt that Mike Moran and the rest of his crew didn't give two hoots about his feelings. Yet, who for a moment would attribute to likable Mike a desire to displease Burt? How many of us, for that matter, believe that supervisors have any desire to displease any of their workers or make them unhappy? Knowing employees' desire to do work of which they can be proud and their desire to please the boss, we can look toward the problem of what they want from their jobs.

THE MOTIVATIONAL DRIVES OF EMPLOYEES

Most, if not all, of our behavior is directed toward satisfying some need or want. Such needs change and vary in intensity. They can be very small, such as stopping at a water fountain when we happen to pass one. We don't think in that situation, "I am thirsty. I must have a drink of water.'" We are barely conscious of the desire for water. It is there. We help ourselves. Yet we can easily see that the longer we are denied the satisfaction of our thirst drive, the stronger that drive becomes, to the point where it could dominate all our behavior. The principle of motivation illustrated here should be highlighted because it is so basic to our understanding. Our drives remain relatively quiet in us as long as they are satisfied; but deny or withhold the satisfaction of any drive, and it will dominate our behavior. It's very easy to see this principle at work in such physiological areas as hunger, thirst, rest, and breathing. But we often forget that the same principle operates with respect to our social and psychological drives. It's a point we'll want to remember as we consider other aspects of employees' behavior and motivation.

The striving for the things we want and need is what the psychologist means by motivation. So we see that motivation is within the individual. It is a highly personal matter. Because motivation is within the individual, we do not control an employee's motivation. Each person's needs are uniquely his or her own, and the values and priorities of one need over the other are his or her own. We can find patterns on which to make generalizations, but we cannot successfully substitute generalizations for a genuine understanding of the individual. As Burt should have seen, Mike Moran did not respond to the incentive of money beyond a certain point. Other members of that crew attached more importance to money, but not enough to disturb the group relationship that they were enjoying. The attitudes of the entire crew must be examined in the light of the fact that they were earning a better wage than the other crews doing similar work. Unless we recognize the principle that people attach greatest importance to things they're not getting, we might conclude that money is not important. Everyone knows that it is one of the prime reasons why people work.

If motivation is within the individual and if we have no control over others' motivation, where do supervisors come into the picture? Their control or their influence on behavior comes in the area of incentives—the satisfaction of drives. Behavior is the result of an individual's striving to satisfy personal needs. We might express it as a formula:

Motivating drive + incentive (satisfaction) = behavior

In terms of supervisory responsibility, behavior is what the supervisor wants to influence. This can be done by providing or denying the satisfactions an employee is seeking. The influence on behavior can be positive (motivating) or negative (frustrating). A pat on the back for a job well done may very well be all an employee needs to continue his or her excellent work or to strive to improve it. Inadvertently overlooking the good work or simply accepting it as something for which the employee is well paid might result in a lack of interest in work. Although supervisors do not control what the employee wants, in most cases they do determine whether or not employees get what they want on the job.

There are almost as many ways of classifying and labeling human drives as there are psychologists. In the long run the classification systems aren't nearly as important as the principles on which they operate. We should, however, have some base from which we can depart in our discussion of the incentives supervisors control and the influence they have on employees' behavior. The following list of needs represents a fair cross section of what we accept today.

Physiological Drives

We are born with needs that are common to all life. These are the drives that concern the requirements of the body. Typical examples of the physiological drives are hunger, thirst, shelter, breathing, elimination, and reproduction. The physiological drives are the most basic of our drives and must be satisfied before our behavior is directed toward satisfying higher-level drives. These drives remain relatively quiet in us as long as they are satisfied, but they will completely dominate behavior if unsatisfied. Supervisors are really not involved with these needs in their employees. In our economy employees are well clothed, well fed, and well housed. We should not lose sight of the fact, however, that the money a person earns on the job buys the satisfaction for the physiological needs. Money, therefore, is the means of satisfying a person's most basic drives.

Security Drives

We all need freedom from worry about our future welfare. Normally we think of this need in terms of job security. Employees want to feel that their jobs are secure—that they will have a job and income until they retire. Security needs, by and large, are extremely well satisfied by the company, the government, and individuals on their own initiative. Examples of how security drives of employees are fulfilled would include unemployment compensation, guaranteed annual wage plans, social security, medical plans, hospitalization insurance, life insurance, and retirement programs. The insurance industry is founded on the needs of the individual for a feeling of security. The ability to satisfy these needs is again out of the supervisors' hands. The fringe-benefit program in a company (amounting in many cases to 25 percent of the payroll) is determined by top management. We can observe the effects on behavior of the desire for security during periods of recession when layoffs threaten a segment of the work force. The union recognizes this need by selling its members and potential members guarantees that it will fight for their security.

Social Drives

We all want to feel that we belong to the group in which we find ourselves. The urge is the social drive. Wherever we find ourselves in groups—the family, community or social activities, our church, fraternal organizations, and, most important to us, the work group—we want to feel that other group members like to have us around. Inability to satisfy this need for belonging will usually cause a person to quit the group if possible. We probably will never have accurate statistics on how many people leave their jobs because of a feeling that they don't belong. There is enough evidence to show that this is a prime reason for turnover during periods of high employment when other jobs can be obtained.

A company in Milwaukee failed for several years to find the reason for its unusually high turnover rates. In exit interviews, people mentioned better jobs or higher pay as the prime reasons for quitting. A new executive vice president with an outstanding reputation in the field of employee relations put his finger on the real cause of their problem soon after he joined the firm. He discovered that most of the people leaving were new employees who felt no identity with the firm. A number of abuses in the personnel department and in the employees' own departments broke down the employees' feeling of belonging. Initiation of an employee orientation program and a supervisory human relations training program reduced turnover the first year to a tenth of what it had been.

The management-minded supervisor exercises a very high degree of control over satisfying the workers' need for a feeling of belonging. Actually no one person in the organization is in as good a position as the first-line supervisor to make the employee feel a part of the work group, the department, the total organization. The supervisor, too, has this drive—really wanting to feel like a member of management. New supervisors who move up from the ranks start acting more like managers as they feel their identity with the management team grow.

Psychological Drives

The individual needs to feel that he or she is important. All of us, wherever we go, whatever we do, want to feel that we are making a worthwhile contribution to the activities in which we engage. This is true both at home and at work. We usually recognize the importance of this drive at work, but frequently fail to remember that our families are human enough to have similar drives. Keeping an orderly, well-run home is just as much a job as running an automatic screw machine, typing invoices, or assembling relays. Recognition of achievements is just as important to the homemaker as to the machinist. Satisfactions for the psychological needs of employees are many and varied. They include such things as: praise for a job well done, additional responsibility, promotion, pay increases, listening to ideas, just listening, delegation, challenging work assignments, and opportunities to participate in the decisions that affect the job. Many supervisors have experienced the effectiveness of an occasional written word of praise to an employee. If done judiciously and when deserved, a written commendation has special significance to the average employee. For satisfaction of the need to feel important on the job, an employee must depend almost entirely on the supervisor. Supervisors are in complete control of the recognition incentive. Management must depend on its supervisors to satisfy this vital and personal need of the employee. The supervisors shoulder management responsibility to satisfy the psychological drive. The payoff is the employee's enthusiasm for improving performance and, in the long run, for working toward a more profitable operation.

Self-Esteem Drives

We all have a deep-seated need for self-respect—to feel that we are accomplishing what we were put on this earth to do. Each of us wants to

reach as near our full potential as possible. All the praise and acceptance of an individual may go for naught if we feel that we are doing less
than we are capable of doing. Some of the more recent research by M.
Scott Myers of Texas Instruments, Inc., has pointed to a breakthrough in
employee motivation by capitalizing on the self-esteem drive. His
findings suggest that we can benefit by allowing much greater employee
participation in the setting of production goals and standards.*

Supervisors should recognize their responsibility to match the
skills and abilities of employees working under them to the requirements
of the job. Further, they need to guard against any actions which might
prevent an employee from making his or her best contribution. The most
common example of such restrictive actions is the failure to listen to an
employee's ideas for improvement of job methods. We need only recall
the success Burt Hall had with Eric Mader in the previous chapter when
he allowed Eric to try his idea for a new fixture. We also remember that
Frank Connors squelched both Eric's ideas and Eric's desire to work.

To summarize briefly, we see that the employee's needs are met
by both the organization (higher management) and the supervisor.
Company programs and policies meet employees' needs in part. But
they are not within the supervisor's control and are usually economic in
character. Supervisors have a great deal of control over the motivational
factors that concern an employee's need to feel important, the need to
belong, and the need for respect of self. We'll come back to what we do
and do not control later when we discuss some of the research done by
Frederick Herzberg and M. Scott Myers.

FRUSTRATION IN EMPLOYEES' BEHAVIOR

Motivation, we said, is the striving for the things we want and need in life.
But what happens when we can't achieve or realize the things for which
we strive? Frustration. Whenever we are prevented from achieving what
we want, we experience frustration. Any barrier that stands in the way of
our satisfying our desires creates frustrated behavior. Just as it is
important for us to recognize motivated (positive) behavior, it is
important that we learn to recognize the symptoms of frustrated
(negative) behavior.

An example can again be found in the previous chapter. Larry
James, we will recall, wanted to get ahead. He worried about his lack of
education and the degree to which it might prevent him from achieving a
better job. We can say that Larry was frustrated. He didn't have the

*"Who Are Your Motivated Workers?" *Harvard Business Review*, January–
February, 1964.

education needed to achieve a promotion. To his credit, he had decided that going to night school would remove that barrier.

Characteristic of frustrated behavior is its emotional nature. Larry was extremely sensitive to whatever was said that might hurt his chances to advance. He reacted emotionally to Burt's comments, which had been intended as compliments, interpreting them as attacks on his work. His failure to respond to Burt thereafter was the result of his frustration. It was Larry's mild-mannered way of exhibiting the aggressive tendencies of frustration.

Behavior, we have said, is caused. It has a reason. When an employee takes an "I don't give a damn" attitude toward the quality of his or her work, what is the reason? Could it be that something needed very badly by an employee, perhaps subconsciously, is missing from the job? Other forms of negative behavior that we might encounter could be excessive absenteeism, careless handling of equipment, frequent complaining and griping, horseplay, slowdowns, argumentative behavior, and sometimes resistance to change. All too often we are inclined to dismiss such behavior as unreasonable, without any attempt to try to understand what is causing it. Identifying the symptoms of frustrated behavior many times produces opportunities to change conditions to the satisfaction of the employee.

Common sense demands that we use caution in analyzing negative behavior by making the effort to determine whether the behavior is due to frustration or whether there might be a real cause for dissatisfaction. An undesirable working condition such as poor lighting may be a genuine cause for dissatisfaction and may be very easily corrected. On the other hand, if the negative behavior is due to frustration, the cause may be much more difficult to determine. There is, as we've said before, no substitute for knowing as much as possible about the individual's background, interests, and ambitions. Empathy helps many supervisors determine the causes of frustrated behavior.

Deep-seated or long-standing frustration may require professional help. If consideration and fair treatment does not produce a desired change in behavior, supervisors should not hesitate to discuss the advisability of professional help with higher management or the personnel director. Unless the cause of frustration is determined and corrected, frustrated behavior will continue and probably worsen.

WHAT PEOPLE WANT FROM THEIR WORK

Having discussed motivating drives, we have already gained a good deal of insight into what people want from their jobs. But let's be more specific. Employees spend at least one-third of all their time in the work environment. They spend more of their alert waking hours on the job than they do with their families or in any other single activity. What do they expect from this occupation which consumes the major portion of their adult years? What they feel toward their work—frustration or satisfaction—cannot help but affect the relationships they experience outside the work environment. A genuine understanding of what employees want from their jobs sometimes eludes the supervisor who is wrapped up in reaching departmental production, cost, and quality goals.

Numerous surveys have been conducted seeking to find what employees want from their jobs. These surveys have almost no value to the supervisor in understanding what people want at a given time because changes in economic conditions, working conditions, and management affect responses. Whenever people are asked to rank what they want to get out of their jobs in order of importance, it is essential to understand that they tend to rank highest those things which they are not getting or which might be threatened. This tendency stems from the fact that an unsatisfied drive dominates behavior.

What we can learn from such surveys is the relationship that exists between supervisory and employee thinking. These surveys also help us remember that people want more from their jobs and from the supervisor than a boost in pay or a pat on the back. One of the most widely quoted of such surveys was published in *Foreman Facts* by the Labor Relations Institute of New York in 1946. Ten thousand employees from a cross section of industries were asked to rank ten factors in the order of importance to them on the job. At the same time, the supervisors of the respondents were asked to rank the items as they thought their employees would rank them—in other words, they were asked to empathize a little. Let's look carefully at the results of their responses (Figure 6).

Most managers explode when shown the results of this study in conferences or seminars. Some accuse the employees of being hypocritical. Others claim that it doesn't check out with their experience. Employees' complaints, they say, are usually about wages, seniority (security), and working conditions, and these things show relatively low ranking in the study.

Now let's take a more objective view. First it's important to understand that these results were published in 1946 and do not apply to conditions today. Wages were going up after the removal of wartime controls, and employment was at a very high level. It's not difficult, then,

COMPARATIVE RANKING OF JOB FACTORS

Employees' Ranking	Job Factors	Supervisors' Ranking
1	Full appreciation of work done	8
2	Feeling of being in on things	10
3	Sympathetic help on personal problems	9
4	Job security	2
5	Good wages	1
6	Interesting work	5
7	Promotion and growth in the company	3
8	Personal loyalty to employees	6
9	Good working conditions	4
10	Tactful disciplining	7

FIGURE 6

to see why security and wages did not at that particular time concern employees as much as some noneconomic factors. However, we should not lose sight of the fact that the supervisors responded to the survey at the same time that their employees did.

It's of particular interest to observe that the supervisors gave the bottom three rankings to those factors which the employees had said were most important to them. Do we not have cause to question how much the supervisors were able to empathize? Of even greater significance, we see that the supervisors ranked first, second, and third those factors over which they had almost no control. Wages, job security, and promotions are factors determined at higher levels, frequently in negotiation with a union. Can we therefore draw the conclusion that supervisors were throwing in the towel on motivation by saying, in effect, "What employees want most is what we can't give them"?

Whether we agree with the employees' responses or not, it's interesting to observe that their top three rankings went to noneconomic factors which are completely within the control of their supervisors. We have already agreed that recognition for good work is an obligation which is almost exclusively the supervisors'. None of us would deny that showing appreciation for good work and making an employee feel that he or she belongs falls fully within the scope of the supervisors' responsibilities. A number of supervisors, however, do take exception to the employees' third ranking item—sympathetic help on personal problems.

Many supervisors state that they feel they have no business poking their noses into the personal lives of the employees under them. We should recognize, however, that there's a vast difference between poking our noses into their personal lives and creating the kind of climate in which employees with problems feel they can discuss it with their boss. A person with a problem often needs to share it with someone. Often it's only a case of listening. Other times it's best to help the troubled person find qualified guidance from a priest, minister, doctor, lawyer, psychologist, or family counselor. An employee's loyalty goes to that person or organization which demonstrates the greatest interest in helping him or her. How often have we seen workers' loyalty won over by the union steward who says, "Bring your problems to me. I'll see that they're heard. That's my job." At the same time the supervisor is saying, "Don't bring your problems to me. They're none of my business." Again it's completely within supervisors' control to create the kind of climate they want to exist in their department.

It is also important to recognize in examining this survey that employees look for *all* ten factors from their jobs. Management's job in trying to motivate improved performance is to see that none of the factors is neglected, or else conditions for frustrated or negative behavior will be created. Needs, in life, are continually developing and demanding satisfaction. Satisfaction frequently is only temporary, and the need arises again and again—or one need arises, and then another. Creating an environment in which all wants and needs of employees are satisfied borders on the impossible. Conscientiously striving, however, to develop a sensitivity to people's needs can't help but improve the supervisor's batting average and elevate his or her stature as a member of management.

NEW INSIGHTS INTO MOTIVATING EMPLOYEES

Some of the most significant and practical research into the problems of motivating employees has been done by Frederick Herzberg of the University of Utah* and M. Scott Myers of Texas Instruments, Inc.† Herzberg found that levels of job satisfaction and productivity in engineering and accounting groups were closely related to two sets of factors—"dissatisfiers" and "motivators." Myers carried on his inves-

*Frederick Herzberg, *Motivation to Work*, John Wiley & Sons, Inc., New York, 1959.

†"Who Are Your Motivated Workers?" mentioned earlier.

tigation of these factors with technical personnel, supervisors, and production employees.

Both found that many of the factors we have considered as incentives or motivators for some time have greater capacity for dissatisfying employees than they have for motivating them. The dissatisfiers are essentially peripheral to the job and include such things as pay, physical working conditions, fringe benefits, job titles and classifications, orientation to the job, work rules, seniority rights, and grievance procedures. It is essential that these factors be maintained at an acceptable level because dissatisfaction can quickly arise where deficiencies exist. These factors have, however, relatively little value in stimulating high achievement or extra effort.

The second classification, the motivators, according to Myers and Herzberg, includes such factors as growth, achievement, delegation, freedom to act, recognition of work done, participation, goal setting, responsibility, and performance appraisal. Myers found that these motivators were primarily associated with the self-actualization of the individual on the job. He stressed that job satisfaction and high production were most often associated with the motivators and that disappointments and ineffectiveness were most often associated with the dissatisfiers.

Of particular interest to first-level supervisors is the fact that research now confirms the key role the motivators play in producing high levels of performance and job satisfaction. Here is proof that supervisors can't wash their hands of the responsibility for motivation simply because they have no control over wages and job security. To be sure, the organization must maintain fair wages, assure job security, provide decent working conditions, and offer competitive fringe benefit programs to prevent widespread dissatisfaction—which is a complicated and expensive responsibility for any employer. But for the most part, the motivators are under the supervisor's control. Management must depend on its front line for the creation of a motivational climate.

NONFINANCIAL INCENTIVES
FOR IMPROVING PERFORMANCE

Good work, extra effort, and motivated behavior occur when a supervisor supplies something outside the employee (an incentive), thereby satisfying something inside the employee (a motive). In carrying out the job of motivating people, a supervisor is likely to be most effective when selecting and tailoring incentives to meet the workers' individual needs. Burt Hall neglected to give consideration to Mike Moran's individual needs, assuming instead that Mike was primarily interested in financial reward. Since we have established that the supervisor's control is essentially over the nonfinancial motivators, let's identify some specifics which can be used in motivating people. Here are some suggestions that many successful supervisors have found helpful.

Treat Employees as Individuals

"Show a personal interest in them," many supervisors have said. Supervisors get so wrapped up in their own problems that they forget that the employee is an individual with feelings and opinions needing the opportunity for expression. Most employees would like the chance to express their opinions, ideas, and feelings to the one person who more than any other is management to them—their supervisor. Remembering that all people want to feel important, the management-minded supervisor finds two easy and natural ways to satisfy that need. First, the supervisor talks with them—listens to them. Most employees like to be able to go home to their wives and say, "I was talking with the boss today, and I told him . . ." Generally speaking, we find that the chance to identify with leadership in the department goes a long way toward satisfying the employee's need to feel important. Second, the supervisor has the opportunity, particularly with new employees, to show them the importance of their jobs to the overall operation. They do make a distinct contribution, or they wouldn't be employed. The easiest, most natural thing in the world is to show them the importance of their job.

Offer Sincere Praise and Recognition

The key to giving praise is the word *sincere*. No one wants praise given "by the numbers." We want to feel that we have earned it and that the boss means it. Praise, we know, ought to be specific. For example, if the quality of a person's work was particularly outstanding, it should be recognized; if finishing a job ahead of deadline was accomplished because of extra effort, praise should include a recognition of the difficulties overcome. Lavish or undeserved praise can have a negative effect and do more harm in the long run than no praise. Many supervisors have found it easier for themselves and for their employees to praise indirectly—that is, to praise the work rather than the individual. Instead of saying, "Jane, you're a top-notch worker. I couldn't get along without you," many supervisors make it more palatable by saying, "Jane, that job you turned in yesterday was really top-grade. It's work like that that makes us all look good. Keep it up."

Listening to employees is an easy, natural way to recognize them. Promotion, increased responsibility, and written commendations are also effective means of giving recognition when they are timely and deserved.

Provide Growth Opportunities Through Delegation

Many managers regard this suggestion as a way of killing three birds with one stone. Delegation demonstrates confidence in the employee, thus satisfying, in part at least, the drive for self-esteem. Delegation gives employees a chance to show what they can do. And the increased responsibility assumed gives them the opportunity to make a greater contribution to the work of the department and increases their feeling of personal worth.

Delegation also provides the supervisor with the chance to strengthen the departmental team by creating growth opportunities for individuals. As the members of a department grow, so does their supervisor. We identified in the first chapter the supervisor's responsibility for the training and development of employees. Delegation is one of the most practical ways of developing people if it is properly handled. It is not without risk—but then what worthwhile things are ever accomplished without some risk? The risk of sharing in a subordinate's mistakes, for example, causes many supervisors to shy away from delegation, saying, "It's easier to do it myself."

The third benefit is the time supervisors can save. Supervisors who will study the activities they engage in and the decisions they make will find many that subordinates can do. This not only makes jobs more meaningful for subordinates but frees the supervisor to do more of the things he or she can't find the time to do. One of the more satisfying aspects of supervision is having subordinates come to supervisors with the solutions to problems they have carefully thought through. When supervisors encourage thinking and problem-solving at the lowest possible level, they are motivating the employees in their departments.

Review Their Performance

Many supervisors say that supervisors should let their people know where they stand. People want to do a good job and would rather please than displease. Common sense should tell us, then, that they need to know how the supervisor thinks they're doing. Imagine the frustration of an employee who really tries to do his or her best day in and day out and never hears a word of evaluation, never has a chance to discuss his or her accomplishments. Most of us know supervisors who operate on the theory that "You're doing all right as long as you don't hear from me." Yet we recognize immediately that anyone concerned about motivating better performance can't afford to operate that way. Some of us have heard supervisors say they can't evaluate or review performance because the company doesn't have a program for review. Few, if any, supervisors would ever be denied the right to sit down informally with an employee and let that person know what they think are the strengths in his or her performance and discuss with him or her how that performance might be improved. Such reviews are just one more way of recognizing individuals and the contributions they make to successful operations.

Provide for Participation

When we discussed resistance to change in a previous chapter, we noted that one of the best ways to overcome resistance was to provide for opportunities to participate in the formulation of the change. Proper motivation of employees is best encouraged when a supervisor can involve the employee in improving his or her performance. Many companies are now experimenting with involving production employees in the setting of goals and standards. Most of those who have tried it report that the employees tend to set higher goals than the management's and to achieve them with less difficulty. Human nature proves time and again that employees who have been a part of formulating a plan, setting a goal, or developing an idea work harder to bring about its success. After all, they are a part of it, and they belong to the group who said it could be done. They don't have to be sold. They sold themselves.

Plan the Orientation of New Employees

New employees tend to be insecure when they face a new job, a new boss, new working conditions, and new fellow employees. The need to feel that his or her work is important and that he or she belongs to the work group, to the department, and to the organization can be most effectively satisfied at the time a person is the most impressionable—during the first hours and days under new supervision. Probably never again in his or her career in the department will a person be more receptive to the supervisor's thinking, attitudes, and suggestions.

Train Them Well

Acquiring new skills and knowledge acts as a spur to better performance. The desire for excellent work grows with the employee's confidence in his or her ability to do the work. Good training and motivation go hand in hand—each contributing to the other. In the next chapter, we shall go into detail on the importance of proper training in motivating improved performance.

Communicate With Them

In a recent study conducted at the University of Wisconsin,[*] the supervisors who said they did not feel that they were a part of management cited lack of communication as the chief reason. The failure of management to communicate does more to tear down employees' morale and to frustrate their behavior than does any other single shortcoming. Every incentive that the supervisor controls depends on communication as the vehicle for its implementation. Praise and credit must be communicated. The devices a supervisor uses to make employees feel that they belong or feel that they are important require communication. Employees want to know what's going on, where they stand with their supervisor, what changes are being contemplated, what their role in the successful operation of the department is, and what they can do to improve. Their feeling of being in on things is the result of how well the supervisor communicates with them.

A MATURE APPROACH TO MOTIVATION

Like communication, motivation is more an attitude and a philosophy than a technique. Every suggested technique for motivating a work group is just so many words unless it is handled well and carried out with sincerity.

For several decades it was felt that the supervisor had very little to do with motivation, even though lip service was paid to his or her responsibilities in that area. The more we learn about motivation, the more we realize that the first-line supervisor is the real key to job satisfaction and high productivity. The importance of that responsibility should therefore motivate supervisors to try to do their best to apply the

[*]From Bradford B. Boyd and Burt K. Scanlan, "Developing Tomorrow's Foreman," *Training Director's Journal*, May, 1965.

philosophy discussed here. Since motivation theory is so intimately tied up with satisfying the needs and wants of others, a giving attitude seems to be the most desirable. In the previous chapter we said that one of Dr. John Schindler's criteria for personal maturity was a giving rather than a receiving attitude. Can we survey our departments, our jobs, and our people and ask ourselves, "What have I to give?" Carry that question to the specific suggestions contained in the preceding section on non-financial incentives, and we see that the opportunities for giving are numerous. Most of those with a genuine concern for giving will experience the satisfaction of witnessing higher morale, unsolicited cooperation, and greater productivity in their departments.

HIGHLIGHTS

1. The first-line supervisor is strategically situated to implement motivational practices which will have the greatest payoff in organizational effectiveness. No other level of management has more control of the incentives that stimulate greater effort on the job.

2. Dwight Eisenhower's definition of leadership—"the ability to get a person to do what you want him to do . . . *because he wants to do it*," serves the management-minded supervisor as a working definition of motivation.

3. Striving for the things we want and need is what most psychologists mean by motivation. Satisfaction of needs represents the control supervisors have in motivating the improved behavior of employees. A person's needs or motivating drives are classified as:

    a. Physiological
    b. Security
    c. Social
    d. Psychological
    e. Self-esteem

4. Inability to find satisfaction for our drives results in frustration (negative behavior) that in work situations may take the form of excessive absenteeism, careless handling of equipment, frequent complaining, horseplay, slowdowns, argumentative behavior, or resistance to change. Before dismissing such behavior as unreasonable, we should try to understand what is causing it; for unless

we understand and remove the cause, the frustrated behavior will continue.

5. People expect a great deal more than money from their jobs. Research has shown that such things as pay, fringe benefits, physical working conditions, seniority rights, and grievance procedures have greater capacity for dissatisfying employees than for stimulating improved performance. The factors which have the best potential for motivating high productivity include growth opportunities, achievement, freedom to act, participation, recognition, goal setting, and responsibility. It is in the latter area that supervisors have the greatest control.

6. Nonfinancial incentives that can be used to motivate employees in the supervisor's day-to-day contacts with them include:

    a. Treating employees as individuals
    b. Offering sincere praise and recognition
    c. Providing growth opportunities through delegation
    d. Reviewing their performances
    e. Providing for participation
    f. Planning the orientation of new employees
    g. Training them well
    h. Communicating with them

7. Opportunities to motivate improved employee performance seem to center on our own answers to the question, "What do I have to give my people?"

DISCUSSION QUESTIONS

1. In your own words, explain what is meant when we say that the supervisor has more control over the incentives that motivate improved performance than the members of any other level of management.

2. Why should employees in India or China differ from those in the United States in terms of what they want most from their jobs?

3. Describe the attitude of an employee whom you have known, who was not primarily motivated by money. What did he or she put ahead of money?

4. What are some specific things a supervisor can do to make employees feel that they belong in the work group and in the department?

5. We say employees need recognition. How many specific things can you list that a supervisor can do to recognize individual employees?

6. Cite an example—either on or off the job—when you thought another person's behavior was unreasonable. Can you now see the reasons behind his or her actions or attitude? Explain.

7. Explain the thinking behind the statement that praise insincerely given can have a negative effect.

8. Is it possible to praise too much? Why or why not?

9. Evaluate the philosophy of some managers that reflects the attitude expressed by the words, "You're doing all right as long as you don't hear from me."

10. Why would employees try harder to improve their performance when they have had a voice in setting the standards that apply to their jobs?

CASE PROBLEMS

THE CASE OF BOB SANDERS AND JACK MINTER

"The trouble with civil service is that it's so cut and dried. It's just about impossible to motivate anyone to do a fair day's work," declared Bob Sanders, supervisor in the post office, to his best friend, a supervisor in one of the local manufacturing plants. "We can't raise their pay and we can't fire them. If you can't do either one, your hands are tied and they know it!"

"What makes you think it's any different in our shop?" Jack Minter asked. "The union negotiates their wages and the union makes it impossible to fire anyone. My employees know who runs the place, and it sure isn't me. Motivation is something our training director preaches, but he doesn't have to run a department with no authority or control the things that really count."

1. Is it more difficult to motivate in government than it is in private industry?

2. What would you tell Bob Sanders about motivating civil service employees?

3. Evaluate Jack Minter's statements about not having any control over things that count.

THE CASE OF JOE SNYDER

Supervising salespeople who can earn practically as much as they want ought to be duck soup. Everything they need to motivate them is right there in our commission setup. At least that's what Joe Snyder, supervisor of sales in the Swim-Time Pools Company, thought when he took over the North Division office. They work, they earn! Goof off and you don't eat. It's as simple as that.

Problem was that sales were dropping off while their competitors' sales were increasing. Joe knew it wasn't price or quality because they were as good as or better than their competition. Swim-Time was still number one but losing ground.

Joe's sales force was made up mostly of young men and women who were enthusiastic about swimming. Their spending time socializing in the store instead of prospecting and following leads irritated Joe. He had seen too many sales lost by salespeople accepting easy-to-overcome objections. He suspected that time away from the store wasn't always spent tending to business. When people don't punch a clock and when they manage their own time, a supervisor has to depend on commissions to motivate them, is the way Joe had it figured. Somehow it wasn't working for him.

1. Is money the primary incentive for sales personnel?

2. What besides money would interest a salesperson in wanting to improve his or her performance?

3. What steps should Joe take to recapture Swim-Time's sales leadershipff

THE CASE OF JAN PETERSON

Laboratory supervisor in the research and development department of Apex Chemicals was a mixed bag as far as Jan Peterson was concerned. She considered herself a scientist first and a supervisor second. The real love of her life was research and experimentation. Her dedication was "rewarded" by the promotion to supervision. It was recognition—a move upward—and it did mean more money. But it took her away from the projects that excited and satisfied her.

Jan soon found that getting others moving was a different ball game. Her attempts to show an interest in the outside interests of her technicians fell flat. Compliments were met with snide remarks about putting it in the paycheck. Her assignments of projects brought frequent comments about favoritism or unchallenging work. Not infrequently her technicians complained of her "snoopervising" when she checked their progress on a project. All she really had wanted was an opportunity to lend a hand or give some new direction to a project.

"I thought supervising would be a challenge," she explained to an associate. "Now I'm afraid it's too much of a challenge. Why can't people be predictable, like chemicals? Everything I've read about complimenting people, showing an interest in their personal lives, and being a buddy to them just doesn't work. Somebody ought to write a book about motivating technical people. They sure are different, and I don't know what to do about it. Sometimes I wish I could go back to my old job."

1. How does motivating technicians differ from motivating other employees?

2. How can Jan improve her relationship with her technicians?

3. What should she do now?

SUGGESTIONS FOR FURTHER STUDY

Bittel, Lester R., *What Every Supervisor Should Know*, 3d ed., Chapter 4, McGraw-Hill Book Company, New York, 1974.

Evans, C. George, *Supervising R & D Personnel*, Chapter 8, American Management Association, New York, 1969.

Shout, Howard F., *Start Supervising*, Chapter 5, Bureau of National Affairs, Washington, D.C., 1972.

Steinmetz, Lawrence L., and H. Ralph Todd, Jr., *First-Line Management*, Chapters 5, 6, and 7, Business Publications, Inc., Dallas, Texas, 1975.

Strohmer, Arthur F., Jr., *The Skills of Managing*, Chapter 3, Addison-Wesley Publishing Company, Reading, Massachusetts, 1970.

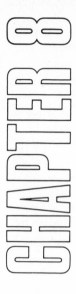

TRAINING FOR RESULTS

CHAPTER 8

THE CASE OF
THE UNTRAINED
TRAINERS

Lack of time was the real reason Burt Hall delegated his training function. Besides, a good supervisor should delegate. It was one way of developing a sense of responsibility. No one had to tell Burt that training employees was his responsibility or that costs, quality, morale, and production are all affected by the kind of training employees receive. But you just can't be everywhere doing everything, and training takes time—a lot of it.

So Burt had delegated the training of employees in the department to three experienced men acknowledged by everyone to be good producers who knew their jobs backward and forward. Each of them had performed a number of different jobs, and among the three of them every job in the department was covered. None of them reacted negatively to the idea of breaking in new people as a part of their jobs, but their reactions were mixed.

Clarence "Squeaks" West, for example, radiated pleasure when Burt first discussed the assignment with him. Squeaks, who got his nickname because of a high-pitched, squeaky voice, was a smiling, gregarious employee, liked by everyone. Burt entertained a few doubts about using Squeaks as an instructor for new employees but decided his experience and popularity would overcome any handicap his voice might pose.

Sam Pitman, the youngest of the three, shrugged his shoulders, grinned, and said, "Yeah, I'll give it a try," when Burt approached him. Sam had come to work in the department right out of high school. He was twenty-seven years old but already was an old hand with ten years' experience. His competitive spirit made him an outstanding producer. It was only natural that Burt had developed a high regard for Sam.

Joe Meyer was the old-timer. At fifty, he had twenty-seven years with the company and fourteen years in Assembly Department B. He had dropped out of school in the ninth grade, knocked around doing odd jobs, and got a stock chaser's job as the company was working its way out of the depression in the late thirties. Joe was fond of calling himself a graduate of the "school of hard knocks" and took great pride in being a steady worker who appreciated the chance to do a job well—an outlook, he felt, that was "missing in the young people we hire these days." Joe wasn't keen about working with youngsters but said he would if Burt wanted him to.

As new people were brought into the department, Burt would greet them and spend about ten minutes in giving them a quick tour of the department. He felt it was essential for him to have this contact with new employees. With those who transferred in from other departments, he skipped the tour, assuming that they knew their way around. With the preliminaries out of the way, Burt turned the new employee over to the one of his training trio who had the most experience in the job to be learned.

"Full responsibility and authority for training these people will be yours," Burt told his trainers. "You know the jobs better than anyone, and therefore you're the best qualified men I have to do the training in our department," he told them as he wound up a brief meeting before putting his plan into operation.

It was only in recent weeks that Burt had come to the realization that almost all rejects and rework were being caused by people who had come into the department since he had taken over as supervisor. At first he had subconsciously written off the problem as one of new people learning the ropes. Recently, in analyzing the roadblocks to more efficient production, it dawned on him that it was those people trained specifically by Sam and Joe who were producing over 80 percent of the work rejected by inspection. Further analysis revealed that a couple of what he referred to as his attitude problems—the gripers—were in that same group.

Rather than blame Sam and Joe immediately for poor training practices, before he was even willing to admit that training was the problem, Burt decided on a course of observation and checking. First he planned to talk with the last person each of the trio had trained and then to observe each of his trainers in action with new people who would be hired in the coming weeks.

Sarah Weeks, obviously nervous when Burt called her in to discuss how things were going on her new job, felt certain that she was going to be called on the carpet for producing too much rejected material. She said that her job overall was all right and that she was sure she would get the hang of it. The first couple of days were pretty hectic, though, she told Burt.

Asked if she felt she had sufficient training on the job, Sarah said no without hesitation. She didn't want to criticize a whiz like Sam, she said, but she just couldn't keep up with him.

As she described her training, these patterns became evident. Sam had demonstrated the job several times, going so fast she couldn't see his hands move. He laughingly apologized for being so slow, saying that the other workers set a pretty stiff pace and that he was out of practice. She was sure Sam thought she was hopeless. She felt both relieved and tense when Sam left her alone. Yes, he had said she could ask questions, but she couldn't think of any before he left her on her own. The other women helped her whenever she asked them.

Al Wagner welcomed the opportunity to talk to Burt, since he was thinking of quitting anyway. To himself, Burt thought he wouldn't mind his leaving at all, since Al was a griper. When they got around to discussing his training, Al revealed an immense dislike for Joe, though he grudgingly admitted that Joe was a good hard worker.

"But you get the feeling that if you don't copy everything he does, you're no good," Al told Burt. "Once he called me a young punk. He pretended he was kidding, but I knew that's what he was really thinking. He went so slowly when he showed me the job, he must have thought I just got out of kindergarten. When I had an idea for speeding up a part of the job, Joe said I should wait until I knew something about the job before I start telling old-timers how to do it."

Al said he understood everything Joe had told him, but he felt that Joe might be holding back a few tricks that would have been helpful. He felt this way because he had picked up a few watching the guys working next to him, and an old-timer like Joe sure could have passed them on if he wanted to. After a few words of encouragement from Burt, Al said he appreciated the opportunity to talk about his job. He promised to be a little more careful about his quality.

Alice Draper thought Squeaks was just about the nicest guy around. She described how he had made her feel right at home, took her down to final assembly to show her where her work fit into the finished product, and introduced her to the other women around her before they sat down at her bench. She particularly remembered how he stressed going slowly at first so that she would only produce quality work. Squeaks had told her that there wouldn't be any difficulty working up to standard after she had been there a couple of weeks. She remembered being all thumbs at first and that she and Squeaks had several good laughs over her clumsiness.

"It's a wonder he didn't go crazy with all my silly questions, but he had the patience of a saint. The first day, I knew I was going to like working here, and I haven't been wrong."

Burt couldn't believe it when he saw identical situations develop as each of the trio tackled their next training assignment. It was, Burt thought, like seeing a movie a second time. Each of them apparently had developed a style he felt worked for him, but Sam and Joe certainly weren't helping build a strong department.

While watching Squeaks work with a new young man, Burt noticed him referring frequently to a sheet of paper in his hand and was puzzled about it. Squeaks seemed a little embarrassed when Burt asked him about it over a cup of coffee that afternoon. "I'm not good enough at these jobs to keep everything in my head," Squeaks explained. "Unless I sit down beforehand and make a checklist, I'm sure to forget something or get things all out of sequence. It's not very fancy. I just jot down each step of the job and anything special along the way that I have to remember. It may not be very professional, but it sure helps me get my thinking organized."

Grinning from ear to ear, Squeaks answered Burt's question about how he liked his instructing assignments. "I ought to be paying the company for that time instead of letting the company pay me. Seriously, Burt, I like it. These new employees are so eager to do a good job, they make me feel I should really learn something about instructing so I could do a better job for them."

As Burt began to evelute his checking and observing of the three trainers, some things were so obvious that he was ashamed that he hadn't seen them before. Sam and Joe weren't contributing much to his goal of quality production. Squeaks, with a humble view of his own instructing ability, was getting results which anyone could be proud of. Burt wondered about several other things.

1.   Should a supervisor delegate the training function to others in his department?

2.   What made Squeaks so superior as an instructor to both Sam and Joe? Squeaks, after all, was the only one Burt had had any doubts about in selecting his trio of trainers.

3.   What do employees really learn from their trainers? Isn't it a lot more than just how to do a job?

4.   Just how important is training in the smooth functioning of a department?

THE TRAINING RESPONSIBILITY OF THE MANAGEMENT-MINDED SUPERVISOR

What Burt Hall was learning the slow, painful way, many have come to appreciate very early in their careers. Unfortunately, some supervisors never learn it. The responsibility for a well-trained work force is just about the most important responsibility a supervisor has. From the top executive to the first-line supervisor, every manager must accept the obligation for training and developing employees. This principle is so vital to the progress of any organization that most large successful companies spell it out as a matter of policy.

The results supervisors achieve in production, costs, quality, safety, morale, and methods are proportionate to the quality of the training employees receive when they begin their jobs and while they are on the job. We all recognize, for example, what a mistake it would be to discount the effect employees' attitudes have on the major areas of supervisory responsibility. Nor can we fail to recognize that the most potent factor in shaping those attitudes is what happens when employees learn new jobs.

More supervisors than we like to admit have a negative attitude toward training because, they say, it takes so much of their time. Yet we see them taking time to correct mistakes, assign rework, and put out the fires that proper training would have prevented. We can always find time to correct those things that we didn't have time to do properly the first time—but sometimes this fact is slow to dawn on us.

Perhaps there is a deeper reason for disliking the job of training. Most of us like best the things we do well. Supervisors who have been deprived of the opportunity to learn how to train have in most cases been deprived also of the satisfaction that any good teacher experiences in working with students. Squeaks West was one of the fortunate few to whom the skill came naturally. The trial-and-error approach to job training yields about the same results that it does in any other area. There will be a few who "luck out," but not many. The odds favor our falling victim to one or more of the common mistakes in training, which we'll analyze soon. When we do make any of these mistakes, dissatisfaction results and the dislike for training deepens.

We can all learn a lesson from a supervisor in a Minneapolis firm whom I'll call George Westphal. He was participating in a supervisory institute at the University of Wisconsin a few years ago when the discussion turned to the benefits of good training to the supervisor. George popped up his hand and said, "It's fun." Almost everyone in the room did a double take and waited for George to explain that remark. Few of the people who were there that day will forget George's little speech.

"The thing I hate most about my job," he said, "is criticizing people. I don't like the look on their faces, and it just plain makes me feel lousy. When I don't train them right, I've got a lot more criticizing to do. That's one thing.

"I don't know how many of you stopped to think about it," he continued, "but a new employee is just about the most anxious-to-please person in the world. They want to do a good job. Sure, they're nervous, but it's mainly for fear that they won't be able to satisfy us. When you know that the impression they get in the first couple of hours is going to stick with them for a long long time, you know your work is cut out for you. That's when the fun starts. They're like putty in your hands. A lot of personal satisfaction comes in feeling that what you're doing is helping people learn the skills that will earn their living for them. You feel the responsibility, too. I guess I just enjoy being with people when they're so darned cooperative."

What a philosophy! Imagine what it must be like to come to work as a new employee and meet George. Imagine, too, what kind of attitudes grow out of George's enthusiasm for teaching people how to do their jobs. This kind of attitude enables a supervisor to be accepted as a true leader and to experience the personal satisfaction we all seek from our jobs.

Empathy is a much-needed quality in discharging the training responsibility. Good teachers need the ability to put themselves in the shoes of their students—to see their needs and to understand their fears and tensions. The ability to empathize will help the supervisor recognize the anxiety experienced by the new employee as he or she stands for the first time in the new work area facing a new boss, new surroundings, new fellow employees. Empathy will help the supervisor see the job from the learner's viewpoint rather than through the eyes of one with years of familiarity with the operation.

A little empathy helps the supervisor see the hopes and expectations the employee has as he or she begins a new job. To the extent that we can generalize about these hopes, the following desires would apply to most people on the day they face a new job, a new boss, a new department or company, and new fellow employees:

The Hope That Their Job Is Important

We've all read and joked about the janitor who wants to be called a sanitary engineer or the trucker who prefers "materials handler" as a job title. Supervisors are proud of having attained a position of some standing in the company. Even the person coming in to do the most routine job wants to feel that he or she is doing something worthwhile. A management-minded supervisor capitalizes on this desire by assuring the employee that the service to be performed is needed. By so doing, the supervisor stimulates even further the desire of the employee to succeed.

The Hope That They'll Get Along
Well With Their Supervisor

We frequently lose sight of the fact that most people want to enjoy friendly relations with the boss. It's good to be able to say, "My boss is a real good egg." These hopes of new employees make the supervisor's job much more pleasant if they are recognized.

The Hope That They Will Do Well in Their Jobs

As we've recognized before, we all need something to work for. We want to feel that we're accomplishing something. The management-minded supervisor who shows employees how to measure their performance builds in self-motivating incentives. Employees want to see what progress they're making, against realistic standards. Through good performance they please the boss and satisfy personal needs for a feeling of accomplishment. This natural need is especially high when an employee is beginning a new job; this need gives rise to the conclusion that new employees are anxious to make good.

The Hope That Their Supervisor Will Set
High Standards of Performance

Every worker entertains the hope that the boss has high expectations of performance. While the supervisor's expectations from employees during the learning period must be moderate, employees want to know that their supervisor has a sufficiently high regard for them to expect them ultimately to perform to high standards. Mistakenly, many managers play down standards to show their consideration, but in doing this they are removing incentives for top-notch performance. High but realistic standards are a compliment to an employee. Being a good guy by suggesting that they want people to take it easy may salve managers' egos, but it does very little for the employee eager to show a boss what he or she can do.

An employee's first few days on the job are full of high hopes and expectations. The supervisor who is able to empathize recognizes these hopes and takes advantage of them. In so doing, a supervisor finds his or her own role as an instructor infinitely more satisfying and more productive.

DELEGATING THE TRAINING FUNCTION

Common practice among a majority of supervisors is to delegate the function of job training to others—lead persons, setup men, older employees, top-producing employees. Burt Hall's approach to training in his department is frequently followed. Unless special steps are taken, experiences like Burt's with Sam and Joe are the result. The problems and concerns discussed in this chapter must be faced by those who do the job training in the department. It doesn't make much sense for a supervisor to know the principles of job training and then not pass them on to the person who will actually train departmental employees.

We should recognize some factors concerning delegation in determining the desirability of delegating the responsibility for training. There are those who say that responsibility can't be delegated. It's a moot point. When a supervisor delegates, a new responsibility is created—that which a subordinate has to the boss. A supervisor does not, however, delegate away the responsibility for a well-trained employee or department.

When supervisors delegate, they give others the right to perform in their name, to make their decisions. They share with the subordinate the results of his or her performance. The subordinate's performance is the supervisor's performance. If there are mistakes, they are the supervisor's mistakes. A supervisor cannot tell the boss that an assistant's poor training of the employee is responsible. The supervisor is just as much responsible as if he or she had personally handled every step in the training procedure.

It stands to reason, then, that the person to whom the supervisor delegates the training function must be adequately prepared to carry out the responsibility. The subordinate should understand the impact that good job training will have on the total results of the department. The trainer's training should include analysis of the learner as an individual, identification of the common mistakes made in training, finding out how people learn, learning techniques for preparing to instruct, and guided practice in teaching a job using a systematic approach.

Delegation is very effective in developing subordinates. Burt Hall, however, didn't appreciate that training requires special skills apart from knowing the job to be taught. Before a supervisor delegates training activities, he or she should understand thoroughly the principles and techniques of good job training. Then those techniques must be taught to the trainers. If a supervisor cannot do this, he or she must at least arrange for the trainers' training and review carefully their performance as they begin to assume the supervisor's responsibility.

Tangible benefits accrue to the supervisor who properly delegates training in the department. That supervisor develops much-needed and extremely important skills in his or her subordinates. Having people specialize in training can result in a higher level of job performance in the department. Finally, the supervisor is freed to accomplish other important work in the department. The risks in delegating are obvious. But they can be minimized by even greater emphasis on *training the trainer* than on training the new employee.

COMMON ERRORS IN TEACHING EMPLOYEES THEIR JOBS

The assumption that anyone who can do a job can teach another how to do it has led to countless errors in the instruction process. Many of us have been the victim of one or more of these errors. Others have seen them committed. Perhaps a few of us have even been guilty of a couple ourselves. Some of the more common mistakes made by supervisors and trainers are listed here. Later we will discuss an approach to training that is designed to eliminate such errors.

Feeding Too Much at One Time

Like the overeager parent who shovels food into an infant faster than he can swallow, a supervisor can heap a multitude of details on the learner so fast that they can't possibly be assimilated. This tendency is an easy trap to fall into, since the trainer knows the job so well. We assume that pictures we carry in our heads are easily and quickly received in the mind of the learner. Lacking sensitivity to the special problems of the learner in digesting new concepts, we proceed on our merry way to compound the confusion.

Telling Without Demonstrating

Anyone who has ever seen the classroom exercise of having a supervisor tell a discussion leader how to put on a coat or open a pack of cigarettes will quickly testify to the fact that *telling alone is not enough*. Semantic problems for the trainee are often major barriers to learning. The learner must receive the words and visualize what is wanted. Being strange to this environment, he or she finds these visualizations extremely difficult. While the mind is trying to understand one concept, two or three more have gone in one ear and out the other. An example or two may dramatize the problems this error can create.

In a Midwestern pharmaceutical plant, a new employee was sent up a ladder to tighten down the cover of a pressure-cooking vat. The cover was clamped down by a stud and a palm-sized wing nut which swung up into a U-shaped projection on the rim of the cover. The supervisor told the employee, "Clamp it down good and tight." The shape of the nut, of course, indicated that he meant hand tight. But, being as eager as most new employees are, the employee got himself an 18-inch pipe wrench and proceeded to get the cover down "good and tight." In the process of following instructions, he snapped the stud off. The delay ruined chemicals with which the vat had been charged, production schedules fell behind, and customer relations suffered, all because the inexperienced employee had tried to do "only what he had been told."

A Chicago manufacturer of small brass fittings provides another example. One of the foremen who had a new employee on his hands had to go to a production meeting. He needed something to keep the new man busy while he was gone. He called the man over, pointed to a large pile of fittings on the floor, and said, "Start cleaning up that pile of fittings, and I'll be back with you in a couple of hours." He intended the employee to clean the burrs off the fittings—a pure, out-and-out make-work assignment. After the boss left, the new man lost no time in securing a 55-gallon scrap drum, a shovel, a broom, and hand truck. Cleaning up the pile took little more than an hour as the employee hauled four loads of fittings to the company dump.

It took a crew of three men the better part of a day to sort out and recover about two-thirds of the fittings from the debris in the dump. Head in hands, the new man could only mutter, "I just did what he told me."

These examples may seem extreme. Yet, who among us can't find many examples, just as ridiculous, of what can happen when the trainer relies on telling without demonstrating.

Lack of Patience

For many, learning is a slow process that demands frequent repetition and careful explanation. To the supervisor anxious to get on with running the department, the temptation to lose his patience is great. Burt Hall, we'll recall, was beginning to see that a learner learns more than the job being explained to him. He or she observes the attitude of the trainer and reacts to it. Impatience on the part of the trainer produces tension in the learner. Tension slows learning. Slow learning taxes the trainer's patience, and so it goes. Sam Pitman's approach was a fine example of this vicious cycle at work.

Lack of Preparation

Good training doesn't happen by accident. Distractions caused by an instructor who has forgotten to have materials, supplies, tools, and prints ready before job instruction begins can only slow the learning process. Inhibition of learning is also caused by the trainer who doesn't present the job in its logical sequence. Confusion is the inevitable result of backtracking during instruction. An unorganized approach to training will create an image of an unorganized boss or department in the mind of the new employee.

Failure to Build in Feedback

The instructor who fails to take advantage of feedback opportunities during instruction is asking for trouble. Imagine the trainer who tells the learner how the job is performed, shows him or her the operation, and then says, "Well, that's all there is to it. You know everything I know. Good luck."

Good luck! They're both going to need it. Who knows at that point what the trainee has learned, if anything? Job training requires effective two-way communication. An instructor who is not oriented to the needs of the student and is concerned only with his or her presentation does only half the job.

How does the trainer build in feedback? It can be done in a number of ways. During the explanation of the job, the trainer is getting constant feedback through the facial expression and attitude of the learner. Any instructor who is sensitive to the student can read that "I don't have the faintest idea what you're talking about" expression on the learner's face. And the instructor can also feel the eagerness that communicates understanding and readiness to try out the job.

Another opportunity for feedback is created when the instructor invites the trainee to explain the job as he or she understands it. It helps to encourage the learner to ask questions about anything he or she doesn't understand. The dedicated trainer recognizes the vast difference between *encouraging* questions and simply saying at the end of an instruction, "Now, do you have any questions?" The latter approach makes questions almost impossible by creating the feeling in the trainee that it would be stupid to ask about anything—or, even worse, that it would be implying criticism of his instructor's explanation. One of the most effective and crucial feedback techniques, which should never be omitted, is to have the learner perform the job two or three times to demonstrate his or her understanding of it.

Failure to Reduce Tension

"Put them at ease" is a phrase we often come across in discussions of how to handle any face-to-face relationship with employees. This concept is especially important in job training. Clear thinking is necessary during the learning process; but tension inhibits learning, and new employees have plenty to be tense about. Usually they have just come from the personnel or employment department, where they have had explanations of wage scales, deductions of many varieties, life and health insurance plans, vacations, hours of work, overtime pay, regulations concerning their joining a union, and countless other considerations which constitute conditions of employment. Their heads are filled with these facts as they face their supervisor, the department, the job, and their new fellow employees.

Why should they be tense with such amiable fellow employees? The problem is that they don't know the other employees yet. Much will depend on how they reveal themselves in those first few hours. How valuable it would be if the members of the department could only see a new employee's mental picture of them during those first hours. A simple concern about what that image might be would undoubtedly cause a majority of them to make some positive adjustments in their approach.

STIMULATING A READINESS TO LEARN

Everyone who had seen his or her children through the elementary grades has been made aware of the principle that children must be ready or interested in learning before real learning can take place. Teachers have cautioned parents not to panic if reading or math doesn't sink in immediately. Johnny has to be ready to learn, they counsel.

Because a job and a means of earning a living are at stake, it is easy to tend to take readiness to learn for granted when dealing with workers. True, new employees tend to be anxious to please, but supervisors cannot afford to overlook the importance of stimulating a readiness to learn. It's as important to job training as explaining the sequence of the job to the employee. Common sense tells us that once the learner is motivated to learn, the supervisor's job becomes easier and training efforts are more effective. Motivation to a large extent depends on the employee's feeling that the job he or she will be doing is dignified and will contribute in a significant way to the overall work of the department and the organization. How often, for example, has a supervisor tried to reassure an employee that a job will be easy to learn but downgraded its importance instead? Instead of stimulating interest, this leaves the employee wondering, "If a ten-year-old can do it, why should I?"

Consider for a moment the approach of a supervisor in an office in Racine, Wisconsin, who made it a practice to greet every new employee with a smile, a firm handshake, and these words, "Betty, am I glad to see you. This job you're going to be doing really needs some attention."

In his very first words he tells the employee that the office needs her and that her job is important. Sincerity, of course, is the keynote in his approach. But it's easy to be sincere when we recognize that people don't get paid for jobs that don't need doing. No matter how menial the tasks to be performed, that supervisor in Racine could voice his greeting with the deepest conviction.

If the job to be taught is menial, routine, and easily learned, the supervisor has a golden opportunity to stress accuracy and quality. Even the sweeper makes an important contribution to good housekeeping, making a better place to work and indirectly contributing to the efficiency of production employees. When the supervisor can see every job in the department as a substantial contribution to the overall effort, he or she is on the way to transmitting this same outlook to individual employees. If people are our most valuable assets, why not communicate that fact to them? Empathy will help the supervisor see employees' jobs as their whole work life. Their standard of living and their feelings of personal worth are tied up in those jobs. A management-minded supervisor recognizes this and cultivates the employee's pride in the work to be done, and in the process conditions the employees to learn with enthusiasm.

HOW TO FACILITATE LEARNING

Having recognized what a vital part of the supervisor's job training is, we might examine the skills that promote effective teaching. Most supervisors can't achieve the skills of the dedicated professional teacher, but they can borrow a few ideas to make the discharge of this key responsibility easier and more satisfying. Translating the principles of the educational psychologist into the commonsense language of the supervisor, we find a number of aids to good teaching. Let's consider what makes learning and the job of training easier.

Repetition

Difficult or complex operations may have to be explained several times and in several ways. A good instructor will find a variety of methods of presenting the job to an employee in order to maintain interest at a high level. For example, the instructor might have the employee observe someone else performing the job as the first step. He or she might then explain the job in words in a logical sequence and follow this with a demonstration of the job which includes telling and showing. Another variation, if further repetition is desirable, might be for the instructor to do the job as the employee gives directions. The last method is particularly useful in the operation of machinery when damage to equipment or injury to the employee might result from faulty handling. The degree of complexity will naturally determine how much repetition is needed. Without insulting the intelligence of the employee, the supervisor or instructor can capitalize on the knowledge that repetition does make learning easier simply by varying the method of presentation.

Arousing Curiosity

A key technique in stimulating thinking or learning is arousing the learner's curiosity. Others will say the same thing this way, "You can't learn them nothing until you gets their attention." In effect, we're using this approach in this book. Burt Hall finds himself in situations that have confronted many beginning supervisors. He is faced with problems they have faced and ponders questions that they have asked. As we think about his problems, we open our minds to the suggestions of thousands of experienced supervisors who have shaped the text of each chapter.

Arousing the learner's curiosity is easily accomplished in the training situation by an occasional query—"Joe, do you have any idea why we do it this way?" "Why do we do it in this sequence?" "What does this part do?" Joe may or may not have an idea, but in either event he will want to know why—his curiosity has been aroused. If he has guessed incorrectly, he will listen carefully to the proper explanation, provided that we haven't belittled his effort. If he says he doesn't have the slightest idea, we can bet he's receptive to the answer. Selecting two or three key points in the operations to pique the curiosity will serve to reinforce learning where it is especially important.

Careful Use of Competition

Most people like to compete, especially if the competition is fair and there's a reasonable chance of succeeding. The competitive urge drives people to try a little harder—something supervisors would like to see in new employees. Competition can enter into job training in a number of subtle ways. For example, if the trainer points out that it takes an average operator two weeks to achieve a certain level of production, he or she has indirectly set a goal the employee will try to reach. A caution, however, is in order. The goal set should be fairly easily attainable lest we produce a frustration that will have a negative effect on the employee's effort. Remember Sam Pitman, Burt Hall's young trainer? Sam had needled Sarah Weeks about how his speed was no match for the performances of the others, and he had given Sarah a hopeless feeling that she could never come up to standard.

Employees can compete against time. If it takes five minutes to complete a unit of work the first time, how long will it take the second, the fifth, the tenth, etc.? Then how many units per hour can be achieved after a week, a month, and so on? Wherevec it is possible for employees to record or graph their production, they have an opportunity to compete with their own achievements.

Knowing the Knacks

Many jobs revolve around certain key points, special timing, tricks, or knacks. A thorough knowledge of the job on the part of the instructor will include an appreciation of these knacks or principles. Teaching will be more effective if he or she can highlight these, convey an understanding of them, and show the balance of the job as revolving around these principles. For example, an instructor might tell a new assembler, "The trick to this whole job is matching these two surfaces." Or the trainer might advise, "Once these two wires are properly soldered, the rest almost fall into place."

When learners see that a particular knack is a key to successful completion of that job, they'll be likely to focus extra effort there. If we have been judicious in identifying the knacks of the job, the employee's extra effort should pay handsome dividends.

Enthusiastic Instruction

It's not very likely that someone will get excited about a job or quality production if no enthusiasm is shown by the trainer. Experience in many fields proves to us that enthusiasm is contagious, and this is especially true in teaching. Positive attitudes toward the job are best developed by supervisors who can communicate those same positive attitudes. The quiet enthusiasm reflected in the attitudes toward instruction shown by Squeaks West and George Westphal is a valuable asset to anyone charged with the responsibility of training another. Common sense tells us that people are far more responsive to the instruction of an enthusiastic trainer.

Satisfaction in Accomplishment

Perhaps the most potent stimulant to learning is the satisfaction employees find in making progress on the new job. As their fears and anxieties are replaced with confidence, their interest deepens and their effort increases. We can easily see this phenomenon at work in children. Even the mildest encouragement brings an immediate response. Tell little Mary you're proud of the way she can sound out words, and she'll try to read everything in sight. Until, that is, she tackles a few words that are too tough—then she backs off to safer ground. Although adults are more sophisticated in their behavior and have learned to disguise their feelings, the inner positive response to praise and encouragement still exists in most of us.

Learners need encouragement. It affects their behavior in a most positive way. It is easiest and most natural to encourage learners when they have actually earned the praise. False flattery is quickly recognized by employees. The real challenge to the instructor is to plan training in such a way that learners have the opportunity to recognize their progress during the learning process.

Helping employees experience satisfaction in accomplishment is not difficult and well worth the effort. The technique is simply one of breaking the job down into sufficiently small elements to allow mastery of each one with relative ease. Working with the learner, the instructor can sense how quickly or how slowly he or she may proceed and still allow the learner to feel progress. Interestingly enough, encouraging the learner is one of the most satisfying aspects of training for the instructor. As learners feel satisfaction in their accomplishments, the teacher's own satisfaction in a job well done grows.

HOW TO INHIBIT LEARNING

Practical experience has taught many training people that they can unknowingly slow the learning process. Without proper preparation for training and without a sensitivity to the problems of the learner, seemingly insignificant factors can become a part of training patterns which have a definitely negative influence on learning. At the risk of repeating some of the points already raised in this chapter, we might profit by identifying what prevents learning efficiency. If learning efficiency is impeded, training effectiveness is reduced.

Fatigue

Learning is hard work. It requires effort. We tire very quickly in learning situations, and the mental processes slow down. To avoid undesirable consequences of fatigue, the instructor should schedule training, whenever possible, at a time when an employee is both physically and mentally fresh. Usually this time is early in the shift. Efficiency diminishes as the day wears on. There is little doubt that the poorest time to attempt any training is during the last hour before quitting time. Many supervisors have suggested breaking up the job and teaching it in segments. Training sessions which go on and on reach a point of diminishing returns.

Monotony

Teaching a neophyte how to do a job that doesn't challenge the trainer's abilities can easily be regarded as a chore, and this attitude will result in a monotonous presentation. A very detailed job which may appear to require a recitation of a great deal of factual information can likewise be monotonous to both instructor and learner. The most logical remedy for avoiding monotony in training seems to be an employee-oriented approach to teaching.

Even the most routine job is new to the employee—it's a puzzle and a challenge. Recognizing this fact helps many supervisors generate enthusiasm for teaching old jobs to new people. The situation is similar in many respects to that of a successful Broadway actor beginning the five hundredth performance of a play. The temptation to give less than his best, to walk through, to recite lines rather than live them, is ever present. The actor continually needs to remind himself, in the tradition of the theater, that no matter how many times he's performed the play, it's still the first performance for the audience.

To those who say, "yeah, but that's what he gets paid for," the supervisor can reply that effective training is his or her job. Fortunately the supervisor's pay comes not only in dollars but in the satisfaction of teaching and in the performance of well-developed employees.

Distractions

Anything that interrupts the employee's concentration during training slows the learning process. Some distractions cannot be avoided. Others can be anticipated and eliminated. When the training is done at the workplace, many distractions must be contended with. For example, the curious eyes of fellow employees at adjacent work stations or desks may distract the learner. This disturbing influence is reduced if the new employee is introduced to everyone in the department before actual job training begins.

Noise from machinery, typewriters, or people generally must be tolerated when training at the workplace. Where the noise level is especially distracting, as much of the job as possible should be discussed in an isolated area. Mockups or models have proved useful in many plants and offices to introduce the employee to job principles.

If the instructor is often interrupted to answer the phone or other employees' questions a real deterrent to learning can develop. If the trainer makes it known he or she is not to be disturbed during training, most distractions in this category can be avoided. All too often, though, the distractions are of the trainer's own making. Any time the training sequence must be interrupted because the instructor has forgotten certain materials, supplies, forms, tools, or equipment, the worst of all distractions is created. We noted before that employees learn a good deal more during the job training than just how to do the job. If they must sit and wait while their instructor is off getting some tool or supplies, what do they think as they idle away their time? The obvious step to remove this barrier to learning is better planning—perhaps a checklist.

Anxiety

We needn't dwell on the obvious. Tension and anxiety are not conducive to thinking or learning. Research in one division of Texas Instruments, Inc., proved conclusively that the removal of anxiety shortened the time it took for operators to reach a satisfactory level of competency.* Special effort was made to minimize anxiety by stressing, for example, the extremely high percentage of people who succeed on the job. This helped new employees to anticipate some of the joking by experienced employees about the high rate of failure. Every assurance of help and consideration was given. In short, each possible cause of anxiety was identified and eliminated before the employee was given instruction on the job to be performed. The results proved, beyond question, that eliminating learners' anxiety will reduce greatly the time needed to reach standard performance.

OPPORTUNITIES FOR TRAINING

If we have created the impression, by frequent references to the "new employee," that training is necessary only with newly hired personnel, let's take a quick look at other opportunities that call for expert training. Any time a new method is introduced in the department, the opportunity arises to reestablish the importance of quality, costs, safety, and housekeeping. The installation of new equipment or machinery provides a similar opportunity. Changes in products, in the model produced, or the addition of new features allow for renewed emphasis on job pride.

It goes without saying that excessive waste or scrap demands investigation and additional training. The same is true of serious accidents or increases in the rate of accident frequency. Poor attitudes; excessive gripes, complaints, and grievances; turnover; higher than usual tardiness; and absenteeism are all conditions which might be improved by training.

With the increased emphasis on automation and technological improvement, many employees will be moved from job to job and from department to department. Every transfer to a new job creates a new opportunity to train for improved employee performance.

*From Earl R. Gomersall and M. Scott Myers, "Experiment in On-the-Job Training," *Harvard Business Review,* July–August, 1966.

A SYSTEMATIC APPROACH TO TRAINING

Many will say, ''All this talk about principles, theories, and suggestions is fine, but give me something specific to guide me.'' Is there a simple system to incorporate the principles of good training and avoid both the common mistakes made in training and the things which inhibit learning? Yes, but the system is a stepwise procedure and, like any four-, five-, or six-step approach, it must be followed with care if it is to be valuable. We often seek such a system, find it, and dismiss it as oversimplification or claim that it's fine for someone else but that our situation is different.

Here, then, is a six-step system for teaching a job—any job. Conscientious application of these six steps will almost guarantee improvement in training effectiveness. We must say *almost* because the final result depends on the care taken in preparation and on the individual skills of the instructor. It will be easy to see how the principles of good training are built in—the system simply organizes our thinking.

Step 1: Prepare the Instructor

Many supervisors, trainers, and educators claim that adequate prepa- ration is more than half the job of teaching and that even the most skilled communicator severely limits his or her effectiveness through in- adequate preparation. Conversely, good preparation can compensate greatly for the lack of a flair for talking.

The instructor's preparation should consider, for example, how much time will be needed to do a good job and when and where the instructor and the learner will be able to accomplish the most. He or she will see to it that all the supplies, materials, and equipment are available to ensure uninterrupted learning.

Perhaps most important is to have a training plan which breaks the job down step by step to tell the instructor *what* to present. The same plan will include points to stress to tell the instructor the *how* of each step, or the knacks of the job. Figure 7 shows a blank training plan which will facilitate preparation. The same essentials can be covered with any breakdown form, even on the back of an old envelope. Remember that Squeaks used a homemade checklist to accomplish the same purpose.

Step 2: Orient the Operator

The instructor should remove the new employee's anxiety and tension by putting the learner at ease. A smiling face works wonders. Helping the employee see where the new job fits into the departmental and overall

JOB TRAINING PLAN

Job _____

Estimate of time required _____

Date and time of training _____

Location of training _____

Supplies needed _____

_____

_____

Tools or equipment _____

_____

Job Sequence (What)	*Points To Stress (How)*
1.	1.
2.	2.
3.	3.
4.	4.
5.	5.
6.	6.
7.	7.
8.	8.

FIGURE 7

picture is important. Instructors can build their teaching on a sound foundation if they find out what the employee's previous experience has been. The key in this step, of course, is to make the employee interested and eager to learn the job. The employee learns a great deal about the boss and the attitudes he or she will be expected to cultivate during this step.

Step 3: Explain the Operation

Here's where the training plan is put to use. The trainer gives a step-by-step explanation of the job in its logical sequence and demonstrates each step as he or she goes along. It is essential that the trainer doesn't proceed so quickly that the learner is lost. Facial feedback is the best clue to how well the learner is grasping an explanation. It may be necessary to repeat the operation several times to ensure understanding. A final test of comprehension is to have the learner explain the job to the trainer.

Step 4: Test Performance

Once the instructor is confident that the employee completely understands each step in the operation—how and why it is performed—it is time for the employee to try the job. Consideration in correcting errors is important. While it is essential that the learner turn out accurate, high-quality work, the trainer can't lose sight of the fact that the learner needs encouragement in abundant doses. The trainer should remain with the employee until he or she has demonstrated that the job can be performed without 100-percent supervision.

Step 5: Release the Operator

The new employee is now ready to strike out on his or her own. Before leaving, the trainer should check again to see whether the employee has any questions, stressing never to go ahead if in doubt about anything. A characteristic of most learners is that they're gamblers. It's nearly impossible for the instructor to cover every situation that is likely to occur on a job, so the new worker should know where to go for help if it is needed. If a fellow employee is designated as a source of help, it is essential that the employee be informed so he or she doesn't show annoyance at requests for help.

Step 6: Follow Up Performance

This is the step that trainers so frequently overlook or where they tend to take shortcuts. Checking several times a day during the first week to offer encouragement, suggestions, and friendship helps the employee develop good work habits and helps him or her recognize the trainer's interest in him or her. As the employee demonstrates competence, he or she is checked less frequently until he or she is a full-fledged member of the work force.

These six steps can be applied to almost any operation—office, factory, or sales. In clerical work modified application of these steps may occur several times as the employee faces a variety of jobs that he or she will be expected to perform. Training is hard work, but it's work that saves work, and little else in supervision is as satisfying as seeing a novice develop into a reliable performer.

HIGHLIGHTS

1. Training is a prime responsibility of the management-minded supervisor, and it greatly influences the results he or she achieves in production, quality, costs, methods, safety, and morale.

2. Seeing the job from an employee's point of view, we recognize the hopes and desires employees bring to it:

    a. The hope that the job is important
    b. The hope that they'll get along well with the supervisor
    c. The hope that they will do well in the job
    d. The hope that their supervisor will set high standards of performance

3. When supervisors delegate the training function, they do not absolve themselves of the responsibility for a well-trained work force. The supervisor should see that whoever does the training in the department knows the principles of good training and has the skill to apply them.

4. Unskilled trainers tend to make these common errors in teaching people their jobs:

    a. Feeding too much at one time
    b. Telling without demonstrating
    c. Showing a lack of patience
    d. Failure to prepare to instruct
    e. Failure to build in feedback
    f. Failure to reduce tension

5. People don't learn until they're ready to learn. They must be motivated by seeing that the jobs they will be doing are important to the operation.

6. Some factors which tend to facilitate learning or make learning easier for the employee are:

    a. Repetition
    b. Arousing curiosity
    c. Careful use of competition
    d. Knowing the knacks of the job
    e. Enthusiastic instruction
    f. Satisfaction in accomplishment

7. Unknowingly, supervisors can inhibit the learning process and make their own jobs tougher. Factors which slow down learning are:

    a. Fatigue
    b. Monotony
    c. Distractions
    d. Anxiety

8. A six-step system for training:

    a. Prepares the instructor
    b. Orients the operator
    c. Explains the operation
    d. Tests performance
    e. Releases the operator
    f. Follows up with checks on performance

DISCUSSION QUESTIONS

1. Explain the effect that good training will have on production, costs, quality, safety, and morale.

2. What, specifically, can a supervisor do to get an employee interested in learning a job?

3. In your own words, explain why empathy is so important for anyone instructing a new employee on the job.

4. What are the advantages and disadvantages of a supervisor's delegating the training of new employees to others?

5. Many offices follow the practice of having the outgoing worker train her replacement. What are the limitations of this procedure?

6. Six common errors in teaching people their jobs were identified in this chapter. Can you identify at least four more?

7. Explain in your own words how the instructor's enthusiasm, or lack of it, is likely to affect the learner.

8. What can a supervisor do to put a learner at ease before beginning instruction? Be specific.

9. Make a job training plan (like the one in Figure 7) for a simple job from your department.

10. Teach somebody a job using the six-step system presented in this chapter. Evaluate your experience using this system.

CASE PROBLEMS

THE CASE OF FLORENCE BILLINGS

Florence Billings knows she has her work cut out for her. Affirmative action programs have always been something she has ignored—"don't cross the bridge until you come to it" has been her philosophy. As supervisor of the steno pool in the United Telephone Company, she has had no minority group members in her department, even though the company had advertised that it was an equal opportunity employer. She had even taken a casual attitude to recent rumors that the personnel department was going to get serious about affirmative action rather than giving lip service to it. Everybody knew the company had been engaging in "tokenism."

Three well-qualified applicants have just been interviewed by Florence—all three black and anxious to work. Personnel has indicated to Florence that they expect her to make her choice from the three young women sent her. Her choice must be made quickly so the other two can be placed in other departments. All three are potentially too valuable to lose to other employers. Any of the three would be an asset to the department, and Florence is certain she would have no difficulty in working personally with the one selected. "I'm not prejudiced," she thinks, "but what about the others I supervise? How much preparing of the group do I have to do? What if they don't accept her? What should I say to the new person about coming to work as the first black in the department? The applicants all have pleasing personalities. I have good teamwork in the department, and I don't want that to change."

1. What should Florence say to the people she supervises about the new employee?

2. How should Florence handle the introduction of the first black in her department?

3. Should the orientation of her new employee be any different than it has always been? If so, how?

THE CASE OF ELTON JACKSON

Harney's was the largest and busiest hardware and building supply establishment in the metropolitan area. Getting a new salesperson started was always a problem for Elton Jackson. There were so many items in their inventory and most of their customers were do-it-yourselfers who needed answers to a thousand questions. The opportunity to hire Ken Randall, who had quit Harney's chief competitor after years of experience, was grasped as quickly as Randall indicated his availability. "A real find," was Elton's feeling when the hiring decision was finalized.

   Randall's knowledge of building materials and tools was even better than Elton had hoped. He ranked immediately with the best salespeople Harney's had on the floor. Because of his knowledge and sales experience, training centered primarily around the store's paper work—sales slips, charging procedures, inventory records, credit identification, handling returned merchandise, and so on. Randall seemed so anxious to prove himself as a salesman that he was frequently preoccupied when explanations about transactions were given him. He said he understood, but repeated errors revealed that he didn't. Frequent interruptions of other salespeople to ask questions already covered in his training proved that he hadn't paid attention and that he had faked understanding. Randall seemed embarrassed when caught repeatedly making errors, but this "anxious-to-please" sales expert was obviously going to have to be taken by the hand and started all over.

1. What might be some of the mistakes Elton made in training Randall?

2. How can you make sure employees understand the basics when they are so anxious to get to work?

3. How should the problem of starting over with Randall be handled?

THE CASE OF MARSHA MARTIN

She seemed so capable and enthusiastic, this Marsha Martin. Her positive attitude shone through her employment interviews and her appearance for work the first morning at the State Highway Department's bridge design and construction office. She'll be a real asset to the department, Donna Wright, supervisor, thought when she turned Marsha over to Frances Carrol for training. Frances's departure in another week would be welcome. Ever since she gave her notice almost two weeks ago, Frances was next to useless. In addition to producing less and less each day, she seemed to resent the added chore of having to break her replacement in.

At the end of this first day, Donna asked Marsha to stop in for a chat before going home. Confusion had replaced Marsha's eagerness. Her smile was lost in fatigue—no more bounce. When asked how the day had gone, Marsha softly said, "Fine, I guess, but I'm not sure I'll be able to keep up. I just don't seem to grasp things as fast as Fran thinks I should. Maybe the first day is always like that. I hope so, anyhow. I just have to get used to all this government red tape."

Donna started to explain that there was good reason for all the procedures, but decided this wasn't the time. Instead she reassured Marsha the confusion was natural and would be short-lived. A good night's sleep, she told Marsha, would restore that bouncy enthusiasm they so admired.

"I can't believe how she's changed in just one day. Something has taken the starch right out of that girl. Will things improve before Fran leaves or is the problem with Fran? I'd better talk with Fran in the morning," is the way Donna was mentally summing up her chat with Marsha as she locked her office.

1. What might be some of the reasons for Marsha's lost enthusiasm?

2. Evaluate the practice of having outgoing employees train their replacements.

3. If Marsha must be trained by Fran, what should be done to ensure quality training?

4. How should Donna handle the situation now?

SUGGESTIONS FOR FURTHER STUDY

Bittel, Lester R., *What Every Supervisor Should Know*, 3d ed., Chapter 13, McGraw-Hill Book Company, New York, 1974.
Broadwell, Martin M., *The Supervisor and On-the-Job Training*, Addi-

son-Wesley Publishing Company, Reading, Massachusetts, 1969.

Ficker, Victor B., *Effective Supervision*, Chapter 6, Charles E. Merrill Books, Inc., Columbus, Ohio, 1975.

Steinmetz, Lawrence L., and H. Ralph Todd, Jr., *First-Line Management*, Chapter 10, Business Publications, Inc., Dallas, Texas, 1975.

Vernon, Ivan R., *First-Line Management*, Chapter 6, Society of Manufacturing Engineers, Dearborn, Michigan, 1972.

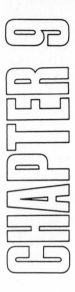

CHAPTER 9

DISCIPLINE AS A WAY OF THINKING

"I'm so mad I could chew nails. Have you got a couple of minutes, Ray?" Burt Hall was standing in the doorway to Ray Ford's office after the shift had left for the day.

Ray motioned Burt in, saying, "Come on in and grab a chair. Frank and I will have things wrapped up in about thirty seconds." Ray affixed his signature to a requisition, handed it to Frank Connors, toolroom supervisor, and turned to Burt, saying, "Now, what can I do you out of?"

Before Burt could answer, Frank started to go; but then he asked Burt, "Is this a private fight, or can anybody get in?" Without smiling, Burt said, "If you've got a few minutes, Frank, stick around. Maybe three heads are better than two, or should I say one. I think I've just lost mine."

"It sounds serious," Ray said. "What's up?"

"It's that Slim Carpenter we hired about a month ago. Rules just don't mean a thing to him. If I could have found him tonight, I'd probably have fired him or given him a week off to think things over," Burt started out. "For the third time in a month he's walked out of the department without checking—without permission. And these last two times he can't claim he didn't know about the rule because I explained it clearly the first time it happened. I don't know . . ."

"Wow," Frank interrupted. "You've really got him. Lower the boom. Teach him a lesson he won't forget so easily this time. You've got to show these new young punks who's boss, or they'll run all over you."

Burt nodded and went on to explain that he had been in the production office just before the end of the shift. He had been given a small but routine rush order that had to be ready for shipping late the next morning. On his way back to the department Burt decided that Slim could handle it if he got at it first thing in the morning. Slim should have finished that Apex order before quitting time. When Burt arrived at Slim's bench, Slim was nowhere in sight. His bench was cleaned up for the night. It was still five minutes before quitting time. Burt asked the man on the next bench where Slim had gone and was told by Slim's neighbor that he wasn't sure. He said that Slim had been talking about wanting to sign up for the softball team just before he left and that maybe he was going to take care of that. "Now how do you like that?" Burt asked Ray. "He just ups and walks out to sign up for softball after two warnings in less than a month about leaving the department. Maybe Frank is right. Clobber him."

"You bet," smiled Frank. "Get tough with him and get him in line."

"Now wait a minute," Ray cautioned. "Cool down. He's your man, Burt. Whatever you decide to do, I'll back you up. But let's be sure we're doing what's best for everyone concerned before we move. If I understand you correctly, we're not sure at this point why Slim was absent from the department tonight. Shouldn't we find out why before we decide to fire him or give him time off?"

Burt somewhat sheepishly said, "I suppose you're right. I only figured it's just like him to pull a stunt like that."

"Let's quit pussyfooting around," Frank snarled. "You'll get a beauty of an alibi. You can count on that. Give a guy like him an inch and he'll take a mile every time. No sir, I say you crack down hard before he gets to thinking he's got you hoodwinked."

"Burt," Ray asked. "What kind of a worker is Slim? Has he given you any other kind of trouble?"

"No, actually he's pretty good. He was a quick learner. I can always count on him to get a job done on time, and his quality is all that anyone could ask. But, Ray, I can't have a guy ignoring the rules in the department without giving everybody the idea that rules don't matter."

"You're right, Burt," Ray admitted. "Rules are made for everybody, and we can't be making exceptions. If we do, we're asking for trouble. Something will have to be done as soon as you find out why he was gone. What about the first two times? What happened then?"

Burt explained that maybe the first time shouldn't count, except that the rule was violated and he had taken the time to explain the rule to Slim. The first week that Slim was on the job he had gone over to the next department during the morning break to buy a candy bar. The machine in Assembly Department B was empty. Burt explained to Slim that the rule about leaving the department included break periods. Not every department took its breaks at the same time, and it wasn't fair to be bothering other departments where people were working. He also explained to Slim that as supervisor it was his job to know where his people were at all times. Slim said that he could see the point. He told Burt that he understood and that it wouldn't happen again. Burt told Ray that Slim was so cooperative that he didn't think of it as a warning and hadn't even made a note of it.

The second incident happened about two weeks later. The personnel department sent a note asking Slim to sign some insurance forms that they were processing. Burt said that this time he'd been waiting for Slim when he got back and that he called him into the office immediately. Slim told Burt that he thought a note from Personnel took care of the rule and that he was only doing what he was told. He hadn't meant to create any trouble, he said.

Burt pointed out that absence from the department for any reason should first be cleared with the supervisor. Burt also told Slim that he accepted his explanation but that Slim could consider their conversation a warning. He told Slim that another violation would force him to take stronger action. Burt concluded by telling Slim that he had confidence that it wouldn't be necessary.

"And now," said Ray, "it seems we have another violation a little over a week later."

"Seems? Hell!" snapped Frank. "What more do you need to prove what I've been saying? If you're smart, you'll let him know what it's like not to have a paycheck coming in."

"We've got a fair investment in him, Burt," Ray said, ignoring Frank's last remark. "But we can't afford to let him disobey rules either. Find out what he has to say in the morning. You decide whether or not he's worth trying to save. Either way, I'll back you up. It's your department. Just as a final check on your decision, you might give some thought as to whether or not it will accomplish what you want it to."

By the time Burt got to work the next morning, he was thinking more clearly. Slim, he had decided, was too good a man to lose in a burst of temper. He actually hoped that Slim had a better excuse than signing up for softball for being absent from the department again. He wanted something that would take him off the hook. He had outlined four alternative courses he could take, depending on Slim's attitude and his reason for being gone. First, if Slim had a good reason, he could let him go with another warning. Second, Burt could send a written warning to become part of Slim's personnel file. That would be stronger. Third, there was a three-day suspension without pay. That would give Slim something to think about. Finally, if Slim's attitude was poor, Burt might recommend discharge. He didn't want to do it, but it was a possibility.

In the office, Burt started out by asking Slim what he had to say for himself. Slim turned red and said that he was sorry and that he had wanted to check with Burt first. Slim said that he had found out yesterday afternoon about the company softball team. Then he found out that the deadline for signing up had passed that noon. The personnel department had told Slim on the phone that Barney Stilwell had the list and was taking it down to the city recreation department on his way home from work. It was 3:00 P.M.; there was no way to phone Barney in the maintenance department, and Burt was gone.

"Gee, Burt, I didn't know what to do. I kept hoping you'd get back in time for me to ask you. I was sure you'd say OK," Slim said apologetically. "I play a pretty good game at first base, and I was sure I could make the team. You know it kind of makes a guy feel he belongs to be able to play on a company team. Well, I finished the Apex job, and it was too late to set up for the next one. Actually, I pushed pretty hard to finish so you could let me run over in time to catch Barney. But you didn't come, and you didn't come. Finally, I had to take the chance that you wouldn't get back before 3:30 and find out that I was gone. Burt, I'm sorry. I shouldn't have left, but it was only six or seven minutes, and I caught him just as he was walking out the door. What else could I do?"

Burt told Slim to go back to his bench until he had time to think. He gave Slim the rush job and told him to come back to the office at break time, when they would decide what should be done. Burt mentally eliminated his fourth alternative—discharge. Slim's attitude was all right. He knew what he had done and was sorry. "But where do I go from here?" Burt asked himself. "Ray and Slim both expect my decision. Why in blazes did it have to be the softball team?"

1. What did Ray have in mind when he cautioned Burt to determine whether or not the decision he makes will accomplish what he wanted it to?

2. What might be the results of implementing each of the three alternatives Burt has left?

3. How should we evaluate Burt's handling of Slim Carpenter up to this point?

4. How should we evaluate Frank Connors' advice to Burt?

5. What objectives should Burt be trying to reach in deciding how to handle Slim Carpenter?

6. What should Burt do under the circumstances?

THE MEANING OF DISCIPLINE

Applying the principles of sound discipline is a difficult job for many supervisors. Most supervisors don't think much about discipline until faced with rule violations. They accept without question the responsibility for enforcing the rules of the organization. And not until an incident occurs that calls for correction does the word *discipline* cross the supervisor's consciousness. At that point there's a strong temptation to react as Frank Connors did when he heard about Slim Carpenter. Crack down, straighten him out, show him who's boss, get tough, clobber him, lower the boom—these and many other thoughts direct the supervisor's thinking about discipline along the lines of punishment.

Rationally, we readily realize that disciplinary action and discipline represent two widely differing stages. It's important to understand that when we reach the point of getting tough, the probability is that discipline has already begun to fall apart. Disciplinary action is the action taken when discipline breaks down. Burt is at a point where he must decide whether disciplinary action must be taken with Slim.

For the purposes of our discussion in this chapter, we should take note of several definitions of *discipline*, keeping uppermost in our minds that the management-minded supervisor wants to stress its positive side as much as possible. The word *discipline* and the word *disciple*, which was originally used to describe the followers of the teachings of Jesus Christ, both have the same source. But the disciples were more than followers. They were also teachers and leaders after Christ's crucifixion. Those who choose to relate modern concepts to biblical origins will say that discipline means either following rules of conduct or leading people and training them. For our purposes both concepts are extremely useful.

The military recognizes the discipline of troops as essential—the unquestioning acceptance of authority and orders. The college professor speaks of his discipline as a field of study. The dictionary meaning defines discipline as the training that encourages self-development and self-control. It is also a system of rules governing behavior; and it is also punishment. Industrial training directors will generally agree that discipline involves controlling employees' performance.

Now let's see whether we can find a working definition that fits the job of the front-line manager. First we can agree that it would be better not to think of discipline as punishment. Since the supervisor is charged with maintaining control of the department, we might simply say that *discipline means control*. If that control includes the idea of people voluntarily following rules of conduct, we might add that *the ultimate goal of discipline is self-discipline*, or self-control. Probably one of the best tests of discipline in a department is to find out what happens when its supervisor is away from it. Does business go on as usual with everyone tending to his or her own job? *Discipline*, then, is *the training that makes punishment unnecessary*.

To summarize what many truly management-minded supervisors have said, we find that discipline is a positive concept involving building and teaching and is not a negative concept with the connotations of punishment and revenge. Good discipline encourages self-control. Discipline actually can be regarded as a morale builder instead of a threat to morale. Truly, discipline is a way of thinking. It requires sound leadership, the creation of a healthy climate, and expert teaching.

With this background, we can begin to see the end of the road that Frank Connors was trying to lead Burt down. Punishment was undoubtedly the focus of Frank's thinking about discipline. He followed the bull-of-the-woods approach, using fear and threats to keep his people in line. We don't have to be told that Burt probably would have lost Slim if he had taken Frank's advice, but more important, he would have sowed the seeds of disrespect among the other members of his department. An unhealthy desire for revenge might have been temporarily satisfied—but at what cost?

Ray Ford demonstrates qualities of a good boss. Without suggesting what decision Burt should make, Ray's first step was to calm Burt down. Anger or temper greatly inhibits the ability to reason. Ray helped Burt see both sides of the problem—Burt's and the company's long-range interest. Without humiliating him, Ray showed Burt the error of making a decision until he knew the facts surrounding Slim's disappearance. And finally, he assured Burt that whatever action Burt might want to take, it would have his full backing.

The implication was there that Ray's support would be forth-coming even though he might not agree with Burt. Clearly, Ray was demonstrating excellent leadership by showing confidence in Burt's ability to make a wise decision. By his example, he was suggesting that Burt should demonstrate the same strength in leading his department. From a management point of view, we can see the wisdom of Ray's suggestion that Burt decide what objectives he was trying to reach with his decision.

If we compare Ray's approach and that of Frank Connors with the definition of discipline we developed, we can see that Ray comes as close as one can to demonstrating that discipline is the training that makes punishment unnecessary. The objectives of members of man-agement are to train, develop, and mold a body of workers in their departments. Every rule violation or incident of misconduct should be regarded as an opportunity for training. Even when strong action to stop an undesirable practice is indicated, supervisors need to think about what kind of action to take in terms of how well it will teach, not how much it will punish.

CREATING A CLIMATE FOR DISCIPLINE

Creating a climate in which employees willingly and naturally abide by company rules is not simply a matter of devoting so much time per week to discipline. Everything discussed so far has a marked impact on how people respond to leadership. Communication, motivation, and training all contribute heavily to building a responsive, responsible work force. The cornerstone for sound discipline is respect for authority. How supervisors handle job assignments, respect the feelings of people, satisfy their needs, keep them informed, and teach them their jobs influence the way their employees conduct themselves.

It would be unrealistic to think that we could ever reach that state of perfection in which no one ever broke a rule. What supervisors do when violations do occur will also help create the climate in which they manage. The great majority of employees accept rules and directions as a condition of employment. They wouldn't think of breaking a rule. These same people, however, will observe and evaluate our conduct in handling those few who may get out of line. Everyone is concerned with getting fair treatment. It is not good for morale either to see someone else get away with violating rules we abide by or to witness unduly harsh disciplinary action. Supervisors should ask themselves whether their disciplinary methods contribute to good departmental control or threaten it.

Common sense and years of successful supervisory experience suggest some practical guidelines to follow in creating a healthy climate for constructive discipline.

Make Sure Employees Understand the Rules

This is so obvious and basic that many supervisors take it for granted. First, of course, the employees need a thorough knowledge of the rules themselves. Not only do they need to know what the rules are, but more important, they need an understanding of why the rules exist. Burt Hall's explanation to Slim Carpenter of the reason for the rule about not leaving the department even during a break was much more effective in building understanding than simply reading the rules out of the book. Burt also was willing to go easy on Slim because the possibility existed that Slim didn't understand or had forgotten the rule. He was much more concerned with the second violation. If we expect people to follow rules, they must know what the rules are.

Enforce Rules Consistently

Rules are made to be followed by everyone in the department. It's extremely difficult for an employee to understand on-again, off-again enforcement. The supervisor's position in relation to enforcing rules becomes quite untenable if the violator can come back with, "Yeah, but you didn't say anything when Joe did the same thing last week." Reprimands may not be necessary with every violation, but it is extremely important that every violation be acted upon. The circumstances surrounding the violation and the intent and attitude of the violator will influence such action. But the supervisor should not overlook the opportunity to demonstrate his or her concern and to teach violators the error of their ways. For example, Burt was quick to explain to Slim that he shouldn't leave the department even during the break. His action couldn't be construed as a reprimand—he didn't even make a note of it—but he did act. Any time a supervisor ignores a violation and does nothing about it, he or she is, in fact, condoning the act. Such conduct can only make it difficult to correct future violations.

Make the Disciplinary Action Fit the Crime

It is a temptation to quote the Gilbert and Sullivan dictum, "Make the punishment fit the crime." When disciplinary action must be taken, it soon becomes common knowledge in the department. A supervisor's actions will be judged by every member of the department. What would Burt's employees have thought if Burt had followed Frank Connors' advice and discharged Slim Carpenter? Burt had to take some action, but few, if any, of us would recommend Slim's discharge. The test of training which would make punishment unnecessary is a good one to remember in considering the disciplinary action it is most appropriate to take.

Most plants have certain rules which call for automatic discharge if violated. Examples of such rules include theft of company property, insubordination, fighting, sabotage, intoxication on the job, and smoking in hazardous areas. Even with discharge authorized on the first offense, a supervisor is inclined to weigh very carefully all the circumstances surrounding the incident before taking such drastic action.

Determining the appropriateness of disciplinary action should come only after serious consideration has been given to (1) the circumstances surrounding the violation, (2) the seriousness of the offense, (3) the past record of the offender, (4) the intent of the offender, and (5) disciplinary action taken in similar situations.

Make Certain That Actions Correct, Not Punish

One plant of the Western Plywood Company, Limited, of Canada is so concerned with teaching their foremen the importance of eliminating punishment from their concepts of discipline that whenever disciplinary layoffs are necessary, the employee is paid for the time spent at home. They maintain that the purpose of the suspension is to give the employee time to think over the consequences of his or her behavior—to decide whether the employee wants to be a part of the team and abide by the rules. Loss of pay is punishment. Time to think without loss of pay tends to be more constructive. Expensive? According to an executive of the company, every time an employee was sent home without pay, a grievance resulted. Under the new program, grievances seldom grow out of suspension since there is no punishment involved. The expense of grievance meetings, he reported, was much greater than the cost of paying an employee for time off while thinking about the future with the company.

It's not likely that many companies will institute such an unusual procedure. It is important to understand the principle behind this method. Even in the case of disciplinary layoffs, the company was adhering to the principle of training and education rather than punishment.

Ray Ford was steering Burt's thinking along similar lines when he counseled Burt to consider what he was trying to accomplish. Constructive discipline requires the supervisor to show the offender how to make the necessary corrections, to explain the rewards for doing so, and to set forth the consequences of failing to conform to acceptable standards. Firm, fair, patient handling of rules violations is much more likely to produce the desired result than impulsive, insulting, humiliating treatment.

Remember to Give Credit

Most supervisors when pressed for an answer will admit that they criticize and correct far more often than they give credit. But they all know that giving credit is much more pleasant and satisfying than criticizing. Why should this be? Some say it's their job to criticize and correct. But isn't it just as much their job to give credit, particularly since creating a climate for sound discipline depends on gaining the respect of employees?

Others will say that they don't know how to give credit. Three considerations will perhaps encourage supervisors to credit good work. First, they should be alert to the opportunities for giving credit. These arise when a worker shows commendable initiative, sets a good example for other employees, performs better than was expected, shows evidence of good planning or good housekeeping, extends help or cooperation to fellow workers, makes a good suggestion, keeps his or her temper under stress, supports management's position to fellow employees. When these and countless other opportunities present themselves, why not give proper credit to the deserving person? Mark Twain once said, "When a man has credit due him, now is the time to give it to him, for he cannot read his tombstone when he's dead."

Second, supervisors should consider the advisability of crediting the work, not the worker. If the emphasis is put on skill, the giving of credit is a business matter rather than personal flattery, and there will be much less likelihood of creating any feeling of embarrassment.

Third, it is possible to give credit indirectly. By asking for suggestions, for example, a supervisor shows respect for the knowledge and ability of the employees. Checking on the progress of work is another method of recognizing the individual. Noticing improvement in a worker's performance, however small it may be, is still another. Most supervisors who credit the performance of their employees find their employees praising them. And that's a nice climate to have!

What to Avoid	*What to Do*
Sarcasm	Consider feelings of employees.
Loss of temper	Cool down, analyze each situation.
Humiliating an employee	Show confidence in the employee's ability to make necessary changes.
Profanity	Carefully explain the nature of the violation and the correction expected.
Public reprimands	*Always* reprimand in private.
Threats and bluffs	Outline specific consequences of future violations, and follow through.
Showing favoritism	Give every employee fair treatment.
Delay tactics	Give prompt attention to violations.
Unduly harsh penalties	Define the objective of disciplinary action.
Inconsistent enforcement	Deal promptly with all violations of rules.

How can we recognize a good climate for constructive discipline? If a department's employees abide by rules willingly and naturally, if suggestions for improvement replace gripes and complaints, if employees are enthusiastic about achieving the goals of the department, if employees are cooperative in helping one another, if employees accept assignments cheerfully, if employees will go out of their way to help the supervisor, if employees generally support management policies, and if employees show initiative in doing the best work possible, the chances are that the supervisor has done an outstanding job of creating the proper climate. Certainly we can see that if the above conditions exist, there's little likelihood of disciplinary problems, and disciplinary action will rarely be necessary.

Frequently new supervisors will ask for the dos and don'ts of creating the proper climate for constructive criticism. At the risk of oversimplifying a complex aspect of our management job, let's consider what to avoid and what to do.

Just reviewing such a checklist can be a reminder of the consequences of poor disciplinary methods. A breakdown in discipline is a great deal more difficult to repair than a breakdown of machinery or equipment. How much easier it is to build a healthy climate than to weather the storms of discontent and disobedience.

WHEN A REPRIMAND IS NECESSARY

If we had reached that utopia where no one was ever guilty of a rule infraction and where cooperation and harmony were the only responses to supervision, then we could forget any consideration of the reprimand. We haven't, though, and rules will be broken—unintentionally or otherwise. Corrective measures must be taken, or else the idea that obeying rules isn't important may take hold.

Fortunately, few people ever need to be reprimanded. But good climate is encouraged by expert handling of those occasions when disciplinary action becomes necessary. The challenge is to correct mistakes without arousing resentment. We're thinking now particularly of those situations that require more than a simple suggestion or a casual corrective remark—those situations when an infraction is serious or when the negative behavior has become chronic. Slim Carpenter's three infractions amounted to what we might call a chronic tendency.

In analyzing how to reprimand, we should remind ourselves that corrective action and not punishment is the proper objective. The reprimand is a training situation. It requires careful consideration of the individual to achieve a positive response rather than resentment. As simple as this may seem, it's very difficult to remember and achieve. When a situation is serious enough to require a reprimand, the supervisor's control is being threatened, his or her leadership challenged, and his or her patience strained. The temptation to resort to impulsive, harsh treatment of the offending person is great. Yet, here in a calm, rational discussion of discipline we can easily see that it is the calm, thoughtful approach that keeps the supervisor in control of the situation and allows moving positively toward the goal.

Since it's generally easier to remember and understand an organized approach, let's think of reprimanding in terms of these six steps:

Control Your Temper

Little constructive disciplining is ever accomplished in anger. We tend to say things we're sorry for and make accusations that are difficult to retract. There's little need for concern about saving face if we control our temper. We don't think clearly when we're angry, and common sense tells us that we want to maintain every advantage we can. We'll recall that Ray Ford's first advice to Burt was, "Cool down." He was telling Burt, in effect, to stop reacting and start thinking.

Be Sure of Your Facts

Gossip, rumors, and hearsay evidence all too often prove to be inaccurate. A supervisor wants to be certain that an employee is deserving of a reprimand before issuing it. Burt was ready to take drastic action before he even knew why Slim had left the department. What were the circumstances of the infraction?

What, specifically, did the offender do wrong? What are the consequences of the infraction? What could they have been? Have there been similar infractions in the past? How long ago? How frequently? The better equipped the supervisor is with the facts, the less likely he or she is to get caught off base. We have probably all known supervisors who have impulsively reprimanded an employee only to discover that the reprimand was not justified. A few such incidents can go a long way toward building a climate of disrespect.

Talk to the Offender in Private

The training objective of our reprimand demands that it be done in private, where the possibility that the offending employee will lose face in the eyes of the group is minimized. Safety violations which endanger other employees or company property will, of course, have to be stopped on the spot; but even in these cases the reprimanding interview can be conducted in private. Humiliation and embarrassment produce tension and make people less receptive to corrective suggestions.

A short postponement of a reprimand interview until it can be done in private gives both the supervisor and the employee some time to cool down. If one or the other, by chance, does allow their temper to flare up, how much better it is to have it occur in private. In fact, the supervisor who possesses a short fuse should make doubly sure that reprimands are handled *only in private*.

Get the Offender's Side of the Story

Empathy helps in trying to understand why a person might have committed an infraction. There is no substitute, however, for allowing employees to explain their side of a situation. Even criminals are entitled to their day in court and, we might add, are considered innocent until proved guilty. By listening attentively and courteously to the offender's full explanation, the supervisor demonstrates concern for fair treatment of the employee. We might recap what Burt learned by listening to Slim's explanation: (1) Slim knew he was violating the rule. (2) He deliberately risked Burt's finding out. (3) He did want to clear with Burt and abide by the rule. (4) He wanted, through softball, to feel that he belonged. (5) He had put forth extra effort to finish his work to make time for his errand.

How strong a reprimand to give and what disciplinary action to take, if any, will be based on the attitude of the employee, the intent when committing the infraction, the understanding of the rule broken, and interest in changing of behavior. It's almost impossible to get this kind of information without listening to the employee's explanation.

Be Firm but Fair

It is to be hoped that nothing in this chapter has conveyed the idea that a supervisor should be anything but firm in dealing with rules infractions. Being firm does not mean, however, getting tough or throwing your weight around. Consideration of the employee's feelings is what we mean by fairness. Being fair also includes explaining why the behavior is unacceptable, how it violates the rules of good conduct, and why the rule exists.

A fair reprimand requires the supervisor to outline for the employee what corrective action or behavior is acceptable. If disciplinary action is to be taken, the supervisor should explain what that action is to accomplish. Even in the extreme case of discharge, there is little justification for humiliating the employee. A highly respected training director has always maintained that the real test in discharging an employee is to do it in such a way that the employee says "thank you" at the end.

Express Confidence in the Offender's Ability to Improve

Since the objective in a reprimand is training, it is impossible to ignore the encouragement that should be given any trainee in learning the job. The sting of a reprimand can be removed by the supervisor's showing confidence in the ability of the employee to modify his or her behavior. Showing confidence in the employee is a strong positive way to conclude the reprimand. We know that employees would rather please than displease. Don't the supervisors need to demonstrate the kind of supervisory behavior that makes pleasing them easy? A supervisor should expect an employee to change behavior and should show confidence in the employee's ability to do so, for the more the supervisor asks of an employee, the more the employee is likely to give.

How can a supervisor be sure that, once the reprimand interview is concluded, the job has been successfully discharged? In the long run, if the employee makes the desired correction without resentment and causes no further difficulty, the supervisor has succeeded. Most supervisors would like a quicker evaluation, however, and answering these questions should help determine the effectiveness of a reprimand:

1. Did I maintain a positive corrective attitude throughout?

2. Did the employee understand and acknowledge what he or she had done wrong?

3. Did the employee realize the possible consequences of the error?

4. Does the employee know what is expected in the future?

5. Does the employee feel that I have tried to help?

6. Does the employee feel that I have been fair?

7. Is the employee free from any feelings of resentment?

Unless the supervisor has handled the reprimand in a way that will make the employee more interested and enthusiastic about the job, rather than hurt or resentful, the use of authority has been harmful to the best interests of the company he or she represents.

STAGES OF DISCIPLINARY ACTION

Most labor contracts outline the steps to be taken in applying disciplinary action. Even in the nonunion organization, supervisory manuals will outline a variation of these same stages. They are designed to ensure fair treatment of employees—to protect them against impulsive, unduly harsh punishment for wrongdoing. In industry, as in society, the rights of the individual must be protected. These steps represent that protection:

First Offense: Oral Warning

It is presumed that the employee did not understand the nature of the wrongdoing. The rule or standard of conduct is explained, and it is made clear that continued misconduct will not be condoned. The employee is warned that future violations will make stronger action necessary. A written record of the time, place, and circumstances of the warning is recommended by nearly all companies.

Second Offense: Written Warning

The employee is informed in writing that his or her misconduct is in violation of rules or standards of good conduct and that another infraction will result in loss of pay or job. A copy of the warning is given to the employee, a copy is put in his or her personnel file, and a copy is given to the superior of the supervisor issuing the warning. If a union exists, the steward and/or the union also receives a copy. In effect, all parties concerned are informed of the action taken.

Third Offense: Disciplinary Layoff

The employee is suspended from the job without pay for a period of time consistent with the seriousness of the offense. Most such suspensions range from one to five working days. Coupled with such action is the usual warning that another violation will call for discharge.

Fourth Offense: Discharge

It is presumed that by this time the employee has been given every opportunity to conform and has little concern for doing so. The best interests of both the company and the employee are assumed to be best served by complete separation.

Obviously, as we noted earlier, some infractions are so serious that discharge is permitted with the first violation. In other cases, the seriousness of the offense or the antagonistic attitude of an employee might dictate a shortcutting of these steps. On the other hand, many supervisors have added a fifth step. Before any of the above actions are taken, they will have a private talk with the employee at the first offense. An example of such action would be Burt's first talk with Slim, after Slim went out for a candy bar. For most employees this is all that is ever necessary.

It is most important to remember that even in disciplinary cases the training objectives of the action be recognized. Our goal is not to fire employees in whom we have a substantial investment, but to train them to be well-disciplined members of the work group. In determining what action should be taken after an infraction has occurred, many supervisors have been guided by asking themselves the following questions:

1.   What is the past record of the employee?

2.   Do I have all the facts that bear on this situation?

3.   Has the employee had a reasonable chance to improve?

4.   When was the employee given a fair warning of the seriousness of misconduct?

5.   What actions have been taken in similar cases?

6.   What effects will this action have on the rest of the department?

7.   Should I consult anyone else before taking action?

The last question particularly is worth turning over in our minds. Discussing contemplated disciplinary action with the boss or with a staff specialist (personnel or labor relations) is not ducking responsibility. These are the people who will be having to support the supervisor's actions. Another person, one who is not emotionally involved and whose judgment the supervisor respects, might very well add another dimension to his thinking. Ray Ford played this role in "The Case of the Disappearing Carpenter."

**DISCIPLINE:
WHAT IT IS AND ISN'T**

In concluding this discussion of discipline, we might benefit by reviewing what a positive, constructive approach to discipline means to the management-minded supervisor. For purposes of comparison we should also identify some commonly held ideas that should have no part in management-minded thinking about discipline.

First and most important, discipline is the training and development of a cooperative work force striving together for the realization of management goals and objectives. Disciplinary action has the purpose of teaching and molding. Planning and implementation of such action should never lose sight of that purpose. Punishment has no place in thinking about discipline.

Discipline is best achieved by creating a climate of respect through sound leadership. The supervisor who demonstrates respect for his or her work group gets respect from that group in return. Many supervisors find it helpful to think of discipline as a program of preventative maintenance—heading off trouble before it starts. Discipline should not be ignored until trouble starts. It is not a policing action that begins only after infractions and misconduct have occurred and must be dealt with under conditions of stress.

Discipline in the work force is best demonstrated by self-discipline—people working in harmony, abiding by departmental rules and standards of good conduct. When discipline is good, cooperation with supervisors and fellow employees is at a high level. Discipline is not the use of fear, threats, and punishment to keep people in line.

Discipline is a means of maintaining and boosting morale. By providing for fair treatment to everyone, equal application of rules, and considerate correctional methods, a supervisor establishes a climate of trust. Discipline is not rigid, unbending supervision that fosters resentment. It encourages rather than discourages, molds rather than destroys, rewards rather than penalizes, creates profits in human relations rather than deficits. It's a way of thinking.

HIGHLIGHTS

1. Discipline means control. Its goal is self-control. It is the training that makes punishment unnecessary.

2. Anger, temper, punishment, and revenge have no part in the management-minded supervisor's concept of discipline.

3. Discipline in the department is largely a matter of creating the proper climate. Practical guidelines to follow in creating a climate for constructive discipline include:

   a. Making sure that employees understand the rules
   b. Enforcing rules consistently
   c. Making disciplinary actions fit the offense
   d. Making certain that actions correct, not punish
   e. Remembering to give credit

4. Naturally, some offenses will occur. Corrective measures against these inevitable rules infractions require skill in reprimanding. To be constructive in reprimanding, the supervisor should:

    a.   Control his or her temper

    b.   Be sure of the facts

    c.   Talk to the employee in private

    d.   Get the offender's side of the problem

    e.   Be firm but fair

    f.   Express confidence in the employee's ability to improve

5. Four or five stages in taking disciplinary action are outlined in most labor contracts and supervisory manuals to guarantee the employee fair treatment. A five-stage procedure might include:

    a.   First offense—private talk

    b.   Second offense—oral warning

    c.   Third offense—written warning

    d.   Fourth offense—disciplinary layoff

    e.   Fifth offense—discharge

6. Discipline should:

    a.   Encourage rather than discourage

    b.   Mold rather than destroy

    c.   Reward rather than punish

    d.   Create profits in human relations rather than deficits

DISCUSSION QUESTIONS

1. Expand on the statement that discipline can be regarded as a morale builder rather than as a threat to morale.

2. List four reasons why it is important for a supervisor to keep his or her temper under control when handling disciplinary problems.

3. Evaluate the philosophy that many managers follow when they support a supervisor in disciplinary actions even though they may not agree with the supervisor's decision.

4. What is your evaluation of the practice of paying employees for time they are away from work for disciplinary suspensions?

5. Would you support the policy of paying employees during disciplinary suspensions in your company? Why or why not?

6. Cite as many reasons as you can for supervisors to give credit to their employees.

7. What, in your opinion, are the main reasons why supervisors don't praise more often?

8. Describe a situation in your experience in which the disciplining of an employee was poorly handled. What, in your opinion, should have been done to leave the employee with a positive feeling toward the job and supervisor?

CASE PROBLEMS

THE CASE OF HANK MUELLER

Like most companies, Southeastern Gas and Electric has strict rules about drinking on the job. Ned Feller, area supervisor, was concerned then to learn that Hank Mueller, one of his gas installation crewmen, was having an occasional can of beer with his lunch. The report came confidentially from a crew member who didn't want to be identified as "squealing" but thought Ned ought to know.

Hank never carried beer in his lunch bucket. So he didn't have it on the truck or in the shop when he left in the morning. If there was a nearby tavern, bowling alley, or restaurant near the job, Hank would buy a can before the crew opened their lunch buckets together. When the rule was mentioned in conversation, Hank would say beer is like any other food and that he was brought up on it.

Upon learning of Hank's practice, Ned decided to "happen to be in the area" of Hank's crew's installation job on a couple of occasions about lunchtime. The first two drop-bys revealed nothing out of line. Hank was drinking coffee. Ned's third visit was different. He walked up just as Hank was finding his place with the seated crew with a cold unopened can of beer in his hand. Ned asked Hank about the beer and Hank innocently said he had purchased it to take home that night. With a half smile, he explained that he didn't have any at home and had only enough change with him for one can.

1. Is Hank in violation of the company's no-drinking rule?

2. Should Ned involve others on the crew who have seen Hank's drinking on the job?

3. What would you say to Hank—how would you handle the situation?

THE CASE OF GRETCHEN WASHINGTON

Gretchen Washington has been doing routine clerical work in the underwriting department of the Hartland Insurance Companies for eight months. Her tardiness record is very poor. She has been late for work on the average of six to eight times a month. Shirley Simms, her supervisor, has talked to her repeatedly. Gretchen always responds by saying she is very sorry and will try to do better. For several days she is on time, and then another late arrival. She has a variety of unusual excuses that demonstrate a very creative mind. Her work is unusually good and would warrant a sizable merit increase except for her tardiness.

The last time Shirley talked to Gretchen, she warned her that something more drastic would happen if she didn't get to work on time—consistently. Now, just a week later, Gretchen walks in, obviously distressed, about fifteen minutes late.

1. What disciplinary action should Shirley take?

2. How should Shirley approach Gretchen after she puts her coat away?

THE CASE OF DALE HILLMAN

"What can I do," asked Dale Hillman of a fellow supervisor in the physical plant department of State University, "when I've got two men whose personalities clash constantly? Most of their work is here in the carpentry shop, and I can't separate them except for short periods of time.

"They argue and they fight—not physically. Their swearing at one another creates a sideshow that disrupts the rest of the department. Sometimes it's funny, but too often it creates tension that we can do without. It's getting to the point where they try to get support from the others in the department. If I don't do something to put a stop to this I'll have two armed camps warring with one another. Who needs that?

"I tried calling them aside to talk to them. Individually they're reasonable guys. Each accuses the other of starting things—you can never pin down where the arguments begin. They both admit it's no fun to work under such conditions, and each promised to cool it if the other guy would 'get off his back.' I tried bringing them in together for a good dressing down and they wouldn't say a word. Things were better for a while, though, while they brooded like a couple of school kids. In a couple of days they were back at it. It seems they absolutely can't refrain from picking at one another. I can't fault the work of either one of them. They're both good craftsmen."

1.   What steps could be taken to correct Dale's problem?

2.   Is disciplinary action appropriate for one or both carpenters?

3.   How can personality clashes in the department be handled?

SUGGESTIONS FOR FURTHER STUDY

Bittel, Lester R., *What Every Supervisor Should Know*, 3d ed., Chapters 17 and 18, McGraw-Hill Book Company, New York, 1974.

Ficker, Victor B., *Effective Supervision*, Chapter 3, Charles E. Merrill Books, Inc., Columbus, Ohio, 1975.

Magoon, Paul M., and John B. Richards, *Discipline or Disaster*, Exposition Press, New York, 1966.

Steinmetz, Lawrence L., and H. Ralph Todd, Jr., *First-Line Management*, Chapter 13, Business Publications, Inc., Dallas, Texas, 1975.

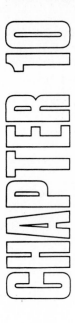

CHAPTER 10

HANDLING COMPLAINTS AND GRIEVANCES

THE CASE OF GRIEVING KAMINSKY

Burt wore a worried look as he joined two of his buddies for a beer before going home Friday afternoon. He had been eager to accept the invitation to have a beer because he wanted to talk. Seated in the booth as Burt dropped into his seat were Jack Holt, supervisor of final assembly, and Kevin "Mac" McNeil, supervisor of the molding department. Both men had over ten years of supervisory experience. Burt hoped they could shed some light on the uncharted territory he was entering.

"What's up, Burt? You look as if you're about to lose your last friend," Jack said.

Smiling weakly, Burt told them that he was about to be slapped with his first formal grievance. Burt's tone of voice, his facial expression, and his general attitude showed that he felt that his ability to manage was being challenged—that this was a black mark on his record. It was clear that he did not relish the situation.

When Mac asked Burt what had happened, here's the story he

told. Boris Kaminsky had been a chronic absentee problem. He had been away from the job eighteen days in the past year, usually a day at a time. Most of his absences were excused for causes that both Burt and his predecessor Harry Gates felt were questionable. Their suspicions were deepened by the fact that twelve of the absences occurred on Fridays or Mondays. A headache or an upset stomach appeared to be a convenient way of extending the weekend to three days. Boris was usually careful to call in, as the rules required, when he was going to be absent. Even so, it was a problem to find a replacement for him or to reshuffle work assignments on short notice.

After the first three absences, Burt began to talk to Boris about the problems his absences created and the obligation of employees to be on the job since they were counted on every day. Burt's lectures seemed to have little effect. Boris usually said he couldn't help it.

Three weeks ago Boris didn't show up on a Monday. As soon as he showed up on Tuesday, Burt called him in and handed him a written warning pointing out that he had been talked to repeatedly about the absences and that any future absences would be cause for considering more severe disciplinary action. Copies of the warning had been given to the union steward and to Ray Ford and placed in the personnel department files.

Boris was clearly angered by the warning. He said it was a dirty trick to give him a warning without finding out what his excuse was. He claimed that his wife and child were visiting her sister out of town and that he was home alone. He said he was too sick to get out of bed to phone in until late in the afternoon, and by then he didn't feel it made any difference. When Burt asked him how he felt, Boris simply said, "I'm here, ain't I?" The written warning was not contested, but Boris brooded for several days afterward.

After ordering a round of beers, Burt told Jack and Mac that he had had a phone call at home from Boris around 9:30 the night before. When Boris said that he wouldn't be in in the morning, Burt asked why.

"My reason is personal," was the answer. Burt explained that he couldn't accept personal business as an excuse and that he would have to know why Boris couldn't show up for work. Boris simply replied again that his reason was a personal one.

Burt admitted that he'd been annoyed. He told Kaminsky again that his not showing up would create a real hardship. "If you had an acceptable excuse, I'd play ball with you. But I'll be darned if I'll swallow 'personal reasons' so you can have another three-day weekend. Now, either you tell me what your personal reason is, or I'll assume it's not legitimate and act accordingly."

"You can't accuse me of goofing off," Boris retaliated. "I'm trying to cooperate by giving you plenty of advance warning. If I tell you it's personal, that's all you have to know. You have no right prying into my personal life. I'm not coming in, and that's all there is to it."

"Not quite," snapped Burt. "I'm giving you a five-day suspension starting Monday if you're not there ready for work tomorrow morning." Burt said that Kaminsky then hung up without saying any more.

"Boris wasn't there this morning, so I had to reshuffle the work of three people and ask them each to work an hour overtime tonight. That's why I was late getting over here. The guys seemed glad enough to help me out, but they weren't very happy to have to be covering for Kaminsky," Burt told his audience.

"What makes you think you've got a grievance on your hands?" Mac asked. "It seems to me you're within your rights. I'd probably have done pretty much the same thing if I'd been in your shoes."

"I'm glad to hear you say that," Burt told Mac. "About the middle of the afternoon Sam Bassett, the steward in my department, came in to say that they were filing a grievance. Kaminsky apparently had called him from home or wherever he was on his personal business. They're claiming that he gave me more than the required advance notice and that I have no right to discipline him. They also are going to claim that it's not our business to pry into his personal life and that a five-day suspension is excessive under any circumstances. I've always gotten along pretty well with Sam. We've leveled with one another. I figure he wouldn't go along with Kaminsky on this thing unless they thought they could win it. I've never had anything like this happen to me. I hate like the devil to run to Ray Ford again. It's going to look as though I can't control my people. What did I do wrong? Don't we usually get beat on these grievances?"

Mac thought that statement was strange, coming from a supervisor, and suggested that Burt sounded as if he was giving up before things really got started. He told Burt that all employees have the right to grieve and that the union has the obligation to represent them.

"Management has the right to manage—to run the plant efficiently and to make a profit," Mac explained. "Now, we're a part of management, and you were doing your job with Kaminsky. You probably won't get the grievance until Kaminsky gets back from suspension. Then you'll have to write an answer to it. This sounds like one the union might take all the way to arbitration if they don't get satisfaction before then. Keep Ray Ford posted, because he'll be in your corner all the way. This will be good experience for you, Burt. Take advantage of all the help you can get from Ray and Personnel."

"Hey, Burt, I've got an idea," Jack said. "Both Mac and I have had grievances go all the way to arbitration. We'll describe the situations. You put yourself in the arbitrator's shoes and see if you reach the same conclusion they did."

"I'm game. Go ahead," Burt mumbled.

"Well, you know me," Jack started. "I've got a fair temper when I get riled up. I had a gal by the name of Sarah Boyle who had a temper like mine. The difference between us was that I'm a fairly nice guy when I'm not mad. Sarah, though, was sullen. We used to say she was sore as a boil most of the time. She did her work but never more than just enough to get by. She seemed to resent orders, and you were never sure if she was going to follow them. We had several arguments. I don't mind saying that I didn't like her and that it was hard to be civil to her. One day we got into a hassle about a job I thought was taking longer than necessary, and she got smart. I lost my head and decided I wasn't going to take any more. I told her that she was lazy—that she had better shape up or ship out. It wasn't hard to see I was getting under her skin. Finally she blew up and called me a damned s.o.b.—loud and clear for half the department to hear. You can guess what happened. I tied the can to her right then and there. We had a grievance before the day was over, and it went through all the steps to arbitration.

"We based our whole case on insubordination, claiming that a supervisor can't afford to have insubordination in his department if he's going to maintain control. The contract permits discharge on first offense. Sarah and the union claimed that I had provoked her outburst, that her record was good, that she had not had any previous warnings or disciplinary action against her, that a short suspension might have been in order—but not discharge. Now, Mr. Arbitrator, how would you rule on that one?"

"Well, from what you've said," Burt mused, "I'd side with the union. It's pretty rough to can a person the first time. I would guess that the arbitrator made us take her back with the loss of some or all of her pay."

"Well, you're wrong," Jack smiled. "The discharge stuck. The arbitrator said that a plant couldn't operate if employees were allowed to curse or abuse their supervisors. He said that control was essential and couldn't be maintained if public abuse were permitted. Then he slapped my wrist for provoking Sarah and said that he probably would have ordered her reinstatement if the incident had occurred in private. It was what you might call a close call, and I learned a lesson. Sarah had more of a following than I thought. It took quite a while for things to get back to normal. OK, Mac, tell him about your trip to arbitration."

"Well, Burt, this happened several years ago," Mac said. "I was really out on a limb."

Burt was already deciding that Mac had won the case because he liked Mac. To Burt, Mac was the ideal supervisor—well-liked by his people, highly thought of by higher management, level-headed, firm but fair, and always in command of his operations. Mac ran a tight ship and was respected by his employees. Burt couldn't remember, either as a supervisor or employee, any disciplinary problems coming out of Mac's department.

"We had a young fellow, Les Harder, who was a wise guy. In some respects he was like your Mike Moran—a good worker, but he found plenty of time to bother other people without hurting his own production. Part of being a wise guy, I guess, was the way he liked to show off. He gave the impression that he knew more than anybody else. Every management policy or rule was a lot of kid stuff to him, and he let people know it. I don't think I ever told him to do anything without getting a lot of smart talk or sarcasm. A couple of times I called him in for a straightforward man-to-man talk about his attitude. I gave him every chance to get straightened out and become one of us. Nothing helped. He just seemed to enjoy making fun of me, of management, of the company, and of anything else that we took seriously. Finally, I recommended to Oscar Palmer, who had just become plant manager, that we fire Harder. Even though he was new to the job, Oscar backed me up.

"Well, the fur began to fly. Harder filed a grievance with full union backing, saying that he never had a written warning of any kind. They claimed there was nothing in the contract requiring him to like his supervisor. His production was never the subject of any criticism, and if any discipline was called for, he should have been properly warned in accordance with mutually accepted disciplinary procedures.

"In our defense we claimed that we didn't have to put up with people who were consistently and openly hostile to management, that Harder's attitude was a disturbing influence on other employees, that he had been given plenty of chances to straighten out, that even though no single incident warranted a warning, his attitude in total constituted grounds for discharge. Remember, Burt, we had no precedent for taking such action. How would you rule on that one?"

"Just because it's you, Mac," Burt smiled, "I'll rule for the company. Seriously, I think an arbitrator would make you take him back. You can't fire a guy for having a poor attitude."

"That's where you're wrong again, Burt," Mac came back. "The discharge was upheld. The arbitrator said that Harder or any other employee has no right to ridicule management and its directives. He said that if Harder hadn't liked his supervisor, he could have asked for a transfer. Since there was no evidence that he had, the discharge was justified. But the thing you have to remember, Burt, is that the next arbitrator might rule differently. We were lucky. Well, let's knock it off. I've got to get home.''

Driving home, Burt felt a little better, and he was sure it wasn't the two beers. Maybe a grievance wasn't the worst thing in the world that could happen to a guy. He was hoping that it could be settled without going to arbitration, but he didn't see how he could back down from the suspension he had given Kaminsky. It was good to know that all arbitration cases weren't decided in favor of the union. Looking ahead to the possibility of going all the way, he decided that every move he made would have a bearing on the case. He'd have to be careful.

1. How should we evaluate Burt's handling of Kaminsky in this last incident?
2. What did Jack Holt mean when he said he had learned a lesson from his arbitration case? What might he have learned?
3. How can we account for Burt's feeling that the union always seems to win out in arbitration matters?
4. What should Burt do now that he knows his handling of Kaminsky will result in a formal grievance? Outline some of the steps he should take.

THE MANAGEMENT-MINDED SUPERVISOR'S ROLE IN HANDLING GRIEVANCES

The supervisor who's doing the best job for the company in the area of grievance handling is probably the supervisor who spends less time handling grievances than any other supervisor. Does this seem like a contradiction? It doesn't if we accept the idea that the most valuable role a supervisor can play is in preventing grievances—notice we did not say squelching them or sitting on them. Certainly the supervisor has a primary responsibility to protect management's interest—management's right to manage. If anyone can do that with sound leadership, fair discipline, and wise administration and can resolve differences before they become grievances, is he or she not fulfilling the role? Management judges a supervisor's effectiveness in terms of how few grievances are generated in that department unless of course a union is looking for test cases.

Misapplication of this criterion has led to mistakes, however. It does not follow that a supervisor with no grievances is necessarily doing a better job than one who has two or three grievances to his or her credit. We could, for example, hardly criticize Burt Hall for taking the disciplinary action against Boris Kaminsky which resulted in a grievance. He was simply protecting management's interest in the regular attendance of its employees. There will always be a few employees who stretch the rules to the breaking point and who become shop lawyers when they are called to account. The real test to be applied to grievances filed against a supervisor is whether or not proper handling of the situation might have prevented a formal grievance. From the evidence we have, we can conclude that Burt did a reasonably good job of trying to get Boris straightened out. If anything, he might be criticized for being too lenient, so that when the disciplinary action finally was taken, it came as a shock. Yet, how many would have let the matter go one more time in hopes of straightening it out?

Enforcement of rules, assigning work, running the department, administering the labor contract if there is one, and in general, representing management—these are considered to be the supervisor's responsibility. Implicit in that statement is the protection of management's right to operate an efficient, profitable enterprise. When misunderstandings (an early stage in the development of grievances) arise, the supervisor is the point of first contact. His or her willingness to listen and understand and to explain and perhaps sell a decision determine in most cases whether or not there will be a formal grievance. A supervisor has the power to eliminate most misunderstandings with employees. Misunderstandings cause grievances. The supervisor therefore plays a key role in preventing formal grievances and minimizing the time spent in hearing them, weighing them, and deciding them at higher levels. But, above all, it is the supervisor's function to safeguard the interests of management.

As Burt Hall was driving home, he looked ahead to the possibility that his grievance would go all the way to arbitration, and he decided that every move he made from then on would have a bearing on the case. Just a moment's thought reveals the wisdom of his thinking. A supervisor's handling of every request, gripe, complaint, or grievance determines the strength of the case he or she may someday have to defend. The supervisor is the defendant in grievance matters. Before an arbitrator the supervisor has to be able to show that his or her actions were fair, considerate, and in good faith. The defendant can expect the plaintiff—the grievant and the union—to take advantage of any and every mistake made to win their point. Day in and day out the supervisor's interpretations of the labor contract or company policy help shape and define the real meaning of the contract. The contract or policy may say one thing, but if everyday administration and interpretation demonstrate a different way of operating, the grievant's case will be strengthened. Many cases have been lost before an arbitrator or have been conceded by higher management when the grievant has been able to say, "Yes, but that rule was never enforced until now."

In summary, the management-minded supervisor recognizes that management's rights in directing the work force are maintained by exercising those rights. The supervisor recognizes the right of the employee to grieve when a misunderstanding develops. The supervisor's job, he or she knows, is to listen with respect, correct any errors, adjust where possible, or explain courteously the reasons for refusal. The supervisor acts with promptness and consideration, acknowledging that no matter how unrealistic a complaint might be, it is reasonable in the eyes of the person making it. The result of this approach in most cases is a minimum of formal grievances and a minimum of time spent arguing them.

THE ANATOMY OF A GRIEVANCE

A fundamental principle of sound employee relations is the provision of a means for employees to express their complaints and have them fairly considered. Through negotiation, unions have been able to guarantee this right for their members by having it written into the labor contract. Service to members is provided by the union through its willingness to represent the employee in any complaints against management. In the nonunion firm which prefers to remain nonunion, formal grievance procedures are a must because they provide this vital right of employees. Management has the right to manage; the employee has the right to grieve.

In its embryonic stage a grievance is a dissatisfaction with some condition of employment which is expressed either in the form of a request or a complaint. The justification for the complaint may be either real or imaginary, but it is vital to understand that from the employee's point of view it is real. Downgrading the importance of a complaint or ridiculing an individual only adds fuel to a fire that is just starting. It is at this stage in the development of a grievance that the supervisor recognizes his or her key role in preventing grievances. Anger and resentment are absent or minimal. Now is the best time to reach an amicable agreement. Ideally the complaint or request should go no further. The supervisor either grants the request, modifies it, or sells the employee on the reasons for the refusal. Some typical examples of causes of complaints include bids for higher-rated jobs, improvement of physical working conditions, clarification of rules or policy, claims of favoritism, requests for pay adjustments, claims of pay inequities, unfair distribution of overtime, and claims of unfair disciplinary actions. There are hundreds of others. These are typical.

Inability to reach an understanding at the first stage results in the formalizing of the grievance—which usually means putting it in writing. It's important to consider the words "inability to reach an understanding." The supervisor should recognize the role of his or her communication skill in creating understanding. Granting every request or bowing to every complaint is not a good way to handle grievances. Safeguarding the company's interests often requires the supervisor to say no. How successful he or she is in getting the employee to understand the reasons for this refusal is the real test of the supervisor's ability. The times when he or she can say, "Yes, you're right. I'll take care of it right away," pose no problem. Getting the employee to say, "I understand why it can't be done," challenges the supervisor's ability and helps determine supervisory effectiveness.

It's usually with the initiation of this second stage that anger and resentment begin to cloud the logical reasoning of either side or both sides. When there is inability to reach understanding, attitudes become more rigid and opinions more fixed, and the opportunity for compromise or agreement goes out the window.

Again the supervisor's response to the grievance at this second stage (for now it is a grievance) will either strengthen or weaken management's position in future stages. Anger, temper, ridicule, sarcasm, or profanity are luxuries the supervisor can ill afford. It is not at all uncommon for a steward or union official to goad the supervisor into a display of temper. Control of the emotions is essential if management is to be represented with dignity. The grievance at this stage is the supervisor's to answer. The decision is the supervisor's, but it should not be made without recognizing that higher-level management might be put in the position of defending it. Burt was reluctant to discuss his problem with Ray Ford—an attitude he should change. He has the obligation to analyze the situation, to justify his action, and to recommend a course of action. But to go it alone would be shortsighted. Once Kaminsky convinced the union that it should support his grievance, Burt should see the wisdom of consulting his superiors and the labor relations people who will be in his corner and whose support he expects. If the answer to a grievance is to be negative at this second stage, a supervisor will want to deal with the issues fairly, setting forth the reasons why a denial is justified. Nothing should be done to add fuel to the fire.

In the eyes of many managers, the next stage really sets the machinery of the grievance procedure in motion. Up to this point the matter is essentially between the employee and his or her immediate supervisor. It is true that the union steward assisted in writing and presenting the grievance. It is also true that the supervisor may have consulted superiors or staff experts in responding. But the grievance was a complaint to the supervisor by the employee, to be answered by the supervisor—the common definition of the first step in the grievance procedure. The stages from this point on, however, invariably involve union and management officials at increasingly higher levels. Then it is really during the second step in the grievance procedure that the wheels get in motion and the machinery starts functioning. We'll discuss the steps in formal grievance procedures later in this chapter. With respect to the anatomy of a grievance, we should note that generally it goes through three stages of development while it remains in the supervisor's domain.

Stage one — A *request:* no anger, under supervisor's control.
Stage two — A *complaint:* some resentment, under supervisor's control.
Stage three — A *grievance:* considerable resentment; under supervisor's control, but generally with consultation.

WHAT CAN BE LEARNED FROM GRIEVANCES

Handling grievances, as disagreeable and as distasteful as it may be, is a learning process. Jack Holt said he had learned from his experience of having a grievance go to arbitration. But what had he learned? More than likely, the "slap on the wrist" from the arbitrator shocked him back to an objective analysis of his role in the development of the grievance. Undoubtedly, his narrow escape caused him to see that his own temper had nearly lost him the case. He might also have come to the realization that it's possible to win an arbitration case and still lose. We'll recall his telling Burt that Sarah had more of a following than he'd realized and that it had taken a while for his relationship with his workers to get back to normal. Perhaps he learned that it had been a very costly victory.

In measuring the cost of handling a grievance all the way to arbitration, there are many factors to be considered. For example, hours and hours of productive time are lost by those who must argue the case. More time is lost by employees who spend time just talking about the problem. The effect on the morale of the department should be weighed. The cost of the arbitration hearing alone is considerable—fees, wages, salaries, and expenses of witnesses. The problem of settling down to normal operations after a hard-fought case can also be costly. Deciding whether or not it was worth it—whether the settlement justified the cost—is truly a learning experience. One such experience may teach us that the "ounce of prevention" adage has much to recommend it.

After every request, complaint, or grievance a supervisor handles, there should be an evaluation of what has been done. Did he or she create understanding, or miss opportunities that would have helped create it? Was he or she fair, objective, considerate, respectful, and courteous in dealing with the individual? Or was anger, ridicule, sarcasm, profanity, or abuse allowed to creep into the treatment of the employee? In short, did the supervisor add fuel to the fire? If mistakes were made, does the supervisor know where they were made? If the supervisor was successful, does he or she really understand why? Were the lines of communication kept open with the employee, the union, and management? Above all, what has been learned that will help demonstrate to the employees in his or her department that all requests and complaints will get a fair and honest hearing? Every request, complaint, or grievance that is handled, regardless of whether it is accepted or denied, should be a building block in the foundation of sound employee relations.

UNDERSTANDING THE UNION STEWARD'S ROLE

The chief function of a union steward in a department is to represent the employees in any complaints or grievances they might have against management. The steward is a specialist in processing grievances. He or she is in the department as the union's assurance to its members that they will suffer no injustices at the hands of management. Grievances are the reason for the steward's job. While the supervisor is concerned with costs, quality, production, methods, training, and a hundred other duties, the steward is concerned about one thing above all else—the grievance.

While there are exceptions, the steward is usually well trained to handle that phase of the job. When an employee has a legitimate gripe or complaint, the steward knows how to present it. If a grievance develops, he or she is an expert in preparation and presentation. Generally, the steward is intelligent enough to perceive when there's no chance of winning a grievance, and can be an ally of management in convincing an employee not to press an issue.

It should come as no surprise that a steward's training in how to handle grievances runs closely parallel to the supervisor's. Where stewards tend to gain an edge is in their ability to concentrate or specialize on this one facet of their job while supervisors are inclined to set it aside as an unpleasant adjunct to the job. The steward would prefer to have grievances to handle—even to the point of looking for them—whereas the supervisor would prefer to avoid them if possible. The steward is trained to listen carefully to an employee's complaint and to be able to document the case. This person is trained in interpreting labor contracts—from the union's viewpoint, of course. Pinpointing the clause in a contract that will help the union member win a grievance is the steward's job.

The steward's training teaches him or her to investigate the facts, get evidence of unfair treatment, find previous decisions that would be precedent for this case, and secure witnesses to build a sound case. To top it off, he or she is trained in how to deal with or handle the supervisor. The steward knows the strengths and weaknesses of the supervisor just as the supervisor should know the steward's. If the supervisor loses his or her temper easily, that characteristic will be known and exploited. The steward knows how and where to look for loopholes and how to use them to advantage. If the supervisor makes mistakes, he or she can expect those mistakes to be isolated and used with full force against management. Both stewards and supervisors are taught to win. In the strength of both sides it is to be hoped that justice and fair treatment for both employees and the company will prevail.

The union is a political organization. In it the steward holds a political office. Stewards are judged by higher officers and their electorate by the quality of the service they render their members. The steward's effectiveness is measured in terms of how well he or she succeeds in gaining concessions on employees' complaints and grievances. Like baseball pitchers, stewards are concerned about their won-and-lost record. This being so, the supervisor can generally count on a steward pursuing with vigor and skill any issue that becomes a formal grievance. The steward may be an irritant. He or she may create friction. A steward may even challenge the supervisor's leadership. But irritants, friction, and challenges have a way of stimulating, polishing, and motivating, and it may be that a good steward will spur the supervisor to more effective supervision.

In dealing with the steward, supervisors might find it helpful to remember a few brief don'ts:

1. Don't lose your temper.

2. Don't stall or pass the buck.

3. Don't get sidetracked from the main issue.

4. Don't use profanity.

5. Don't ridicule or use sarcasm.

6. Don't guess—have the facts.

7. Don't bluff or make threats.

8. Don't be afraid to stick to your guns.

THE GRIEVANCE PROCEDURE

An effective grievance procedure, whether it be in a union or nonunion firm, makes it possible for employees to express their complaints without fear. Management finds that when a grievance procedure is working properly, it is an effective means of locating and correcting legitimate causes for dissatisfaction among employees. The procedure makes it possible to handle disputes peacefully—minimizing heat and friction. A good grievance procedure provides a way of preventing minor complaints or problems from growing all out of proportion into major grievances. For these reasons, most companies have found it advantageous to spell out and guarantee the procedures whereby employees can have their complaints or grievances heard fairly by the top authorities in the organization.

Essentially the principle on which an effective grievance procedure is built is the right of an employee to have his or her grievance heard at the next higher level if not satisfied with the decisions rendered.

Grievance procedures should be written and published so that employees understand their rights and supervisors know their responsibilities. In the unionized company the grievance procedure is well known—after all, it is the union's stock-in-trade. In the nonunion organization, however, the procedure frequently does not get the same publicity. The supervisor can contribute to better employee relations by making certain that new employees are informed of the existence of a grievance procedure. The procedure assures the employee a sympathetic hearing and fair treatment. Nonunion organizations that have successful procedures for enabling employees to adjust their difficulties continually emphasize the need for assuring employees that no reprisals will result from the use of the grievance procedure.

Grievance procedures, of necessity, vary in their structure. No one standard procedure could be devised to fit every business enterprise. Size, organization, type of operation, kind of personnel—all affect the problem of tailoring the grievance procedure. The purpose of all grievance procedures is to assure employees that they can get a fair, sympathetic hearing without fear of reprisal and to spell out the steps by which employees can carry their grievances to the next higher authority if not satisfied at the first level.

The number of steps in a grievance procedure will usually vary from three to five. For our purposes let's look at a four-step procedure. Our prime concern will be to consider the role supervisors play in each step and to understand that a supervisor loses some control over the problem with each successive step. We should understand management's genuine desire to have grievances settled at the lowest possible stage. This desire, coupled with the structure of the grievance procedure, puts the supervisor in a strategic position.

Step One: The Employee, With or Without Representation, Confers With the Supervisor

The grievance may be spoken or in writing. Many procedures call for a written statement before a complaint is considered a grievance. This is, whether written or spoken, the critical step. Supervisors have complete control to grant or deny a grievance—a responsibility not to be taken lightly. They are the first point of contact. The willingness to listen courteously with genuine interest, to investigate and weigh the facts conscientiously, and to respond with respect for the employee's feelings are the hallmarks of effective grievance handling. The scope of the supervisor's authority is sufficient to settle most grievances. The best practice is to settle employees' complaints quickly, before heat and friction are generated.

A large Midwestern manufacturing company, plagued by a backlog of hundreds of grievances every time it entered contract negotiations, decided finally to embark on a comprehensive program of settling all grievances at the first level. Higher-line management and staff specialists were put at the disposal of their foreman to help them reach a satisfactory settlement. Prompt, on-the-site, settlements became the rule rather than the deliberate delaying procedures previously used. The foreman was the key. He had, however, all the support he felt he needed to reach an equitable acceptable agreement. Concentration on early settlement with support from above worked. The backlog of grievances was eliminated, and negotiations from that time on were begun in a much healthier climate.

The complexity of the grievance will determine how much investigative work must be done before a supervisor can respond to a first-step grievance. All facts that might have a bearing on the case should be gathered. A thorough understanding of the rule or contract clause being contested is needed. Knowledge of any previous actions, decisions, or rulings that might provide a precedent is necessary. The supervisor can be sure that the union will also be very thorough in making similar preparations.

In the handling of the first step the supervisor should remain objective and use an analytical approach. It's possible to be deliberately goaded into a display of anger in the hopes he or she might say something that can be used in the employee's case. The supervisor would do well to be wary of such tactics.

The supervisor's response to the grievance, after thorough investigation, should be firm, specific, courteous, and respectful. There should be no doubt as to what the decision is—nor should there be any room to doubt that a fair sympathetic hearing was given the employee's complaint. If the grievance does go beyond the first step, the handling of the initial phase will provide the basis for future discussions.

Step Two: The Employee and His or Her Representative
Present the Grievance in Writing to Next Higher
Authority (Usually General Foreman or Superintendent)

If the supervisor has done a good job of communicating, this step will come as no surprise to the boss, who will have some knowledge of the issues in dispute. It is assumed that since the boss is in a position of greater authority, he or she will be able to call upon broader experience which might lead to a satisfactory agreement. The supervisor's hope is that on having the full support and backing of higher authority when the decision is challenged in this second step. Thoroughness and judicious handling of the first step will ensure this backing, but the supervisor must recognize now that the decision is out of his or her hands. He or she can influence that decision, but reversal or support is for the boss to decide.

Step Three: The Employee's Grievance, With the Support of Higher Representation, Is Taken to Top-Line Management

In an organized company the top grievance-handling arm of the union represents the employee. This might be the chief steward, the business agent, the president, or a grievance committee. On management's side the grievance is directed to the general manager, plant manager, branch manager, or president. The company's labor relations staff and the union's grievance specialists become involved in hearings and discussions. If only selfishly, the supervisor should note that his or her handling of the first step is under direct and close top-management scrutiny. Perhaps this is what Burt had in mind when he decided he had better be careful about how he handled his first grievance. Everything possible will be done by employees or their representatives to present the case in the best possible light. This means challenging everything the supervisor has done and said.

Management at the top level has just as great an interest in supporting the supervisor as the immediate boss. The supervisor is, after all, a member of management. If one has followed sound human relations practices and protected management's right to manage, he or she can expect management's support. The supervisor needs to be realistic enough to understand, however, that at the top level the perspective is somewhat different.

The effect of granting or denying on the entire organization must be weighed. The risk of having the grievance go to arbitration has to be calculated. It is possible that the long-run interests of the company will best be served by a reversal of the supervisor's decision. Again the possibility of a reversal is minimized by the supervisor's thoroughness in examining all facets of the problem before reaching a decision.

In a nonunion company, this is usually the final step. Provisions for hearing the grievance by an outside party are not usually made. The top manager makes the final determination, and the employee must accept the decision. Management must understand that the employee is relying entirely on its fairness and impartiality.

Step Four: The Grievance Is Taken to Arbitration or Conciliation

If agreement on the disposition of the grievance cannot be reached, it is taken to a disinterested outside party for consideration. Arbitration is commonly specified by contract as the means for final settlement of the dispute. In arbitration both parties agree on an arbitrator to hear the grievance, and both parties agree in advance to abide by the decision of the arbitrator. Conciliation, on the other hand, is the attempt of a disinterested outsider to help the parties find a basis for settling the dispute. The conciliator does not make the decision. He or she simply facilitates and recommends avenues of agreement. The failure to reach agreement in conciliation leaves the courts or the National Labor Relations Board as the remaining recourse for the grievant.

An arbitrator will conduct a hearing similar in some respects to a court trial. The degree of formality will vary with the individual arbitrator, but that arbitrator will require a specific statement of charges, hear witnesses, weigh evidence, and render a decision. Because of the interest both parties have in winning their points, they are usually represented by legal counsel in the arbitration hearing. Obviously, with so many people involved, the supervisor's control over the grievance's disposition is nil. The supervisor is now simply a witness. He or she can only hope that his or her judgment in the first step will be confirmed.

The grievance procedure, in summary, is designed to guarantee employees a fair hearing in their complaints against management. Everything contractually possible is done to protect this right and ensure a fair hearing. We can see that the attitude of both parties and the spirit in which they deliberate contributes significantly to the effectiveness of the procedure. In this brief consideration of the formal procedure, we can see the wisdom of preventing grievances or settling them at the first level, where the supervisor's control is the greatest.

TIPS ON HOW TO HANDLE COMPLAINTS AND GRIEVANCES

Complaints in even the best-managed departments are to be expected. In fact, a complete absence of complaints, say many experts, is an indication that people are afraid to voice their feelings and concerns. Enough has been said of the key role the supervisor plays in preventing complaints from becoming grievances. We can clearly see the importance to any management of having those grievances that do arise settled at lowest possible level. Here are a few tips on handling complaints and grievances at the supervisory level gleaned from thousands of successful and management-minded supervisors.

Listen With Interest

Listening is perhaps the best way in the world of sizing up another person in a disagreement. Listening is a way of showing respect. It helps the listener understand the depth of feeling employees have about their gripes. It's the supervisor's first chance to start developing an understanding of what is really bothering the person.

Consider the Complaint Important

Many complaints and gripes are without foundation and are the result of an overactive imagination. Still, to the employee the complaint is real. It took considerable thought and courage to express it to the supervisor at all. The least the supervisor can do is demonstrate to the employee that he or she considers the complaint important and that it will get full and sympathetic attention.

Keep Calm

Effective handling of complaints and grievances requires clear thinking. Most complaints challenge methods of supervision. The temptation to become angry is great, but anger may add fuel to the fire. The supervisor's objective is to stay in control. When losing one's temper, one tends to lose not only control, but dignity as a member of management.

Get All the Facts

The pressure is on the supervisor to make a decision as quickly as possible. Yet a decision should not be reached without the benefit of factual information. There is always the possibility that a complaint might develop into a full-blown grievance. A supervisor must be certain of possessing the complete story. He or she can ask the employee questions, check records, review rules or contracts, check previous decisions for precedents, and investigate anything that will lead to an intelligent decision.

Give or Get a Direct Answer

Stalling and hedging are annoying. It's safe to assume that anyone coming to a supervisor with a complaint or a grievance would like a direct answer. If it's within the scope of a supervisor's authority to give an answer, he or she should want to give it in clear, definite, understandable terms. A decision outside the supervisor's authority should be sought and communicated to the employee as soon as possible. If the answer is slow in coming, the supervisor will want to keep the employee posted on any progress or the reasons for the delay. Since the complaint is serious to the employee, the longer he or she must wait for an answer, the deeper his or her concern and convictions become.

Sell the Decision

It's no problem to tell employees they are right and that their request will be granted. The test of the supervisor's skill is in telling employees no and in getting them to accept the decision. The employee should be made to understand that the complaint was given very serious consideration. Reasons that are understandable from the employee's point of view should always be a part of rendering a negative decision. A hard, cold no does nothing to strengthen future relations. This, we know, is the critical point in preventing a complaint from becoming a grievance or a grievance from going to a higher level.

The handling of complaints and grievances demands the sharpest human relations skills from beginning to end. This skill can frequently make the difference between a satisfied, cooperative employee and an employee who is a constant source of irritation and trouble.

HIGHLIGHTS

1. Every employee has the right to grieve, complain, or question when a misunderstanding develops. Supervisors are the point of first contact for the grieving employee. Their job is to prevent complaints from becoming grievances while safeguarding management's interests.

2. A grievance usually develops in stages. It starts as a request, becomes a complaint, and, if unsatisfied, develops into a grievance. Resentment and anger, absent in the first stage, tend to increase throughout the process.

3. Grievances provide learning experiences. Every request, complaint, or grievance handled, whether it is accepted or denied, should promote sound human relations.

4. The union steward is a well-trained specialist in handling grievances. A steward's training is similar to the supervisor's with regard to processing and winning grievances. The steward's job is to

demonstrate to the employee the value of the union in getting a fair hearing.

5. Grievance procedures are clearly defined to guarantee the rights of an employee to be heard at the next higher level without reprisal if not satisfied. A typical four-step grievance procedure would permit employees, with or without representation, to carry their grievances to higher levels:

Step one: To his or her supervisor
Step two: To a superintendent or middle management
Step three: To top management
Step four: To arbitration or conciliation

6. Here are a few tips on how to handle complaints and grievances properly gleaned from practical experience. A supervisor should:

   a. Listen with interest
   b. Consider the complaint important
   c. Keep calm
   d. Get all the facts
   e. Give or get a direct answer
   f. Sell the decision

DISCUSSION QUESTIONS

1. Explain why it is so important for a nonunion company to have a formal grievance procedure.

2. Discuss with a union steward his or her ideas of the steward's grievance-handling responsibility. How does the steward's thinking differ from yours as a supervisor?

3. Evaluate the statement that a complete absence of grievances in a department does not necessarily mean that a supervisor is doing a good job of managing employee relations.

4. What is your opinion of the statement that the union is a political organization and that the steward holds a political office? How does this influence the approach of unions and stewards to grievances?

5. Do you agree that a good tough steward can make a supervisor do his or her job better? Why?

6. Why is it so important to avoid profanity, ridicule, sarcasm, and threats when handling grievances?

7. Why should a supervisor be careful to make written record of a spoken warning on a first offense?

8. Describe, from your own experience, a grievance that went to the second or third level. Would it have been possible for the supervisor to have settled it without compromising management's rights?

CASE PROBLEMS

THE CASE OF RUDY BORNOVSKI

"I'll admit I was wrong, but five days without pay is too much. I've learned my lesson and I won't do it again," Rudy Bornovski, an estimator for the Williams and Garret Construction Company, argued.

"Stealing is stealing," Harold Chambers, office manager, countered. "As an estimator you know better than anyone else what our costs are and that pilfering has to be stopped. I'm going to make an example of you. You're lucky I didn't fire you. The suspension sticks. I'm sorry."

The theft was discovered as Rudy was leaving the office with a package wrapped in brown paper under his arm. Just before quitting time Chambers had observed Rudy in the supply room, which was open to everyone in the office. He correctly suspected that Rudy's package contained office supplies and asked to see the contents. After stalling and weak refusals, Rudy finally gave in and revealed two packages of bond paper, a dozen new lead pencils, four new typewriter erasers, and two bottles of white opaque correction fluid. At first he tried to say it was for some office work he was doing at home, but finally admitted that it was for his daughter's high school typing course.

Harold told Rudy he needed time to think over what he would do and sent Rudy away to await a decision the following morning. Rudy expressed regrets and apologies as he departed. "It's getting tougher and tougher to make ends meet. I didn't think anybody would really mind," he said.

Now with Harold's decision firmed up and no appeal except to one of the owners, Rudy had only one course left open to him. Six months ago he and the other office workers had joined the construction workers' union. Joining the union at the time didn't make Rudy happy, but he went along. He never did feel the union would do him any good, but now he told Harold, "If that's your decision, I guess I'll just have to get the union to file a grievance. Five days is too much for a first offense."

1. What should the penalty be for Rudy's first theft?

2. Evaluate Harold Chambers's handling of Rudy.

3. Faced with a probable grievance, what should Chambers do now?

THE CASE OF ROD TROIA

"I've taken as much of this as I can stand," Rod Troia, manager of sporting goods in the city's largest department store, stormed. The cause of his outburst was the recurrence of Sue Jones and Bill Ferger chatting in a corner while customers milled around waiting for service. Rod suspected a romance in the making since the two young clerks seemed more interested in each other than in serving customers.

Approaching the two, he snapped, "I don't know how many times I have to tell you two to knock it off. You can both punch out right now and don't bother coming in tomorrow either. We'll see if a couple of days without pay will teach you something about why you work here. This store has built a reputation for good service, and I'm not going to have it ruined in my department by a couple of lovebirds. You've probably cost us a couple hundred dollars in lost sales already this week. We might find we don't need either of you."

"You can't do that," Bill retorted.

"Who in hell said I can't! I've just done it. Now punch out!" Rod exploded. Sue started to cry and Rod, even more angry, shouted, "Don't pull those tears on me. Just get out of here before I lose my temper and fire the both of you."

Consoling Sue as they departed, Bill said, more for Rod's hearing than Sue's, "Maybe we better find that union organizer who was around last week trying to get us to sign up."

"That's all I need," Rod moaned to himself. "If there's one thing the old man wants more than a profitable operation, it's to keep a union from getting in here."

1. Evaluate Rod's handling of his two salespeople.

2. Was his action fair after several apparent warnings?

3. What should Rod do now as the situation stands?

THE CASE OF AL BAUER

Regents Bank and Trust Company had recently promoted Al Bauer from supervisor in one of its operations departments to manager of one of its largest branches, with the title of assistant vice president. Al was elated with the promotion. He had worked hard preparing himself for it. But the occasion was clouded by his last decision in the old job.

Two people, Helen Withers and Jerry Marks, both were vying for promotion to the job Al was vacating. Their desire for the promotion was known by everyone in the department and it was generally felt that consideration of Al's successor had boiled down to the two of them. In fact, it had. Both were qualified by knowledge, experience, and ability to fill Al's shoes. Al had no reservations that either of them could more than adequately handle his job and that both had earned a chance at it.

The bank was anxious to move women into positions of responsibility. Its record on promoting women wasn't particularly commendable in the past. Nominating Helen Withers, tantamount to appointment, would have been the easy way out. No problems! Al knew from working closely with both of them, however, that Jerry Marks was better qualified and would serve the bank better than Helen. He also knew that Marks was destined for higher management and would move up in a short time.

Al's nomination of Jerry Marks for the supervisory job sparked an immediate outcry of discrimination from Helen Withers. No amount of persuasion to bide her time could calm Helen down. She said her sex was the only reason for being passed over. A grievance to top management would be filed and if that didn't work she said she would go to the Equal Employment Opportunity Commission (EEOC) or whoever looks out for women's rights. "It's about time I stand up and fight," she declared.

1. How justified is Helen in her claim of discrimination?

2. Should an organization appoint a qualified woman to a supervisor even if a more qualified male is available?

3. What should Al Bauer do now after learning of Helen's threat to fight his decision?

SUGGESTIONS FOR FURTHER STUDY

Bittel, Lester R., *What Every Supervisor Should Know*, 3d ed., Chapters 14 and 18, McGraw-Hill Book Company, New York, 1974.

Shout, Howard F., *Start Supervising*, Chapter 10, Bureau of National Affairs, Inc., Washington, D.C., 1972.

Steinmetz, Lawrence L., and H. Ralph Todd, Jr., *First-Line Management*, Chapter 13, Business Publications, Inc., Dallas, Texas, 1975.

Stessin, Lawrence, *Practice of Personnel and Industrial Relations*, Chapter 4, Pitman Publishing Corporation, New York, 1964.

Trotta, Maurice S., and Walter W. Bishop, *Grievance Handling for Foremen*, Bureau of Industrial Relations, University of Michigan, 1969.

PART THREE

JOB KNOWLEDGE

The knowledge we have acquired
ought not to resemble a great shop
without order and inventory; we ought
to know what we possess, and be
able to make it serve us in our need.
GOTTFRIED WILHELM VON LEIBNITZ
(1646–1716)

PERFORMANCE OBJECTIVES

A supervisor's ability to function with the necessary job knowledge and administrative skills can be measured against the following criteria:

1. To be able to set down action steps for the accomplishment of departmental objectives.

2. To know how personal time is spent and how to spend time most productively.

3. To be able to identify where plans have failed when objectives are not accomplished.

4. To be able to take special assignments and projects and develop plans for their successful completion.

5. To have created a climate where employees' response to orders is one of voluntary compliance or cooperation.

6. To have at least two delegated activities being performed by subordinates at all times.

7. To be able to analyze failure to get performance expected when orders are given.

8. To be able to give the great majority of orders in the form of a request.

9. To have identified measurable criteria for job performance in every possible job in the department.

10. To have established controls for monitoring progress toward accomplishment of each departmental objective.

11. To have identified a specific objective to be accomplished before each performance review interview.

12. To have carefully implemented the eight steps in conducting all performance reviews.

13. To be able to quickly identify and define problems in the department before they magnify.

14. To have practiced the listing of many alternatives in analyzing problems.

15. To have actually planned the best possible implementation of a decision once it is reached.

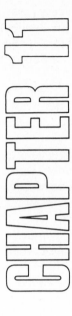

PLANNING AND ORGANIZING WORK

THE CASE OF
CARLA'S CONFUSION "Burt, I need some help. Have you got ten minutes you can spare me?" Carla Cramer, wearing a worried expression, was standing in the doorway to Burt Hall's office. It was 3:35 P.M. Burt was cleaning off his desk before leaving for home. The woman with the worried expression was the supervisor of the production testing department.

"I've got things pretty well wrapped up for the day. Come on in, Carla, and take the load off your feet." If things had gone well, and today they had for Burt, this was the part of the day Burt liked most. He could sit back and reflect on a day of accomplishment. It was a good feeling, and Burt was in a good mood. "What's on your mind, Carla? You look as if you've just lost your last friend."

"To tell the truth, Burt, I don't know which end is up. I'm getting to the point where I'm wondering whether I should throw in the towel and give up this rat race. Ray Ford just chewed me out in his gentle way and suggested that I might get some help talking with you. Frankly, the suggestion didn't set too well with me at first, but I am going in ten different directions at the same time. Ray felt that you were usually pretty well organized and on top of things. I guess he was telling me that I'm not, and what hurts is that he's right. If you can help me get straightened out, Burt, I'd appreciate it. If not, then maybe supervision isn't my cup of tea. Life is too short to live with all this pressure."

Burt was wondering what he could possibly do to take the pressure off Carla as he said, "That's a pretty tall order, Carla. I sure don't know what Ray had in mind, but if I can help, I'll try. Why don't you tell me more about this pressure?"

"Well, I told you I seem to be heading in ten different directions at the same time. There aren't enough hours in a day. The harder I work, the less I seem to accomplish. Ray said that the job seems to be running me instead of me managing the job. I honestly don't know whether it's me or the whole doggonned system. What do you think, Burt?"

"It can get pretty hectic at times," Burt said. "And I don't have a magic wand or formula to cure your problems, Carla. What happened that you and Ray got into this hassle?"

Carla began to explain that it wasn't what would be called a hassle. She knew that Ray was annoyed because some arrangements for a semiautomatic testing device coming in the next week had not been made. The equipment had been ordered three months before. Deciding where it was to be located and arranging the production schedule changes during the installation had been Carla's responsibility. She told Burt that the three months slipped by without her doing the necessary planning. She hadn't forgotten. Practically every day she meant to get at it, but one thing always led to another, and time got away from her. When Ray stopped in that morning, it was to tell Carla that the equipment was arriving in a few days and to find out what arrangements had been made for it.

"He just caught me by surprise," Carla moaned. "I hadn't done a single thing. Yesterday I started to check out one area I had in mind—you know, measuring the area and seeing how much other stuff would have to be relocated. On the way I saw Jack Adams getting ready to set up a machine that I wanted some repair work done on. I got him going on something else and went back to my office to call maintenance. Before I could get away from the office, I had three more calls for information, and two people came looking for help on their jobs. By the time I got the information and returned the calls, the afternoon was shot. I was determined that nothing was going to stop me this morning, but it was the same old story. Ray was there wanting to know my plans before I had a chance to step outside the door. When I told him I hadn't had time to get to it yet, you might know that he'd remind me that I'd had three months. It sounded weak even to me when I told him I had just been too busy. But doggone it, Burt, I've been running my tail off, and I get farther behind every week. I don't know where the time goes. How in blazes do you keep up with it? Have you got some kind of a system? Ray seemed to think you have.''

''I don't know if you could dignify it by calling it a system, but Harry Gates passed a couple of ideas on to me before he left. They've worked pretty well, too, except when somebody louses me up. Harry warned me that unless I took some time out each day for planning, I would be ready for the men in the white coats inside of six months. You seem to be getting ready to be a candidate, Carla.''

''Time for planning,'' Carla groaned. ''Where do you find it? Everything takes time, and I'm fresh out.''

Burt tried to explain that it was time well invested and that it saved much more time in the long run. He said that he came in at 6:45 A.M. every day and spent fifteen minutes listing the things that had to be done that day. As the day went along, he crossed off the things that had been finished. What didn't get done was carried over to the next day. He also told Carla that he stayed half an hour late on Friday to block out the following week in rough form. The morning sessions refined the weekly plan.

''One of the things that the list does,'' Burt pointed out, ''is show you where to delegate some of your work. It took me quite a while to catch on to that part of it because I had to know what I was doing before I could parcel out any of my work.''

''Delegate! That's a laugh.'' Carla grunted. ''You've got to have someone to delegate to. The way things are, I've got to do everything myself if it's going to be done right. Everybody in my department is so darned busy that I couldn't pile my work on them if I tried. Besides, Burt, it's easier to do it myself than to take all the time to show somebody else how to do it.''

''You're right about that, the first time through,'' Burt countered. ''But how about all the times after that? The payoff comes when you have somebody who can do the job every time it occurs. Believe me, Carla, it's worth taking some extra time to help a person do the job right for you the first time through.''

''Yeah, but I never seem to find the time to do it that first time. All my jobs are rush jobs, and I don't have time to play nursemaid when I can do them in half the time myself. What I can't see, Burt, is how making a list of jobs every day is going to help much. I don't know when that blasted phone is going to ring or when one of my people is going to have trouble on a job that I'll have to straighten out. It seems that that's where most of my day goes. I never get around to the important things I want to do. I go from one crisis to another, and I just can't see how you can plan for a problem that hasn't happened yet."

"When you put it that way, I don't know either, Carla." Burt scratched his head. "I'll have to admit that I get upset when somebody fouls me up. Maybe that's the big disadvantage to planning. Once you determine what you want to accomplish, you want to do it. I find myself cursing anything that gets in my way. In the long run, though, the system does a pretty good job for me—especially if I don't try to cram too much into a day. Maybe that's the answer—keep it loose."

"Frankly, Burt, I had hoped for something more," Carla said. "There's so much confusion in my department that it's going to take more than a daily checklist to straighten things out. My people are getting as jumpy as I am. Every time I catch hell for missing a deadline, I pass it on, and I know that's wrong. It's not helping morale any. Every breakdown, shortage of material, or rush order turns out to be my fault. Our costs have been going up. I haven't heard from topside on that one, but I will. Ray didn't actually say it, but I thought you had a real system for streamlining your whole operation that I could use in my department."

"For your sake, Carla, I wish I did," Burt replied. "My morning planning just seems to keep us all on track. We have a pretty good idea of where we're going and when we're going to get there. It's like starting out on a trip. You have a hundred miles to go, and you know it will take you about two hours if you don't stop. Gassing up, coffee or lunch breaks, or side trips add time to that two hours. It's the same here. We've got just so much time, so many people, and so much equipment to get the work done. If there's too much work, something has to give—adjustments are made—push back the deadline, work overtime, farm out some of the work, or add more people. With the daily and the weekly plans I can usually see the need for an adjustment before it's down around our ears—a crisis. Those morning planning sessions give me a feeling that I'm making things happen instead of having them happen to me. Do you know what I mean?"

Carla halfheartedly said that she did and asked Burt why he did his planning in the morning instead of during the day. Burt said that he thought deciding on the best time was an individual matter. The important thing was to find a time when there were no interruptions. Burt told Carla that Harry Gates always did his planning at the end of the day, but Burt felt that he did a better job in the morning when he was fresh. For some reason, he explained to Carla, he still liked Friday afternoon to look at the whole week. One thing was certain, no one hung around to bother a person on Friday afternoon.

"You mean the way I'm doing now," Carla said. "Seriously, Burt, I'm almost as confused about how your system could work for me as I am in trying to keep up with my job. But a drowning person will grab at anything. I'll give it a try."

"That's the only way you'll find out if it will help, Carla. After you try it a couple of days, maybe we can compare notes. Don't expect miracles. It will probably take a while to adjust to planning—that is, if you can call it planning."

1. How much of Carla's confusion could be attributed to a lack of planning?

2. Burt seemed to have doubts as to whether or not his system could really be considered planning. Was it?

3. How should we evaluate Carla's reasons for not wanting to delegate?

4. Is there a relationship between supervisory planning and employees' morale?

5. Burt said that a disadvantage to planning was getting upset when he couldn't always achieve his objective. Is he right?

6. What did Burt mean when he said that his morning sessions made him feel that he was making things happen rather than having them happen to him?

PLANNING AND THE MANAGEMENT-MINDED SUPERVISOR

For decades we have been stressing job knowledge as one of the most important assets of a supervisor. To most of us, job knowledge means a mastery of the procedures, techniques of production, people or machine capabilities, and properties of materials. Job knowledge, as we commonly think of it, is acquired either through technical education or long experience with a variety of operations performed in the department. Great emphasis has been placed on this concept of job knowledge in selecting supervisors for many years. A supervisor's knowledge of the job can be fairly safely evaluated, but it has limited value for predicting success in supervision.

Many have been handicapped by such shortsighted selection procedures. Supervision is management! Job knowledge for a supervisor should mean a knowledge of how to manage—not simply how to produce. As a new supervisor in the production testing department, Carla Cramer was technically qualified beyond a shadow of a doubt. But her conversation with Burt Hall reveals her to be woefully weak in knowing her job as a manager. Management is the achieving of results through people, and Carla was completely lacking in this particular management skill. Every supervisor, if he or she is to experience the satisfaction of successful supervising, will have to learn the job knowledge of management—planning, organizing, motivating (directing), and controlling.

In Chapter 1 we identified the seven major responsibilities of the management-minded supervisor as (1) production, (2) quality, (3) costs, (4) methods, (5) training, (6) safety, and (7) morale. Application of the management process to people and work produces the proper results in those seven areas. It should not be difficult to see how excellence in any of these seven major areas of responsibility is dependent on good planning. For example, programs for the improvement of quality, costs, safety, or methods must be carefully planned if improvements are to be realized. It doesn't happen by chance.

Carla Cramer was typical of so many supervisors who remain producers instead of becoming managers. Most, if not all, of her time was occupied in doing routine work and jumping from one crisis to another. Her thinking was centered on things and details rather than on planning and directing. Her technical knowledge provided a security that wouldn't permit her to trust her people. Work makes people feel productive. A mental barrier limits many supervisors who have never learned the techniques of planning, directing, and controlling the work of others. For most, it takes some time to let go of the producing activities and find satisfaction in the management functions. Management-mindedness in supervision is reflected in a supervisor's ability to plan the activities in his or her department.

What is planning? Some have said that planning is merely deciding in advance what is to be done. Burt Hall said almost the same thing when he told Carla that his morning planning sessions gave him the feeling that he was making things happen instead of having them happen to him. Others have said that planning is the substitution of thinking for worry. If Carla Cramer survives as a supervisor, she will, in time, come to appreciate that definition, for good planning surely does minimize the need to worry. Our purposes will best be served by defining planning as the determination of what needs to be done, who will do it, and when it has to be done in order for major responsibilities to be fully carried out.

In "The Case of Carla's Confusion" we found evidence to support the idea that good planning on the part of a supervisor tends to build respect for that person as a manager. Employees, like supervisors, want to be a part of an organization that is accomplishing things—that knows where it's going. Burt Hall's people knew that Burt was running things and respected him as a manager. Carla, on the other hand, let the job run her, became what is known as a "crisis manager," and earned a sizable disrespect from the employees under her. Many executives have gone so far as to say, "If you can't plan, you can't manage." Ability to plan is therefore one of the first distinguishing characteristics separating a producer from a manager—a characteristic that employees are quick to sense in their supervisor. There seems little doubt that a lack of planning skills has been sufficient reason why many supervisors are not promoted, for each move up the management ladder requires a higher degree of planning skill. If that skill is lacking at the first level, a supervisor is not likely to be advanced to a more responsible position.

Management-mindedness demands more of the supervisor than a personal ability to plan. It challenges the supervisor to demonstrate an enthusiastic willingness to participate in the plans of others with whom he or she coordinates. Much of a supervisor's planning must fit into plans that are developed at higher levels. The supervisor's responsibility is to implement those plans as efficiently as possible. For example, a manufacturing manager calls a meeting to announce a plantwide cost-reduction program. The manager sets forth general guidelines for the program, suggests areas that should be attacked, and sets up time limits for achieving a certain percentage of reduction. The supervisors have been given the job of implementing the plan. They must now develop their own plans—setting their own goals, determining who will do the work and when it will be done. Obviously, the more thorough the planning is at the supervisory level, the more likely it is that the plant will reach its goals.

Frequently a supervisor will be asked by the boss or by staff departments to participate in planning special projects or programs—more demands on his or her time. Yet a mark of management-mindedness is the degree to which he or she is cooperative in participating in the planning of others. The supervisor's responsibility is for his or her department, but there is also an obligation to contribute to the overall operation by making sound suggestions when plans are being formulated and by carrying out any personal assignments that might develop within the designated time limits.

**MANAGING
PERSONAL TIME**

Carla Cramer is an example of a supervisor who has no concept of the critical need to manage time like any other resource. Those who make the familiar complaint, "If I only had more time," fail to recognize that they have all the time there is. They'll never get any more or have any less—twenty-four hours a day. What a person accomplishes in the approximately eight hours a day allocated to the job is dependent on how well he or she manages. It's a simple matter to recognize that if a person takes ten hours to do eight hours' work, those extra two hours must be taken from family, rest, or recreation. There's no way to recover a wasted hour or day, yet tomorrow is ready to be managed or used in any way we choose.

How often, like Carla Cramer, have people said to themselves, "I don't know where the time goes"? The first step in effectively managing time is to find the answer to that question. Just how am I spending my time? Am I chasing around putting out fires? Is half of my time consumed in answering the phone and chasing down information? Am I losing precious hours by arriving late, leaving early, extending breaks, and engaging in nonproductive bull sessions? How much of that forty-hour workweek is consumed in attending meetings, in routine clerical work, or in locating tools and materials? Many supervisors would be surprised at the ratio of their producing time to their managing time. Until they make an effort to find out how they spend their time, there's little likelihood that they will disturb themselves sufficiently to take corrective action. As in the solving of any other problem, they need the facts.

Burt Hall told Carla that it was necessary to spend time to save time, and so it is with respect to managing personal time. It will take some time for a supervisor to determine how he or she is spending time, but that job can be made easier by using a chart like the Personal Time Analysis Chart shown in Figure 8. A precise time study isn't necessary. By using a check mark for each ten minutes, a supervisor can get a fairly accurate picture of how most of his or her time is spent. For example, if he or she attended a production meeting from 9:00 to 10:00 A.M., in each of the 9:00 and 9:30 blocks under "Meetings" the supervisor would put three check marks. If the first half hour was spent on scheduling and instructing an employee on a job, he or she might put two marks under "Scheduling" and one under "Instructing." It takes only about a minute to mark the sheet for the previous hour or two. Estimates of how much time was spent on the phone or talking to employees will have to be made, of course. The supervisor simply wants an approximate idea of how the time is being spent. No one else will ever

PERSONAL TIME ANALYSIS

Time	Meetings	Personal Contacts	Scheduling and Assigning Work	Inspecting	Instructing	Planning	Paper Work	Personal; breaks	Miscel-laneous	Comments
7:00										
7:30										
8:00										
8:30										
9:00										
9:30										
10:00										
10:30										
11:00										
11:30										
12:00										
12:30										
1:00										
1:30										
2:00										
2:30										
3:00										
3:30										
4:00										

FIGURE 8

see the analysis unless he or she chooses to show it. The same sheet can be used for the entire week, or individual sheets might be used each day. Generally, one sheet for the full week carries a greater impact at week's end. The total check marks for the week in each column multiplied by ten provides a good idea of how many minutes are spent in a week on each activity.

The column headings in Figure 8 are for purposes of illustration only. Each supervisor will have to determine those which best cover his or her own activities. After a day or two he or she might want to modify the headings. For example, if the job involved large amounts of time spent in personnel contacts, a supervisor might want to break that down into types of contacts—safety contacts, grievances, personal problems, etc.

By the end of two weeks, the supervisor should have better than a fair idea of where the time is going. To say the least, the analysis should be revealing. One can ask, ''Am I wasting an hour or more a day in idle conversation and on breaks?'' ''How much of that time could be saved?'' ''Am I doing so much paper work that I might more appropriately be called a clerk than a supervisor?'' ''Am I a slave to the telephone and to my role as an expediter?'' Many supervisors, for example, find in making such an analysis that they spend literally no time in planning. Carla Cramer would certainly be one of them.

After a supervisor has found patterns in his or her use of time, he or she should then start to determine how to spend the time most profitably. Somewhere in that workday should be set aside a period for planning and creative work—the function of a manager. But how, and where?

Burt Hall set aside fifteen minutes at the beginning of each day to make a list of things that he wanted to do that day. He hesitated to dignify what he was doing by calling it planning, but that's exactly what it was. Determining what was to be done, who was to do it, and when it was to be done fits our definition of planning perfectly. Burt was managing his day rather than having things just happen. He found, too, that if he tried to cram in too much detail, he couldn't fulfill his plan. There must be some flexibility for emergencies, breakdowns, or demands from the boss or from other departments. No one is free from demands on time imposed by the boss or others in the organization.

Each Friday afternoon, Burt found the quiet after everyone had left an ideal time to look at the next week. Figures 9 and 10 are examples of forms he might have used to project some of the jobs that he wanted to accomplish—jobs which many supervisors put off until they get more time.

PERSONAL PLANNING SHEET

Week ending _____

Work Activity	Mon.		Tues.		Wed.		Thurs.		Fri.		Sat.		Comments
	A.M.	P.M.	A.M.	P.M.	A.M.	P.M.	A.M.	P.M.	A.M.	P.M.	A.M.	P.M.	

FIGURE 9

In a chart like the one shown in Figure 9, a supervisor would simply list in the "Work activity" column the jobs that he or she wanted to accomplish the next week; for example, review John Jones's performance, revise filing system, call departmental meeting on eye and foot protection, and study method of reporting waste materials. To this, of course, should be added any regular known demands on his or her time, such as weekly production meetings, preparation of periodic reports, conferences with the boss, periodic inspections, and training meetings. With the listing of each activity, he or she will put an X in the appropriate column—Monday, A.M., Wednesday, P.M., etc. Rather than trying to do everything tomorrow, a supervisor should work to evaluate activities, set priorities, and schedule each activity when it won't be crowded by a dozen others. During the week as each job is completed, he or she will put a circle around the X. If the job didn't get done, he or she can use the "Comments" column to explain why it didn't get done

PERSONAL TIME PLAN

Week of _____

Hour	Monday	Tuesday	Wednesday	Thursday	Friday
7:00–8:00					
8:00–9:00					
9:00–10:00					
10:00–11:00					
11:00–12:00					
12:00–1:00					
1:00–2:00					
2:00–3:00					
3:00–4:00					
4:00–5:00					

FIGURE 10

and reschedule the job. The advantage of this kind of planning is that the explanations or alibis for not accomplishing the job are made only to oneself. When a supervisor gets tired of explaining, self-discipline should be used to get the job done by setting less important things aside.

Figure 10 combines a daily and weekly plan by identifying each hour of the day for a week at a time. The principle, however, is the same. Some will find one more convenient. Others will find perhaps even another method more convenient such as the monthly pocket calendars which are so popular. Simplicity and flexibility are important. Tying oneself down with too much detail puts a person in the position of spending more time revising the schedule than the system is worth. The objective is to save time and use it more effectively, not to spend it as a slave to a system.

To those who might ask, "Is this really planning or managing?" let's review it in terms of our definition. By this method the supervisor can determine *what* has to be done by analyzing how the time is spent and can decide how to make better use of it. *Who* will do the job is determined when he or she puts it down on paper—either the supervisor will do it personally, or assign it to a subordinate. *When* the job is to be done is designated by the time at which it is scheduled in the daily or weekly plan. Having established that this is planning, we can ask, "Is this managing?" First of all, let's recognize that the first function of management is *planning* and *organizing*. *Directing* is accomplished when the supervisor says, "This is what I will do and when I will do it." *Controlling* enters the picture, when at the end of the day or the week, the supervisor looks to see if what was planned has been accomplished. If corrective measures are needed, he or she plans them, and then goes through the cycle again.

Many supervisors, like Carla Cramer, acknowledge that managing personal time sounds good in theory, but they back away when they look at the countless activities in which they engage every day. Feeling that it's hopeless, they never start. They put personal time planning far down on the mental list of things they will do as soon as they get more time. Several supervisors have reported at university seminars that they were able to bridge this initial hurdle by making their first plans for weekends at home. It works the same way and with much less pressure. How many odd jobs are there waiting around the house for us to get more time—screens to be painted, garage to be cleaned, closets to be rearranged, tools to be sharpened, appliances to be repaired, a room to be painted, shrubs to be trimmed? Scheduling a few of these jobs for particular weekends until the list is whittled down has proved to be an excellent exercise in personal time planning. Oddly enough, the exercise has also contributed positively to domestic relations when tried.

CONSEQUENCES OF POOR PLANNING

Where planning is poor or lacking in a department, it can be said that the department is operating without management. Certainly the supervisor who can't plan can't manage. Carla Cramer's department provides an excellent (or should we say miserable) example of what happens in the absence of good planning. A supervisor hopelessly bogged down in a never-ending deluge of details, Carla was ready to give up. Life, she said, was too short to endure the pressure of the job. Let's take a look at some of the specific consequences of poor planning and organizing.

Lower Production

It stands to reason that lack of coordinating, overlapping activities, shortages of materials and equipment, and poor scheduling can't help but result in lower productivity. With production as one of the supervisor's major responsibilities, failure to plan is to cheat the supervisor and to shortchange the company.

Dissatisfaction Among Employees

Employees want to feel a satisfaction in accomplishment. If poor leadership creates chaos and denies them this opportunity, the natural result is discontent. A supervisor who gives sound direction to his or her work force will build respect. The ability to give that direction is dependent on sound planning. Carla Cramer and Burt Hall are examples of the effect of supervisory planning on the morale of their work force.

High Costs

When productivity is lowered, morale is poor, rework is high, and costs inevitably rise. Another of the supervisor's major responsibilities is sacrificed to poor planning when unit costs increase and profits diminish.

Misunderstanding and Confusion

Not knowing what kind of performance is expected is disconcerting to the employee. Employees want direction, not a lot of ifs and maybes. Standing around because materials aren't available or equipment is missing adds to the confusion. Carla Cramer was confused. Her confusion, as hard as it was on her, was no greater than the confusion her employees experienced.

Pressure From Above

Here poor planning really hurts the supervisor. He or she was put in the job by management to get results and results are expected—not alibis. Few supervisors haven't had the experience at one time or another of having these words stick in their throats, "Boss, I just haven't had time to get at it." When poor planning yields poor results, the pressure from above mounts, and well it should.

Poor-Quality Work

Quality, say some manufacturers, is built into their products; but quality, too, must suffer when confusion reigns in a department. Complaints from customers are inevitable when quality drops off, and what a way that is to draw attention to the supervisor in whose department quality has suffered because of poor planning. Quality improvement must be planned for just like any other improvement.

Accidents

Confusion and dissatisfaction in the work force tend to take people's minds off what they are doing, thus creating conditions ripe for accidents. Lack of planning often results in hurrying, poor housekeeping, substituting improper tools, using makeshift equipment, and taking chances—all known contributors to accidents.

Lessened Chance for Promotion

All functions in the management process are geared to the planning function. Directing and controlling are effective only when planning is thorough. The supervisor who can't plan can't manage. Common sense tells us that the supervisor who can't manage won't be promoted and will be penalized when salary increases for merit are considered.

BENEFITS OF GOOD PLANNING

Other than avoiding the consequences of poor planning, what benefits to the supervisor and to the organization accrue as a result of good planning? Let's enumerate just a few.

Better Coordination

Most departments relate to other departments and functions. Close coordination of activities is required. The planning which enables the supervisor to live up to deadlines, maintain standards, honor commitments, and render outstanding service marks the supervisor as a good team person.

More Effective Control of Operations

As we shall see when we discuss how to plan, the early stages call for establishing the goals or defining the desired results. Goals, results, objectives, or standards are the basis for the controlling function of management. Until, through planning, the supervisor sets objectives, he or she has little against which any effectiveness can be measured. If a supervisor seeks as a goal to increase productivity 6 percent, he or she has established a basis for control.

Easier Delegation

Planning leads to organizing similar activities, setting priorities, and analyzing the personnel available. Good planning will point to the potential opportunities for delegation. When a supervisor sees what jobs can be delegated and who might be capable of doing them, some of the initial barriers to delegation have been hurdled.

More Economical Use of Resources

By pinpointing duplication of effort, uneconomical use of materials, and overlapping functions, planning contributes to more efficient use of the resources under the supervisor's control. Defining skills required to perform specific operations enables the supervisor to utilize lower-level skills on some jobs.

Increased Personal Effectiveness

When we compare a supervisor who can plan with one who can't, the accomplishments of the planner stand head and shoulders above those of the nonplanner. Carla Cramer and Burt Hall are cases in point. As simple as his planning was, Burt overshadowed Carla by far in what he was able to achieve in a day or a week. Burt was managing his department; he gave it direction; he controlled it. Carla was batted back and forth by circumstances. Neither Carla nor any of her people approached their full potential.

Tendency Toward Improvement

There's a tendency on the part of a good planner to want to do a better job next time. As a supervisor implements a plan, he or she finds out what works and what doesn't. The supervisor retains what is successful and seeks to improve what is lacking. If a supervisor achieved one hundred units of production this month, the tendency is to shoot for an increase next month, and the month after that. When improvements are a part of the supervisory pattern, the supervisor's worth to organization rises to new levels.

TYPES OF SUPERVISORY PLANNING

There are those who claim that a first-line supervisor really does no planning and is not expected to. Their reasoning is that production standards are set at higher levels and are simply given to the supervisor to carry out. Further, they point out, staff specialists have taken over the planning responsibilities and the authority of the supervisor in the areas of quality, safety, personnel, methods, and labor relations, leaving little more than an expediting function. Of course, it is these same so-called "experts" who claim that today's supervisor is not a manager. Those who have been a part of supervisory development hold quite opposite views. The supervisor is management, and if he or she is a manager, planning is a part of the job. What does the supervisor plan? Let's look at some of the activities that call for planning on the supervisor's part.

Participation in Setting Goals

Higher-level management is dependent on front-line supervision for the accurate determination of realistic goals. The supervisor is frequently asked to participate in planning production schedules and requirements. The person in the best position to know the capabilities of present production facilities is the supervisor. This role in the critical area of goal setting is significant.

Improvement Programs

We're all familiar with quality-improvement drives, cost-reduction programs, housekeeping campaigns, accident-prevention programs, and methods-improvement programs. Whether a supervisor produces any concrete results in these improvement programs is determined by the effectiveness of his or her planning of departmental efforts. For example, in a cost-reduction program one may set a goal of so many thousand dollars or a general 3 percent reduction as part of an overall attack on costs. From that point the supervisor must plan how the goal will be reached and who will do what. The supervisor also determines how to measure the improvement against the results anticipated. The supervisor who, like Carla Cramer, doesn't have to plan these programs and hopes that something will improve is more likely to find the situation deteriorating instead of improving. These improvement programs, which are constantly recurring, provide an excellent opportunity for a supervisor to exercise and sharpen planning skills.

Personnel Management

The organizing of activities so they are performed most efficiently by qualified people requires expert planning. Determining how many people are needed so that there is sufficient help to get the job done with no extra people standing around calls for a high degree of planning. Disciplining an individual, reviewing the performance with that person, handling a grievance, and discussing a change in job assignments should all be carefully planned to avoid misunderstandings.

Production

Production planning in a supervisor's department may call for a variety of planning activities. Scheduling and routing of production are planning functions. Having the necessary materials, equipment, facilities, and manpower available calls for detailed planning in many operations. Movement of materials or data in and out of the department requires planning. The degree of production planning required by the supervisor will vary with the nature of work performed in the department. For example, a job shop will call for substantially different plans from those required in a production line operation or a data processing department.

Organization of Work

The problem at the supervisory level is not to develop detailed organization charts, but rather to answer the question, "How should the work of my department be divided and grouped?" While a supervisor may have inherited the basic organization of the department and may have had other changes dictated, he or she is still responsible for productivity and must set up a well-organized department. The supervisor is in the best position to know when a shift in job assignments will accomplish the work of the department most efficiently. The company may very well have organization specialists. At the first level, though, it's academic to try to separate the planning and organizing function. The basic purpose of organizing is to group the work to be performed to utilize personnel most effectively. This is done at the same time as the planning function.

Maintenance

Only the most reckless, foolhardy supervision operates expensive equipment until it breaks down or falls apart. Proper maintenance planning ensures a longer service life of equipment and provides uninterrupted production cycles. Determining when a machine needs service, the best time to do it, and the extent of the maintenance (for example, lubrication or complete overhaul)—all demand careful planning to ensure the least possible interference with production.

Paper Work and Reports

So many supervisors complain that an unreasonable amount of their time is consumed by paper work and reports. Generally they have no choice but to generate the information needed by other departments through this paper work. Good planning, however, can contribute significantly to a reduction of the time spent on paper work. Consideration can be given to delegating the paper work as a means of developing subordinates. Reports which are planned to present the information required in the most concise, usable form help both the recipient and the reporter.

Changes

Increasingly supervisors are faced with initiating changes in their departments. Resistance to those changes can be minimized by the proper planning of their initiation. Chapter 4 deals in some detail with the need for planning changes.

Communications

Effective department management depends on good communication. Important communications should be carefully planned. Chapter 3 discusses the need for careful planning in communication.

Personal Time

Because the key to having sufficient time for performing our job is the planning and organizing of our own personal activities, a major portion of this chapter has already been devoted to the subject. A supervisor cannot overlook the fact that he or she must be personally well organized to have a smoothly operating department.

In summary, almost every function the supervisor performs calls for planning to some degree. Short- and long-range plans are participated in daily. He or she is involved in carrying out standing plans and in formulating single-use plans. Planning gives purposeful direction to the management of a department.

KEY STEPS IN FORMULATING PLANS

A dynamic organization depends on planning, and it cannot ignore the basic fundamentals. Any plan must ultimately include the answers to some basic questions. We have seen them grouped so often that they seem deceptively simple: *what, when, where, who,* and *how.* Let's consider the role these questions play in planning.

What

Is the supervisor's goal clearly in mind? How will he or she know whether the objective has been achieved unless the objective is spelled out? Answering the question *what* is the beginning of the planning process and is at the heart of the "management by results" concept. Goals are vital in planning. They give direction to the supervisor's efforts. Examples of goals one might set include: producing so many units of production; reducing the amount of time to complete a project; having a trained replacement available at all times for key jobs; reducing the percentage of scrap in a month or a quarter; reducing overhead labor costs to a certain level; reducing the percentage of turnover, tardiness, or absenteeism; eliminating defects; reducing by minutes, hours, days, weeks, or months the time usually required to do a job. Setting goals in terms of the desired results gives the supervisor a beginning and ending point to his or her plan. Administrative control of the operations depends for its effectiveness on specific objectives that measure progress.

When

Plans are designed to accomplish objectives in a given amount of time—on schedule. How long will it take to do the job and each part of the job? When is the best time to move from one phase to another? When is the best time to start? What is the completion date?

Where

The supervisor should determine the most effective place to accomplish the objective of his or her plan. Should a potential method of improvement, for example, be tested in the department or in some controlled environment like the experimental laboratory? Should a meeting be a tailgate session, held in one's office or taken to the conference room to achieve maximum results? Should special clerical work be performed in the office or outside the company?

Who

A key determination in the formulation of any successful plan is who will carry it out. Who will give the best results? Who is best qualified? Who can benefit most by the experience the project offers? How many times does the supervisor fail to give consideration to these questions and by default wind up doing the job personally, adding to an already heavy burden of work? The opportunity for delegation and timesaving becomes most apparent when careful consideration is given to the *who* in our plans.

How

The methods the supervisor chooses to implement his or her plans will have very real impact on the results achieved. Should a job be done by traditional methods and procedures? Is there room for creative or novel approaches? The less one specifies specific methods when delegating, the more opportunities for growth are created. Can staff specialists assist in finding a better method for reaching a goal? Their help may be well worth considering. That's why they are there.

As an exercise in formulating plans, it would be well to determine whether or not all these questions have been answered. The chances are, that if they have, it is a reasonably well conceived plan. Another check on planning skill would be to analyze a project gone wrong to determine which of these questions were ignored or improperly answered in formulating plans. In the final analysis these questions are the key to sound planning no matter how elementary they might seem.

DIFFICULTIES IN PLANNING

Supervisors ought to recognize that they face some genuine difficulties or limitations in their attempts to plan the work in their departments. The pressure of many jobs and responsibilities limits the time they have for planning. Supervisors lack control over some factors in their plans, such as goals which may be set for them. The frustrations of many supervisors are reflected in the following difficulties in planning:

Lack of Know-How

Many supervisors shrug off their planning responsibility with the comment, "I haven't the faintest idea of how to go about it." For the great majority there's no reason for having to go it alone. This chapter contains some suggestions on how to handle basic planning; supervisors can also always find help from the boss, other good planners, or staff specialists. That Carla Cramer went to see Burt Hall is a good example of a way of getting started.

The Time Required

Planning inevitably requires time. Invariably it will save the supervisor much more time than it takes. Unfortunately planning time must be spent before the activity begins. It's too late to go back to plan after things go wrong. Planning is deciding in advance what is to be done.

Pressure of Other Work

Planning is a mental activity. Current work demands the supervisor's attention. When faced with day-to-day decisions, he or she tends to give planning secondary priority. Planning is difficult at best when the planner is interrupted by having to make on-the-spot decisions. That's why Burt did his daily planning before the shift began and his weekly planning on Friday afternoon, when things had quieted down.

Absence of Similar Problems

The expenditure of time and effort sometimes doesn't seem worth it when the problem or project isn't likely to recur. Why develop a plan that will never be used again?

Tendency Toward Inflexibility

Many supervisors report that plans limit their freedom of action, and well they might if supervisors don't retain their flexibility. Burt Hall became annoyed when things interfered with his projected plans. Once his plans were set, he was determined to accomplish his goals, perhaps even sacrificing time that might be required by more important developments. Sometimes supervisors have a tendency to rely forever on a good working plan. They think that if it worked for them last year, it's good this year and should be next year. This type of thinking naturally stifles creativity, but it's more a deficiency in the individual than it is in the concept of sound planning.

In summary, it is important to recognize that planning is frequently the difference between the haphazard, chaotic operation and the smoothly functioning department. Planning separates the manager from the doer. If one can't plan, one can't supervise!

HIGHLIGHTS

1. Job knowledge for today's supervisor is only in part a knowledge of the technical aspects of the work done in the department. More

important are knowledge and skill in implementing the management process—planning, organizing, directing, and controlling. Management is planning.

2. Planning is determining what needs to be done, who will do it, and when it has to be done.

3. One of the keys to a supervisor's effectiveness is his or her ability to manage personal time. Personal time management starts with an analysis of how time is currently being spent. Additional suggestions include finding some time each day for uninterrupted planning, laying out the work he or she wants to accomplish, setting priorities, and delegating.

4. Some of the consequences of poor planning are:

    a. Lower production
    b. Dissatisfaction among employees
    c. Higher costs
    d. Misunderstanding and confusion
    e. Pressure from above
    f. Poor-quality work
    g. Accidents
    h. Lessened chance for promotion and advancement

5. Benefits of good planning include the elimination of the undesirable consequences of poor planning and in addition these positive results:

    a. Better coordination
    b. More effective control of operations
    c. Easier delegation
    d. More economical use of resources
    e. Increased personal effectiveness
    f. Tendency toward improvement

6. Examples of the types of planning a supervisor gets involved in are:

    a. Participation in setting goals
    b. Improvement programs
    c. Personnel management in the department
    d. Production planning
    e. Organization of work in the department
    f. Maintenance
    g. Paper work and reports

   h.   Changes
   i.   Communications
   j.   Personal time

7. Planning is fundamentally a matter of answering the key planning questions:

   a.   *What* is to be done (goals, results, objectives)?
   b.   *When* will it be done?
   c.   *Where* will it be done?
   d.   *Who* will do it?
   e.   *How* will it be done?

8. Some of the very real difficulties faced in doing a better job of planning in a department are:

   a.   Lack of know-how
   b.   The time required
   c.   Pressure of other work
   d.   Absence of similar problems
   e.   Tendency toward inflexibility

DISCUSSION QUESTIONS

1. What is your opinion of the attitude often expressed that if a person has leadership ability, he or she doesn't need job knowledge and can supervise in any department?

2. Do you agree or disagree with the statement that a supervisor who can't plan can't manage? Why?

3. Make a list of as many activities and duties as you can that occupy a supervisor's time during the day. What suggestions could you make to find more time for planning?

4. Are there any disadvantages to planning carefully all the department's activities?

5. Why should a supervisor's inability to plan have any effect on dissatisfaction among employees in that department?

6. What reasons might there be for the statement that there's a tendency on the part of a good planner to want to do a better job next time?

7. If you were planning a departmental housecleaning campaign, what are some of the considerations you would take into account in your initial planning?

8. Suppose you were planning a new program to get everyone to cooperate in wearing eye protection. Outline how you would answer the planning questions *who, what, where, when,* and *how.* Make whatever assumptions you like.

CASE PROBLEMS

THE CASE OF PHIL AMHERST

"Honey, there just aren't enough hours in a day," moaned Phil Amherst, supervisor of the data processing department of the Carstairs Manufacturing Company. "I'm doing three times more work than anybody in my department, and I'm supposed to be boss. I can't figure it out. I've got to start darn near every job, and my people just stand around waiting for me. Sometimes, I swear I'm supposed to be in four places at the same time. It used to be that I'd have a day like this once in a while but lately every day is like this—rush, rush, rush!"

Phil looked across his late supper at a bulging briefcase and several more hours of work to be tackled before bedtime. His irritation mounted as he thought over the day's activities. Near losses of temper twice because Jean and Chester sat waiting for him to get them started on projects. There was plenty they could have done to accomplish something while they waited. They seemed almost to be taking advantage of his being snowed under—no initiative on their part whatsoever. The phone had rung almost continuously. Other departments wanting answers to questions about a thousand things like procedures, when were they going to get this or that, was he sure of the accuracy of their data on a run, could he handle a "little special job," and on it went.

The night shift wasn't giving him any peace either. Three and four calls a night at home were becoming commonplace. Phil was careful not to show annoyance when Jeff called because he didn't want them taking chances. On the other hand, Jeff could have figured out the answer to more than half of the problems he called about. Poking at his food, Phil had just decided he had best open that briefcase when his wife called, "Phone for you. It's Jeff."

1. What could be some of the reasons for Phil's being snowed under?

2. What is likely to happen to Phil if he continues on his present course?

3. What steps should Phil take to get himself and the department straightened out?

THE CASE OF ANGIE McDONALD

Angie McDonald was the subject of a critical discussion in the state's expanding Department of Industrial Relations. As supervisor of mail operations, she was one of the persons being considered for the position of assistant director of the administrative division.

"It would be nice if we could promote a woman into that position. We ought to be setting the example on affirmative action for the rest of the state offices," Jim Easton, the division manager, was saying.

"Yes, but her sex is about the only thing she's got going for her. That and the fact that she really is a conscientious, hardworking woman," countered Sam Sampson, whose departure was creating the vacancy. "No one in this whole division works harder than Angie, but I don't think she's management material. She probably would try harder and work harder than anyone we're considering. If anyone deserves a promotion, it's Angie for the dedication she gives to her job and her department. But you'd be making a lot of work for yourself, Jim. She's just not on top of things. With some halfway decent planning that department could run itself. Angie's got some good people down there, but she doesn't use them. Has to do everything herself."

"Maybe we should level with her about her one big weakness and get some training for her. What do you think?" Jim asked.

"I guess I really never could bring myself to talk to her about her poor planning. She tries so darn hard. Training would take time and she still might not measure up. I'd say we'd better pass her up this time until we find out if she can learn to plan. It's too risky to throw her into this job until we see what improvements she can make," Sam said.

"Suppose you're right. Let's look at Henry Sanderson. Doggone, I sure would have liked to promote a woman to that job," Jim sighed.

1. Who bears the responsibility for Angie's apparent inability to plan?

2. Should Angie be given the chance at the promotion?

3. What should Angie do when she learns why she has been passed over?

THE CASE OF NINO DiLORENZO

Owner-manager Mike Keller had built his appliance sales and service business into the largest and most successful in the entire metropolitan area. Mike was convinced that his business held its leadership position because of prompt quality service. "We back everything we sell with better service than any manufacturer could ask of a dealer," Mike was proud of telling his business friends. "You don't have to be constantly running gimmicky sales if your customers know you take care of them after the product is in their homes."

Nino DiLorenzo, his new service manager, was giving Mike genuine cause for concern. Nino had been with Keller the longest of all of his repairmen and was really good on customer relations when he made his service calls. New sales frequently resulted from Nino's calls. Nino was the only person considered when Mike had to name a new service manager three months ago. "He's a natural," Mike said at the time.

Mike's problem seemed to be that Nino was inflexible and unorganized. He expected every job to go smoothly and take only the time he felt he would have required if he had done it personally. He scheduled service calls unreasonably close together, the repairmen claimed. He chased them from one side of town to the other and back again and never allowed enough travel time. The repairmen complained that they were forced to take shortcuts and not check things out the way they should because of Nino's wild promises.

Customers, too, were calling to complain about poor service—repairmen arriving hours and sometimes days later than promised. Repaired units not functioning satisfactorily or breaking down again a short time after repair were commonly cited by Mike's unhappy customers. One of his valued customers said it looked to her like the squeaking wheel got the grease when it came to service and that she figured it was time to start squeaking. Repairmen substantiated what she said by saying they frequently were told to change the sequence of their calls to "take care of this one right away." Mike had decided that his business could go downhill in a lot less time than it had taken him to build it. Something would have to be done about Nino.

1. What are the key reasons an outstanding sales-service person like Nino was having trouble?

2. What are some of the consequences of Nino's inability to plan and schedule?

3. What should Mike do about Nino?

SUGGESTIONS FOR FURTHER STUDY

Bittel, Lester R., *What Every Supervisor Should Know*, 3d ed., Chapters 26 and 38, McGraw-Hill Book Company, New York, 1974.

Shout, Howard F., *Start Supervising*, Chapter 3, Bureau of National Affairs, Inc., Washington, D.C., 1972.

Steinmetz, Lawrence L., and H. Ralph Todd, Jr., *First-Line Management*, Chapters 2 and 8, Business Publications, Inc., Dallas, Texas, 1975.

Webber, Ross A., *Management*, Chapters 12 and 13, Richard D. Irwin, Inc., Homewood, Illinois, 1975.

CHAPTER 12

GIVING DIRECTIONS AND ORDERS

It had been four days since Burt Hall had delegated the supervision of a thirty-day housekeeping campaign to Sam Pitman. With over ten years' experience under his belt, Sam was an old-timer at the age of twenty-seven. Burt liked Sam, even though Sam rubbed a lot of people the wrong way. Sam was eager and enthusiastic. A top-notch producer, he had developed into a reasonably good trainer after some sad early experiences. Sam jumped at this new assignment as an opportunity to show what he could do. Perhaps he had been perceptive enough to see that Burt was trying him out on a job requiring supervisory responsibility.

Before Burt had even finished explaining that the campaign was to be plantwide, Sam was popping with ideas of what could be done in Assembly Department B. He would divide the department into three sections and have one person in charge of each section. Of course, he personally would supervise the overall campaign, but it would help to have someone closer to the work carrying out his assignments. Burt

271

gave Sam full authority—within reason, he said—to make their department the sharpest in the company.

That same afternoon Sam came back to Burt with the organization of his campaign all set. He would put Phil Knudson in charge of the north section. Arnie Ross could handle the central section, and Gus Schulz could take charge of the south section, where Sam worked.

Burt asked Sam if he had cleared the assignments with the three "deputies." He hadn't. "Don't worry about that, though," Sam assured Burt. "Getting their cooperation is my responsibility. You don't have to fret, Burt. They'll do what I want them to do."

It was clear to Burt that Sam relished this assignment. What was it he had been told about delegation? You have to give subordinates freedom of action and decision if they are to develop. Well, if Sam says not to worry about it, then maybe a hands-off policy is best, Burt thought. But, doggone it, it sure requires some confidence in your subordinates.

Burt didn't see much of Sam after that, but he knew Sam was busy. It almost seemed that Sam was avoiding him to prove that he was capable of running the campaign without help. Burt's pleasure at seeing Sam take charge outweighed his uneasiness in letting go of the reins in a project where Burt wanted to make a really good showing. As each day passed, Burt showed less concern about the campaign, confident that Sam would come for help if he needed it. Also there was evidence that cleanup activity was under way. His choice of Sam, he was now convinced, had been a good one.

Arnie Ross gave Burt the first clue that things might not be going as well as he had hoped. Four boxes of subassemblies that Burt had set aside for future use and that could now be utilized had been thrown out. They were perfectly good, but they had not met the government specifications for which they had originally been produced. Burt, rather than scrapping them, had saved them because they could be used on nongovernment orders. The production order calling for their use had reached Arnie, and he came in to tell Burt that the four boxes had been junked.

Burt asked why, and Arnie said it was orders from Sam. He asked Arnie if he hadn't told Sam that the parts were being saved for an order that was sure to come. "How could I?" Arnie countered. "You just said to store them over in the corner. You didn't say why."

A little impatient, Burt said, "For heaven's sake, Arnie, if I told you to store them, you should have known it was to use them. At least you might have checked with me before you junked them."

"Now wait a minute," Arnie said. "I don't like getting caught in the middle. I just do what I'm told. You said to store them in the corner. OK, I stored. Sam comes along and says to get rid of them. Sure, I started to question it. But Sam says they go out, and he's running the cleanup. So what am I supposed to do? Besides, I don't like the way Sam is bossing me around. He says you put him in charge, but a little bit of authority sure went to his head. He gives orders like my old drill sergeant. It burns me up being told to do things like a little kid. You've never been that way, Burt. Why does he have to be? Honestly, I thought of checking with you, but then I figured that Sam probably had already checked and that he'd get sore at me for second-guessing him. So I just do what I'm told—no trouble that way. If you've got a beef, see Sam—not me. I was just following orders, and that's what I'll keep on doing the best I know how.''

Burt apologized to Arnie. He said that Arnie was right and that they would just have to write the whole thing off to experience. He complimented Arnie on the improved appearance of the central section, asked him to pass the good word on to the others, but asked him not to say anything about the problem of the scrapped subassemblies. The order would just have to be held up until they could be replaced.

It was Arnie's comments about Sam's way of giving orders that concerned Burt most. It was inconvenient not to have those subassemblies. The delay would be more costly than the dollar value of the parts. But if Sam's order-giving pattern was being repeated in the other sections, more trouble could be expected. Checking up on people behind their backs is a sneaky thing to do, Burt thought. But it might be wiser than sticking your head in the sand and hoping nothing would happen. Heading north out of his office, Burt decided on a little talk with Phil Knudson and a brief informal inspection of the area.

Improvement in the appearance of the area was obvious as Burt glanced around, and he was smiling as he walked over to Phil's bench. Phil really was one of the old-timers, and as steady as they come. Any time you needed cooperation, Phil could always be counted on. Before Harry Gates retired Burt had thought that Phil would be the new supervisor. It was only the difference in their ages that had tipped the scales in Burt's favor; Phil had just turned sixty.

After a couple of friendly exchanges about the improvement in the appearance of the area, Burt decided to come directly to the point of his visit. ''Sam is really going after things,'' Burt commented. ''How are you two making out? He's not moving too fast, is he, Phil?''

Phil looked at Burt several seconds, weighing his answer. Then he smiled and said, ''Maybe you're going to have some trouble because of him, Burt, but it won't be from me. He's an eager beaver, but he does have a head on his shoulders. What he lacks in tact he makes up in enthusiasm. You can get along with Sam if you know how to take him. He gets carried away with a program like this and kind of shoves his ideas down your throat—do this, do that. You know what I mean. Most of his ideas are pretty darned good, so I just overlook his manners, and we get along fine. We've gone him a couple better than he expected, and everybody feels good. Both the fellows and the girls want to show him they can do a better job than he ever thought of. He's quick to give them a pat on the back, and he fakes a big surprised look when he comes around and sees what they've done. They like him now, and the important thing is that things are looking better than they have for quite a while.

"Burt, I don't like to carry stories out of school," Phil continued. "But you may have a problem developing down at the other end. Gus was up here yesterday afternoon, and he was just plain mad. He claimed he was going to knock Sam's block off. You know what Gus can be like when he gets his dander up."

"Say no more, Phil," Burt replied. "I know you don't want to be telling tales. I'll look into it right away; and, Phil, I do appreciate the cooperation you've given us up here. Things really do look good." Deciding not to waste any time getting to Gus, Burt started walking down to the other end of the department. As he passed his office, Arnie, who answered the phone in his office, flagged him down. "Hey, Burt, Oscar Palmer was just on the phone asking where that stuff for the Allied job is. Everything is ready in final assembly except for our stuff."

"That should have gone down an hour ago," Burt said as he walked by. "I'm on my way down there now. I'll check on it." Burt wondered whether the truckers had fouled things up. The job had been pretty well along when he had checked it last night and promised Oscar that things wouldn't be held up on their account. Sam and Gus were engaged in heated debate when Burt approached. At a glance around the area, Burt could see that the Allied job hadn't progressed from the previous evening. Another hour, possibly two, would be needed to finish it up. Several employees were engaged in cleaning activities and were apparently enjoying the argument between Sam and Gus.

As Burt walked up, Gus was saying, "Don't hand me any of that 'That's what I mean' jazz. We're doing exactly what you told us, and you made it pretty damned clear that you didn't want it any other way. Now get off my back so I can get my cleaning done."

"I'm ordering you to get back on that Allied job and get it finished before Burt gets down here," Sam shouted.

"You're too late," Gus sneered. "Here he comes now. And who

in hell do you think you are, ordering us to do production work? Are you the foreman now that you took over the cleaning detail?"

Burt had heard enough to know that a number of the employees were putting a priority on cleaning over production in order to spite Sam. Quietly he suggested to both Gus and Sam that they get hustling on the Allied job. Stopping at the workplace of each person who was involved in Allied work, Burt asked them each to drop what they were doing and rush the Allied subassemblies as much as they could. He explained to them that it was an extremely hot job and that all the other components were in final assembly waiting for them to finish. Each one seemed to be eager to cooperate and relieved to see the tension subside.

With everybody working on the rush job, Burt walked over to Sam and quietly asked him what had been going on. Sam said that every time he had tried to get any cooperation from Gus, he met with resistance. He got so fed up with the lack of cooperation from the whole gang that he ordered Gus and the rest of them to get the cleanup started no matter what—"I meant that I didn't want any more alibis and excuses." Sam told Burt that he was sure that Gus got them to set aside the Allied job just to make a fool of him.

Burt asked Sam if he could bring his lunch down to the office at noon and eat with him. The appointment confirmed, Burt stopped next at Gus's bench to get his side of the story. "For two cents I'd bust that smart aleck in the teeth," Gus blurted out, nodding his head in Sam's direction. "I hate to say it, Burt, but you really pulled a boner giving that punk any authority. He's another Hitler. He's been pushing us around ever since you gave him that cleanup job. There's not a one of us here that doesn't figure we could show those guys up at the other end, but we can't take Sam's bossing us like grade-schoolers.

"This morning before the shift ever started, he blew his stack. He said he didn't give a damn what we were doing, that we better get this place cleaned up or there'd be hell to pay. He acted as if he meant it, so I got the guys going. I think he just remembered the Allied job when you came up, because then he said we'd better get going on that. I told him we hadn't finished cleaning, and he blew his stack again."

Burt again asked Gus to put all his effort on rushing the Allied job along and simply said that they would get things straightened out as quickly as possible. Gus was industriously working, with a smile on his face, before Burt could finish his statement. Hurrying back to the office, Burt decided what he would say to Oscar Palmer when he called him. Then his thoughts turned to delegation. "It sure is a tricky business," he thought. "This is the second time I've gotten burned—and both times Sam Pitman has been involved. I've got to admit that I was to blame the first time for not teaching him something about training. This time it wasn't my fault—or was it?''

He was still talking to himself as he walked into his office, shut the door, and picked up the phone to call Mr. Palmer.

1. How should we evaluate Burt's selection of Sam Pitman to take charge of the housekeeping campaign?

2. What are some of the strengths and weaknesses in Burt's delegating techniques?

3. How can we account for the varied responses Sam got to his orders from Phil, Arnie, and Gus?

4. What principles of order-giving can we identify from Burt's and Sam's instructions to the employees in Assembly Department B?

5. What should Burt say to Sam at lunchtime?

MANAGEMENT IS DIRECTING

Once a supervisor has planned and organized the work of the department, the next step—the vital step—in the management process is to put thes plans in motion. Giving directions unleashes the plans and begins their implementation. At this stage of the management process, everyone acknowledges the key role of the supervisor. Even those who play down the supervisor's role as a manager admit that he or she initiates the action in the department by the orders given.

So much of what we have discussed thus far in this book culminates in the order-giving process. A supervisor's skills in motivation are reflected in how he or she gives directions. Good orders are a matter of communication and the creation of understanding between the one who gives the order and the one who receives it. It would be difficult to differentiate between giving directions and instructing. The principles are the same for training as they are for giving directions. Maintaining a positive climate for giving orders depends in part upon a supervisor's knowledge of individual differences and the philosophy of discipline. The process of giving orders and directions involves not only issuing an order but that part of the management process which gives direction to the entire department. Direction is the reason for a supervisor's being a part of management.

Giving orders is so basic to supervision we tend to take it for granted. Every supervisor gives orders. It's the job! How often does a supervisor evaluate the effect of his or her orders on personnel? Burt Hall took Sam's order-giving skills for granted, and the results were nearly disastrous. If anyone asked Sam if he knew how to give orders, Sam would have been insulted. Of course he knew how to give orders. He'd told Burt not to worry, hadn't he? We can all communicate—give orders, give directions—so we forget that this can be done more or less effectively. This chapter reviews the critical elements of giving good orders.

THE ORDER-GIVING CLIMATE

Everyone who holds a supervisory position has been placed in a position of authority. The supervisor has been given the authority to make decisions and gives orders to subordinates. The supervisor is in charge or in command of the department by decree from higher management. Most supervisors start their supervision only with the authority of rank. People do what the supervisor tells them because they know he or she is the boss. Unfortunately, many supervisors never graduate from that level of authority. Sam Pitman was starting off down this road—order, demand, command. "Do it because I say so." "I am in authority." Unless Burt lets Sam see the consequences of such tactics, the chances that Sam will be able to mature in supervision will be slim. Using rank or authority only is the mark of immature management, and the resulting climate in the department is clouded by tension and hostility.

In contrast to Sam's first supervisory directing, Burt demonstrated that he had earned for himself an authority based on respect rather than rank. Burt had authority because he was Burt, not because he was boss. The authority of respect grows as employees develop confidence in their leader. It grows out of fair treatment and firm direction. The existence of respected authority in a department results in a climate of co-operation—voluntary effort by employees to achieve more than is asked or expected.

As an exercise in analyzing climate, a supervisor might first look at how he or she feels toward the orders, directions, and instructions received from above. Is the feeling the supervisor has toward the boss the same feeling as he or she would want from subordinates? Answers, of course, will vary. What kind of climate exists now in the department, as a result of the orders given? Can the supervisor empathize—put himself or herself on the receiving end of directions? How would a supervisor feel and react toward the orders he or she gives? This exercise alone has caused many to modify the language or the approach they use in their instructions.

Generally we recognize three levels of climate, according to how a work force is directed. Let's identify each level and relate it to the case of Sam Pitman.

Climate of Cooperation

When people accept a direction willingly and follow it enthusiastically by giving more than is asked or expected, we can assume that a climate of cooperation exists. We found evidence of the climate of cooperation under Phil Knudson's direction. Phil's was an informal authority born of respect. Here we saw employees giving more than they were asked. Most supervisors would naturally like to have this kind of response to their orders.

Climate of Compliance

At this level people do what is expected of them—what they are told to do. They seldom do more or less than is ordered. Compliance is automatic, without any questioning of authority. There is no enthusiasm in this climate. Unintentional mistakes are frequently made because people do exactly what they are told. Arnie Ross responded in this manner to his direction from Sam. He said, "I was just following orders, and that's what I'll keep on doing the best I know how." He might have added, because he was thinking it, "Don't expect me to do anything on my own without being told." In a climate of compliance initiative on the part of workers and the creativity that results in ideas and suggestions for improvement are lacking. Compliance is compliance—no more, no less.

Climate of Hostile Compliance

Stormy weather! This response to orders is one of compliance with harmful intent. The employee who receives orders complies because he or she must bow to the authority of rank. He or she waits for an opportunity, however, to do exactly what is ordered and embarrass the supervisor in the process. Gus Schulz's attitude is a good example of hostile compliance. He had bucked Sam's orders until Sam told him to clean up no matter what. Gus's thinking probably would have sounded something like, "Ah-ha, did you hear what he said? 'Clean up no matter what.' Now we'll get this son of a gun. Let the Allied job sit. He said no matter what. OK, wise guy, we'll clean; and you can explain to Burt, or Ray, or Old Man Palmer why the Allied job didn't get finished. We're only doing what you told us, Sammy boy." There are very few of us who could give every order in such a way that an occasional one couldn't be followed in a hostile manner. Supervisors have to trust that their supervision will never create such an unhealthy climate.

UNDERSTANDING DELEGATION

Among the concepts of management that are frequently misunderstood and misapplied, delegation probably ranks first. Delegation can be the answer to many supervisors' problems, such as gaining time for managing, extending their effectiveness and influence, and developing subordinates. Misconceptions of what delegation means have produced results that can lead supervisors away from it rather than make them explore its full potential. For example, the supervisor who regards delegation as a means of dumping any unpleasant task soon finds his or her subordinates resisting rather than seeking it. This is also true of the supervisor who puts so many conditions on an assignment that he or she really isn't delegating at all because no freedom of action is permitted.

CHARACTERISTICS OF DELEGATION

What is delegation? Basically, it's the entrusting of an activity to another person. It may be for an extended period of time or, as in the case of Sam Pitman, for the completion of a project. When we come right down to it, delegation means giving others the right to make our decisions for us. It's within the context of this last statement that we see the elements of risk that cause many managers to shy away from delegation.

Freedom of Action

Delegation does not mean sending someone off on an errand or getting that person to perform some routine menial task. It means giving another the right to act, to decide, and to direct in our place. One characteristic of delegation is that the individual has freedom of action—that the employee makes the supervisor's decisions. Most executives point to their responsibility for having to make decisions as a key factor in their growth. By encouraging a subordinate to make decisions, a supervisor puts an employee in a climate where he or she will grow. Growth is one of the prime objectives in delegation, but growth can't be realized unless freedom of action is allowed. A supervisor delegates by the results wanted, leaving the method of reaching the goal in the hands of the subordinate. Sure, it's risky! Burt found that out when he turned the housekeeping campaign over to Sam Pitman.

Shared Decisions

The subordinate's decision becomes the supervisor's decision. If mistakes are made, they are the supervisor's mistakes. If the subordinate does well, it is a reflection on the supervisor. Many managers want it one way—share the credit, but pass on the blame. Still other managers see it another way—good decisions show them up, and poor decisions demonstrate how indispensable they are. They are the fearful ones to whom the risks of delegation are too great. gone of the truly satisfying experiences in supervision occurs when a subordinate does an excellent job. An example of the shared decision can be found in Arnie Ross's junking the subassemblies on Sam's orders. Sam made a decision, and Burt shared in that decision as if it were his own.

Shared Responsibility

We often hear the statement that responsibility can't be delegated. If a supervisor means to be absolved of responsibility by delegating it, then responsibility cannot be delegated. One cannot rid oneself of one's responsibilities by giving them to another. One does, however, create new responsibilities when delegating. The subordinate becomes responsible to the supervisor while the supervisor retains responsibility to higher management. In this sense the supervisor does delegate responsibility. Burt was responsible for the success of the housekeeping campaign whether he delegated its execution or directed it himself. Sam was responsible to Burt, and Burt was responsible to the plant manager. Both must take responsibility for the success or the failure of the campaign.

Granting of Authority

Responsibility can't be created without bestowing commensurate authority. No one ever wants to be held responsible for an activity over which he or she has no control. Many supervisors today are deeply concerned about being responsible for the quantity and quality of production when they have no authority to make decisions that affect production. Whenever a supervisor delegates an activity to a subordinate, some of the first considerations should be whether or not he or she is giving the employee the authority needed to perform the task.

Defining delegation in terms of these four characteristics demonstrates the potential risks and rewards inherent in the process. Enhancement of promotional potential is certainly not the least of the potential rewards. Many successful supervisors regard the opportunity to increase their personal contribution to the organization as reward enough for proper delegation. Why, then, do so many resist delegation? Let's look at just a few of the reasons:

1. Fear of costly mistakes by subordinates

2. Fear that subordinates might perform too well and show up the supervisor

3. Fear of losing control of an activity

4. Fear of loss of prestige or status

5. Reluctance to give up activities that a supervisor performs well

6. Having no one to delegate to

Not having a subordinate to delegate to is commonly given as the real reason for not delegating. If it's an opinion shared by many supervisors, perhaps we should consider the problem of finding people to whom we can delegate. It is not necessary for a supervisor to have a person designated officially as an assistant before one has a candidate for delegation. There may be several people who can perform an activity in an enlargement of their jobs. Figure 11 suggests a technique for finding potential employees to whom we can delegate. It's a simple inventory of the activities a supervisor performs, why these are performed, who is able to perform them now, and who can be trained to perform them.

Burt Hall might have used such a technique to help him find assistance on his job. In Chapter 8 he picked out three men to perform the second activity listed in Figure 11. When the time-consuming housekeeping campaign was announced, Burt selected Sam in order to test his potential for supervisory work. If a supervisor can think in terms of the ability of several employees to perform a variety of activities instead of in terms of one assistant, he or she may be in a better position to ease into the practice of delegation.

WHAT TO DELEGATE

Activity	Why Is It Performed?	Who Can Do It Now?	Who Can Be Trained?
1. Plan job assignments.	Utilize manpower; give everyone a chance to do his best.	Smith	Jones
2. Train new employees.	Increase productivity; improve job satisfaction; improve work quality.		Smith Brown
3. Make out production reports.	Inform management of department's progress; provide basis for corrective action and decisions.	Smith	Olson

Figure 11

DELEGATION TECHNIQUES

Here are some suggestions on how to delegate that have been gleaned from a large number of supervisors who have experienced the pleasure of watching their subordinates develop through the process of delegation.

Assign as Many Tasks as You Safely Can

There's a double advantage to this that should be obvious. First, it frees a supervisor for more real management activity and creative work. Second, the more people one has carrying out delegated activity, the more the growth in the department.

Expect and Accept Some Mistakes

If mistakes can be looked upon as an opportunity for further training, delegation becomes a challenge rather than a threat.

Give Sufficient Authority to Complete the Task

If a supervisor can empathize and see the situation through the eyes of the subordinate, he or she will very quickly see the need for that authority. A supervisor can't do the job without it—one shouldn't expect subordinates to.

Delegate According to the Results Desired, Not According to the Method People Should Use

Here is the heart of successful delegation. For subordinates, the chance to demonstrate what they can do depends on the freedom of action they are allowed. Little real growth is likely when activity is narrowly and rigidly restricted.

Let Others Know to Whom the Task Has Been Delegated

To give subordinates every possible chance to succeed, a supervisor will want to let anyone concerned know who is authorized to act in his or her place. Although Sam Pitman took advantage of his delegated authority and perhaps overstepped the bounds of good judgment in giving orders, there was little evidence that Burt had let people know that Sam was in charge of the campaign. A supervisor can do much to pave a path of cooperation by letting others know that he or she wants the subordinates to receive the same help and cooperation the supervisor usually gets.

Call for Progress Reports, and Schedule Reviews

In other words, the supervisor shouldn't delegate and forget it. Mistakes can be minimized by inviting frequent progress reports until both the supervisor and the subordinate have confidence in the progress being made. Even though the supervisor has given a subordinate the right to make his decisions, the subordinate is accountable to his or her superior. The progress and review discussions provide the opportunity to coach the subordinate—to give guidance.

The art of delegation is a delicate one. Trying to find the line between too much delegation and too little is difficult. How much freedom to allow has to be balanced against giving sufficient direction to guide subordinates. Too much direction tends to cause subordinates to lean on their supervisor. So that supervisor must give enough, but not too much, direction. Effective delegation requires a knowledge of the individual to whom a supervisor delegates and a clear idea of what the supervisor hopes to accomplish when delegating. Successful delegation allows the supervisor to fulfill the role as a manager who has a prime responsibility for the development of his or her subordinates. By being relieved of the burden of routine, the supervisor will be in a much better position to spend time on the management functions of planning, directing, and controlling. Management-minded supervisors delegate. In the process they increase their management-mindedness.

ORDER-GIVING TECHNIQUES

Sam Pitman said, "Get going on this cleanup right now—no matter what." And a little later, "I'm ordering you to get back on that Allied job and get it finished before Burt gets down here." Burt, on the other hand, asked each of the group to set aside the cleanup activities and get things going on the Allied job. Then he asked Sam to have lunch with him. Within the span of a minute or two they demonstrated the two most common techniques used in giving orders—the demand and the request.

To be sure, many variations often make the distinction between the two more difficult. A request may be stated with such an emphasis and tone of voice that it is received as a demand with no questions asked. Experience indicates that the milder, more tactful request is a much more pleasant form to use. By and large it gives better results, and with good reason. The request, even though it is an order, gives the receiver a sense of participation in an activity. It dignifies that receiver's position by allowing him or her to decide whether or not to comply. For example, "Joe, will you see that those three boxes get down to shipping before three o'clock so they can go out today?" Joe responds in the affirmative; the boxes get to shipping; and the order goes on its way.

If there is some reason why Joe might have trouble carrying out the order, it is much easier to modify a request than a demand. Some supervisors feel that they weaken their position by framing their orders as requests, that no room for debate should be allowed the receiver, and that action is quicker when commands are given. But those who use the request find that it works well. It gets the work done and establishes a pleasant relationship between them and their subordinates without any relinquishing of control of the department. As a supervisor's relationship with his or her people matures and confidence in his or her management ability develops, the supervisor will use the request form of order-giving almost exclusively.

Is there a place for the demand or the command? Of course there is. Emergency situations requiring quick reactions call for commands. An employee who has consistently resisted orders may very well justify the demand. For example, an employee who refuses to follow safety rules may be ordered to do so. The lazy, the careless, the indifferent, the chronic griper, the gossip—all may need more rigid direction. But by and large a supervisor will want to use the request as a means of getting better results in a climate more enjoyable for the supervisor and the subordinate.

CHARACTERISTICS OF A GOOD ORDER

The enthusiastic response and hostile compliance are the extremes in the reactions of employees to the orders they receive. The case of Sam Pitman illustrates both extremes. Everyone wants cooperation and enthusiasm to result from his or her orders, but what criteria determine whether an order has been good or not? The following five characteristics of most good orders offer an evaluation checklist. A supervisor might ask, "How do my orders measure up, and where might I improve them?"

Orders Should Be Clear

An order is a communication. The purpose of all communication is understanding. The supervisor's idea of what is wanted when giving an order is very clear. It's a challenge to see that the one who receives the order gets the same idea. Remember the blacksmith who told his new apprentice, "I'll hold the shoe on the anvil. When I nod my head, you hit it with the hammer." The result was a broken skull.

Making an order clear to the receiver is almost always helped by explaining why the order is given. Wanting to do well, employees can cooperate better and use their initiative more if they know why they're doing a job. For example, Burt told Arnie to store the boxes in a corner without telling him why. If Burt had told Arnie what he had in mind, there's no doubt that Arnie would have checked with Burt before scrapping the parts.

A supervisor's language should be as simple as possible, and the orders issued in words the receiver will understand.

Orders Should Be Concise

Too much detail can be just as harmful as not enough. Why waste time by giving more detail than is necessary to accomplish the desired results? Employees tend to respect a supervisor who can say what he or she wants clearly and concisely.

Orders Should Be Complete

As we noted in our discussion of delegation, giving orders requires a balanced approach. We have just said that supervisors should not burden an order with too much detail—that they should be concise. Yet the importance of giving all the information that is necessary remains. How much is too much? When the order has been issued, an employee ought to know what is to be done (that is, the results expected) and when it is to be done. The employee should understand what standards of performance will apply in evaluating the completed job. In a previous example, Joe was asked to take some boxes down to Shipping. He knew his performance would be judged satisfactory if Shipping had the boxes by 3:00 P.M. That way they could be shipped that day.

Orders Should Be Considerate

It would be more accurate to say that someone giving an order should be considerate. Courtesy and consideration make the one who gets an order more kindly disposed toward the assignment. If an employee feels he or she has a part to play in determining the successful execution of an order, cooperation (the highest level of response) is most likely.

Orders Should Be Reasonable

Surely this goes without saying. A moment's reflection, however, might reveal that an order that is entirely reasonable to the giver may not at all be reasonable to the receiver. Are the time, materials, and equipment available to do the job? Is the job within the scope of the employee's ability to perform? Has the employee had experience? Has the employee been taught? Have the standards of performance the supervisor has set taken into consideration the employee's abilities, experience, and training? Many supervisors have found that the effect on employees' morale of issuing unreasonable orders can be disastrous. This is particularly true when the practice is repeated frequently. Empathy can provide valuable measures of the reasonableness of orders.

THE ORDER-GIVING PROCESS

Early in this chapter we took note of the similarities between giving orders and instructing. They are both forms of communication. They both seek to create understanding and to achieve results through others. Therefore in analyzing the steps in the order-giving process, we can expect to find similarities to instructing. Following these common-sense steps in giving orders should improve effectiveness: (1) plan, (2) explain, (3) check, (4) release, and (5) follow up. To the experienced manager accustomed to giving orders and direction, these steps are done automatically without much conscious thought. More complex orders require more attention to each phase. Failures in giving orders can generally be traced to the neglect of one or more of these steps. Let's look at them in a little more detail.

Plan

The planning questions (what, when, who, where, why, and how) are considered almost instantaneously on a short, uncomplicated order, but they are considered. Let's take an example. "Joe, hand me that wrench, will you?" The supervisor has determined *what* he wants—the wrench near Joe. In a split second he decides *who* is to do the job—Joe, because he's nearest to it. His tone of voice and inflection revealed that now is *when* he wants action. Deciding that he wants the wrench in his hands right here answers the *where* question. *How* was determined, and he asked Joe to hand it to him, not to throw it. In getting ready to give any order or direction, we decide what action we want, who we want to act, and what kind of order we should use, such as a spoken request or a written directive.

Explain

The receiver of the order must know what performance or outcome is expected. What the supervisor has planned is now communicated to the receiver, who wants to know what is to be done, how to do it, and when and where to do it. The employee is likely to be more cooperative and use initiative if the supervisor has explained why he or she wants it done. The supervisor ensures quality by giving an explanation as to what standards the performance will be judged on. For example, "There shouldn't be any streaks or smudges on the windows when you've finished." If the order is complex, the supervisor's plans may very well call for the same type of step-by-step explanation discussed in Chapter 8 under instructing.

Check

The feedback principle again! The supervisor should be certain that the order has been understood the way he or she intended it. Asking and encouraging questions helps check on understanding. Getting employees to repeat orders gives a good check on their understanding and provides an excellent chance to correct any misunderstanding. The supervisor takes unnecessary risks by giving an order and then failing to check the receiver's concept of what is wanted before releasing the employee.

Release

In most cases the release is accomplished with a few simple words, but only after it is certain that the order has been received and understood. Action is initiated with such simple statements as: "OK, let's go." "Get it started right away, will you?" "Check with me if you're not sure." "Good luck." "I'll see you when you've finished." Sometimes encouragement is needed, sometimes a challenge. But in this step the supervisor demonstrates confidence that the employee will be able to carry out the directive.

Follow Up

The final test of whether or not a supervisor's orders and directions have been successful is the degree to which the goals have been achieved. There are other considerations, however, which will guide future orders. How did the receiver perform during the execution of the order? Were there difficulties that can be remedied the next time around? What adjustments are needed, if any? Evaluating the effectiveness of instruction will lead to the improvement of techniques in giving orders.

To these steps which describe the process of giving an order, we might add the advice of several hundred supervisors who have debated the problem at University of Wisconsin Supervisory Institutes in recent years.

Be Sure to Identify the Results Wanted

The supervisor should give the employee something to zero in on. The employee will be able to come to his or her superior and say, "I've done it!"

Condition the Person Receiving the Order

The supervisor should get the employee interested in carrying out the order. Motivation is the key to the enthusiasm with which assignments are handled. There's no more critical time to practice motivational skills than in the order-giving process.

Explain the "Why" of Directions

Man is a reasoning animal. A supervisor helps the subordinate respond by explaining why the action ordered is wanted.

Build in Feedback

Why take chances? Feedback assures a supervisor that the objectives will be accomplished, and it's so much easier to get a quick reading on understanding than it is to require the work to be done over.

Identify Controls and Procedures for Reporting Back

The supervisor should let the employee know what should be done when the assignment is completed. Is the employee to report back, bring a receipt, write a memo, call the supervisor over, call an inspector? If the employee's performance is to be evaluated, then he or she ought to know the standards by which this performance will be measured. The employee will be more likely to excel if he or she can measure progress while performing the task.

Maintain an Attitude of Helpfulness

How easy it is for a supervisor to take the attitude that employees exist to do his or her bidding and to give orders without concern for their feelings. The supervisor should remember that subordinates want to make him or her look good. Maintaining an attitude of helpfulness in giving orders is bound to benefit the supervisor in the long run.

In the management process, the directing phase starts the wheels in motion. Directing or giving orders is the dynamic phase—the action phase. The best plans can be upset by faulty orders. Fulfilling management responsibilities requires expert direction, and no matter how often or how long a supervisor has been giving orders, a frequent reevaluation of his or her skills will pay off. Complacency has no place in developing management-mindedness.

HIGHLIGHTS

1. Direction in the management process is the step that puts plans in motion—initiates the action.

2. Giving orders is so basic and fundamental in supervision that there is a tendency to take it for granted.

3. How orders are carried out depends on climate. All supervisors start on their supervisory jobs with the authority of rank. As they develop confidence and gain the trust of their subordinates, they acquire a different kind of authority—the authority of respect.

4. There are three levels of response to orders:

   a. Cooperation
   b. Compliance
   c. Hostile compliance

5. Delegation means giving others the right to make our decisions for us, and it is characterized by:

   a. Freedom of action
   b. Sharing decisions
   c. Sharing responsibility
   d. Bestowing authority

6. Common reasons why supervisors avoid delegation include:

   a. Fear of subordinates' mistakes
   b. Fear that subordinates will show the supervisor up
   c. Fear of loss of control over an activity
   d. Fear of loss of status or prestige

7. Order-giving techniques generally fall into one of two classifications—a request or a demand. The former usually yields better results and is a more pleasant approach to use.

8. Good orders or directions are:

   a. Clear
   b. Concise
   c. Complete
   d. Considerate
   e. Reasonable

9. Giving orders is a five-step process. These steps are usually carried out with little conscious effort. The steps are:

    a. Plan
    b. Explain
    c. Check
    d. Release
    e. Follow up

DISCUSSION QUESTIONS

1. Explain this statement in your own words: "Giving orders is so basic that we tend to take it for granted."

2. Describe a supervisor you know who through his or her way of giving orders creates a climate of cooperation. What are some of this supervisor's typical attitudes?

3. Describe a supervisor you know or have known who has come close to creating a climate of "hostile compliance" in his or her department. What attitudes and actions on this supervisor's part produced that climate?

4. What possible risks does a supervisor face when delegating part of his or her job to subordinates?

5. Which is a better practice—giving orders by asking or by demanding? What are the advantages and disadvantages of each approach?

6. Why should the reasons for an order be explained to the employee?

7. Five characteristics of good orders and directions were identified in this chapter. Can you cite any more?

8. Write a memo giving directions on cleaning up a work area to a second-shift employee. Make any assumptions you wish. When you have finished, check it against the criteria of a good order.

CASE PROBLEMS

THE CASE OF SCOTT McFARLANE

Northland Community Hospital's building maintenance supervisor, Scott McFarlane, had finished the book on delegation given him by Jess

Doyle, the hospital administrator. "It sounds good, but it doesn't deal with hospitals; and we're a lot different from private industry," Scott said to himself. "It's fine to say you have to trust your people and give them the freedom to make mistakes, but we're dealing with human lives here. A breakdown here could cause needless pain and suffering—or even death. It's a tremendous responsibility.

"I know Jess thinks I should delegate more, and I suppose he's right about having several people qualified to do my job. But what does he think is going to happen to me? I've worked hard to know every piece of equipment and to improve what we have on a limited budget. I'm proud of the way I've handled this job—my people are well trained in their jobs, they're reliable, and morale is as good as you can expect it to be considering our pay scales.

"Delegation sounds to me like giving the best part of the job to someone else. Talk about job pride—what would I have to take pride in if I delegated everything I do? It takes time to delegate and I'm so darn busy now—it's just easier to do my job myself. Besides, if there are any mistakes made, we know how to pinpoint them. I take the blame for what I do and give hell for any mistakes my people make. I just can't see why Jess isn't satisfied with the way I do my job. It's a supervisor's job to train, give orders, and keep people happy—what more does he want?"

1. Evaluate Scott's thinking on delegation. What would make him feel that way?

2. Are the principles of delegation different when applied to hospitals, industry, government, or banking?

3. What should Scott do about Jess Doyle's suggestion to "do a little delegating?" Why would Doyle make such a suggestion?

THE CASE OF LISA ENDRES

"They act like they don't want to work here," is the way Lisa Endres, supervisor of check verifiers at First Madison National Bank, summed up the behavior of Wendy Hanson and Judy Patrick. "I've always felt that a good supervisor doesn't have to be a drill sergeant giving orders and commands. If you treat people with respect and ask them to do something, they ought to respond. I just don't like bossing people around. It's not my style," said Lisa to her boss.

Wendy and Judy were taking advantage of her good nature, Lisa felt. When she asked them to do a job they would have a hundred questions. When did she want them to start? Should they finish what they were doing first? How long would they have to work at that? Could they take their break first? Could they start after lunch? Lisa felt that asking them to do anything was like starting a debate.

"I don't know whether they just want attention or if they really don't understand why they have to do what I ask them. Lately I've been on the verge of telling them to quit the damned stalling and get to work. That would be out of character for me, but my patience is wearing thin. Their questions are unnecessary, and they know it. It's almost like they're testing me. I know if I get tough with them they'll get in line, but I'm afraid they'll hate me for it. I'd rather not do it that way. What should I do, boss? You tell me, please!" Lisa pleaded.

1. Why would Wendy and Judy respond as they did to Lisa's order-giving style?

2. Is Lisa right about not wanting to boss people around? Explain.

3. How should Lisa handle the situation?

THE CASE OF BRAD ROSS

"At his age he's not going to change. I guess I either learn to live with it or start bucking for a transfer," Universal Airlines counter agent Ira Stein was telling his partner. "I'll follow his orders to the letter if he'll only be more specific. But it burns me up when he gives me vague orders and tells me to work out the details myself. Then he turns right around and bawls me out for not using my head or for not following orders."

Ira's supervisor, Brad Ross, was notorious among his subordinates for his vague instructions. The speculation was that the customer complaints on his shift were the main reason that Brad had never advanced beyond his present position. Brad's oft-stated philosophy was that if people are going to grow they have to have freedom to operate and that they learn from their mistakes. And that it's a supervisor's job to help people grow.

"The trouble with old Ross is that he wants you to use your head so he doesn't have to use his. He's pretty good at second-guessing and criticizing, though. When he fired Joyce Long for her mistakes, he should have fired himself. I felt so sorry for her I was tempted to walk out with her. Believe it or not, he told me after she left, 'If you can't stand the heat, get out of the kitchen—or get thrown out.' The more I think about that character, the more I think I ought to get out. He's never going to be promoted and I don't want to be stuck with him forever. I wonder if I could work a transfer to Denver or Dallas.''

1. How could Ira go about getting more specific orders from Brad Ross?

2. Was Ross confusing order-giving and delegation? What is the difference between the two?

3. What are some of Ira's alternatives?

SUGGESTIONS FOR FURTHER STUDY

Bittel, Lester R., *What Every Supervisor Should Know*, 3d ed., Chapter 16, McGraw-Hill Book Company, New York, 1974.

McConkey, Dale D., *No-Nonsense Delegation*, Amacom, New York, 1974.

Shout, Howard F., *Start Supervising*, Chapter 6, Bureau of National Affairs, Inc., Washington, D.C., 1972.

Steinmett, Lawrence L., and H. Ralph Todd, Jr., *First-Line Management*, Chapter 3, Business Publications, Inc., Dallas, Texas, 1975.

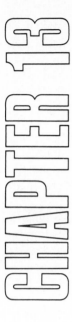

CHAPTER 13

CONTROLLING EMPLOYEE PERFORMANCE

THE CASE OF THE INEPT INTERVIEWS

Burt Hall sat looking at the pile of completed performance-appraisal forms on his desk. In ten minutes Norm Wiley would be in to discuss his performance of the past six months. Wiley had been scheduled first because Burt had wanted to get things off to a good start. After Wiley, the number two person would be Del Burns in the afternoon. That's the way it would go—one in the morning, one in the afternoon until he got through the whole department. By the evening of the first day, with two of his better employees reviewed, Burt felt that he could analyze his results and improve as he went along.

This would be Burt's second round of performance appraisals since becoming supervisor of Assembly Department B. The first time around could hardly count, and Burt was determined that this time he was going to do a better job. His predecessor, Harry Gates, didn't have much patience with the whole idea of performance evaluation and review. He filled out the appraisal forms for Burt as his last official act and left the review interview for Burt to do. His advice was to just tell each employee what his rating was and give him a chance to object if he wanted to. Harry felt that the quicker you got it over, the quicker you could get back to concentrating on production. He kept the ratings on the high side, he told Burt, because then there wouldn't be any difficulty with the employees and because it made the department look good by comparison with others.

That entire first review had gone without incident. Everyone liked Burt. They felt that the ratings were Harry's, and signed the forms acknowledging the interview without much comment. When he had finished, Burt was relieved. But he was concerned that nothing much seemed to have been accomplished.

Determined this time to show his employees that he knew what he was doing, Burt had spent a considerable amount of time preparing the forms. He worked on them three evenings at home in addition to the time spent in his office. Generally the individual evaluations were quite high, but they were deserved. The production results were right there to back them up, and quality in the department was excellent. Naturally there had been a few problems and problem children over the past six months, but on the whole Burt felt good about the evaluation of his department's performance represented by the completed forms on his desk. Burt regarded this job as a chance to get really close to his employees. That was why he scheduled Norm Wiley and Del Burns first. They were easy to talk to; they were cooperative; but most of all they had won high ratings from Burt, and it would be a pleasure to tell them so individually.

The procedure outlined by the personnel department called for the supervisor to make his evaluation of each employee, bring each employee in to discuss the evaluation, and get the evaluation form signed by the employee to show that the discussion had taken place. The signing of the form did not mean that the employee agreed with the rating but simply that it had been discussed with him or her. The employee had the opportunity to register any disagreement with the evaluation either on the form or by contacting the personnel department. There hadn't been a single such objection on Burt's first round six months ago.

The form was a simple two-page booklet calling for an evaluation of the employee's quantity or volume of work, quality or accuracy, reliability, cooperativeness, versatility, loyalty, strengths, weaknesses, and promotability. Training necessary to make the person a more valuable employee was to be covered in the last section.

Burt hadn't been satisfied with Harry Gates's off-the-cuff rating on all factors the last time—especially on quantity and quality of work.

Since production records were available on almost all his employees, Burt pulled out the achievements of each and based his quality and quantity ratings on "the facts," as he called them. His evaluation of reliability was based on tardiness and attendance records even though he felt that a less objective rating was wanted. The rest of the form required him "to play God," as he said. Being human, he was never sure that his ratings were free of his personal bias. Whenever he could, Burt found specific examples to back up his ratings on cooperativeness, versatility, loyalty, strengths, and weaknesses. Many times he wondered, though, how much his choice of examples might be reinforcing his bias. He had done his best, however, and now he was ready to begin. Burt was so anxious to get started on the right foot with Norm that he trembled just a little bit when Norm poked his head in the office door and asked if the time had come.

Shaking hands with Norm at the end of the interview felt awkward to Burt, but it seemed to be the only way to signal the finish. Doggone it, the whole interview was awkward. It hadn't gone at all as he had wanted it to. From the time Norm walked in, he wasn't himself. He seemed to freeze up. His manner was pleasant enough. There was no disagreement with Burt's evaluation. Burt began to feel that they were like a boss with a rookie employee rather than two friends discussing a subject of mutual interest. Burt had wanted informality, but the result was formal and consequently uncomfortable for Burt.

Burt had avoided looking at the evaluations from the last period. He wanted to be certain that he was not influenced by them in any way. He was surprised to find Norm disappointed with the new ratings. It turned out that in most cases they were lower, even though Norm's performance had improved. His quantity of production, which had definitely improved, now had a lower rating. Burt's explanation that nobody rated any higher, and that he was using a new system based on factual information, had a hollow ring. Norm accepted the rating, but Burt had the feeling that he might go to the personnel department to explain that he hadn't really slipped.

For some reason, the whole tenor of the interview was more negative than positive. Burt had intended it to be very positive. He had wanted to tell Norm how pleased he was with his progress, but he wound up several times trying to justify the lower ratings. Burt explained to Norm that his philosophy was to rate a little low to stimulate improvement and that he actually thought more of Norm's work than the evaluation showed. Thinking about that after the interview, Burt felt that it was a stupid thing to say.

Burt rated Norm about midpoint on promotability. The definition on the form at that point said, "shows promise; could be promoted." There were two places above and below to make checks, so that Norm felt that Burt's rating really said nothing. His disappointment was obvious when he told Burt that he did hope to get ahead in the company. Burt wondered, as Norm talked, how many more would feel the same way. He had been very careful to avoid letting a high rating on promotability trap him into making a commitment. His thoughts so occupied him that he wasn't really listening when Norm said something to the effect that another department might possibly offer him a better chance for promotion. The affirmative nod of Burt's head brought another disappointed look to Norm's face, and the subject was dropped.

After that there were some offhand remarks from both intended to terminate the interview, but neither felt that he wanted to accept the responsibility for bringing it to an official conclusion—perhaps because no conclusions had been reached. The awkward pauses at last caused Burt to extend his hand to Norm and thank him for coming in.

A meeting, five phone calls, and a minor breakdown kept Burt from any mental analysis of the interview until it was time for Del Burns to arrive for hers. In the back of Burt's mind he knew that he himself had been responsible for the unsatisfactory interview in the morning. He knew he had missed an opportunity to motivate Norm and to build his interest in the job.

The interview with Del was almost a replay of the morning. Sure, the questions were different; the words were different; it was a different person across the desk. But the coolness was still there where warmth had been wanted. Disappointment masked Del's face the same as it had Norm's. Tension got a firmer grip on Burt's feelings and strained his reasoning powers even more. The same awkward handshake terminated the interview and left Burt wondering how he would ever get through the rest of them.

"Why, oh why," he thought, "didn't I compare these ratings with those from the last period? Just because I wanted these to be my own, I risked antagonizing two of my best people."

Del had shown the same disappointment at the lower rating that Norm had. After getting Burt's explanation of what he was trying to do in quantifying the evalution, Del said, "Sure that's fine, but how do they know that in Personnel or in Palmer's office or wherever they decide on our raises? They look at this form and the last one and see my rating down. What chance have I got to get a raise?"

Burt explained that these evaluations weren't used to determine raises, but the words were hardly out of his mouth before the realization struck him that he really didn't know whether they were or not. Del promptly asked what they were for if not raises, and Burt said he thought it was to be sure everybody got a chance to find out where they stood. Again, he wasn't certain that what he was saying was true. Del mumbled something about not standing very well right now and Burt hastened to assure her that she was one of the best people in the department.

That last statement caused a wry smile to cross Del's face, and she said, "Then a couple of others are in for a rude awakening, because they figure they've been doing a lot better the last few months. They thought they got better than they deserved last time, so they've been looking forward to this time and getting what they deserve. Ha!"

Burt wasn't sure that he had said enough or too much, but when Del was willing to sign the form, it seemed to be a good place to cut it off. Again there hadn't been any arguments. The real disappointment was that he hadn't achieved so much of what he had hoped for in these first two interviews. What had he hoped to accomplish? Well, he really couldn't put his finger on anything specific. He just wanted the relationship between him and his employees to be a lot better, and instead they seemed to be getting more strained.

Why, he wondered, when he was so pleased with his employees' performance, was he creating the impression that he was dissatisfied? Why, he asked himself, should good positive relationships suddenly become so strained at appraisal time? How could anything designed to be helpful and constructive have just the opposite effect? Burt put Del and Norm's evaluation forms in an envelope along with those of Phil Knudson and Arnie Ross, whom he was going to talk to tomorrow. He would study them at home. Somehow he was going to have to find a way to improve his techniques. As things stood now, he was better off just going through the motions the way he had done the first time.

1. What strengths do we find in Burt's approach to appraising and reviewing his employees' performance?

2. How can we explain the results Burt had with his first two reviews in the light of his high hopes?

3. What objectives did Burt have for each review? What objectives should he have had?

4. How can he get better results from the reviews with the rest of his people?

MANAGEMENT
IS CONTROLLING

We have defined the management process as planning, organizing, directing, and controlling. In the first chapters of this section on the supervisor's job knowledge, we discussed the planning, organizing, and directing phases of the cycle. Now we turn our attention to the final phase—control. The purpose of the control phase is to assure that what the supervisor has planned and directed is accomplished. Effective control is dependent on skillful execution of the planning phase of the management process, for plans provide the standards against which performance is measured in the control phase.

Management-minded supervision recognizes the controlling function as one of the most critical. Through the years with all the changes in the concepts of what supervision is, it has always been acknowledged that a supervisor controls the department, the people, the processes. A supervisor wants to know what the quality and quantity of production is. If he or she is not meeting standards, corrective action is taken to bring production back in line. The process of setting standards, measuring performance against those standards, and making the necessary corrections is what we mean by control. Even when the standards are set by higher-level management, the supervisor still functions as a controller in the measuring and adjusting activities.

The supervisor's control extends to a wide variety of departmental activities. First and foremost, production is the supervisor's concern. In addition he or she wants to be sure that the use of equipment, tools, materials, supplies, and services yields the desired results. Control activities keep him or her abreast of the costs. One of the main items under the supervisor's control is the performance of subordinates. Individual improvement programs, such as cost-reduction and methods-improvement programs, also require control. To illustrate how often supervisors are engaged in control activities, here are but a few types of controls most of them use frequently: production schedules, production reports and records, time-and-motion studies, a wide variety of inspections for quality, blueprints and specifications, procedure manuals, standard costs, budgets, special cost reports, work measurement, audits and inventories, and employee performance appraisals. Most of the reports to members of higher management become the controls they use to measure progress on company plans.

It would be impossible to discuss specific controls in view of the wide variety of control activities supervisors engage in daily. For example, quality controls range all the way from proofreading a stencil in the office to 100-percent inspection of parts, to highly refined statistical quality-control programs. Our purposes will be adequately served, it seems, if we identify the key steps in the control function, relate control to other management functions, and finally analyze one major control system which is troublesome for many supervisors—employee performance appraisals or merit ratings.

Planning activities involve setting goals and objectives. These goals and objectives become the basis for control systems. For example, in planning a cost-reduction program, a supervisor may have set an overall goal of reducing costs by $10,000 in a six-month period. This supervisor has a target! At the end of six months it will be known whether the goal was exceeded or whether it fell short. But why wait for six months to pass? Controls should give a means of determining progress throughout the cost drive rather than indicating failure after it's too late to do anything about it. The supervisor might decide to shoot for a $2,500 savings in each of the first three months, $1,000 the next two months, and $500 the last month. Now by comparing total achievement to date against the goals, it will be known how successful these efforts are at any time during the cost-reduction drive. Thus he has performed the first two steps in the control function: (1) setting goals and standards at key points in a process, and (2) measuring performance against those standards.

The third step in the control function is taking corrective action or making adjustments. For an example, let's go back to our cost-reduction program and assume that midway through the six-month period total savings came to $4,500. At this point, the supervisor had expected to achieve $7,500. With only three months to realize the remaining $5,500, there is going to have to be an increase in effort, a change of strategy, or a call for help.

The control function is a questioning activity that keeps the supervisor returning to the planning function in the management process. Planning and controlling are so integrated that it is difficult to set them apart. Planning sets goals; these goals become the basis for controls. If in the evaluation of progress the supervisor finds it necessary to revise these goals or standards, he or she is both controlling and planning. Plans are based on what controls have told the supervisor in past experience is reasonable and possible, and controls are set up on the basis of what is planned. The two are so completely interwoven that it is difficult to discuss them separately.

Management-minded supervision and effective controlling are the same thing. The comment, "He's a supervisor who really knows what's going on in his department," is high praise. It is also an indication of effective control. Every supervisor wants to be regarded as a manager who is really in charge of things. Being in charge, being a manager, and being an effective controller are synonymous.

PERFORMANCE APPRAISALS: WHY?

Burt Hall, like many supervisors, has begun to wonder how performance appraisal, intended as a management control or tool, can have such devastating results. Intended to be constructive and helpful, it can blast morale to bits. The performance appraisal *is* a management tool, but like any tool, it must be properly used. Burt was using this tool with a deep-seated desire to use it well. It wasn't because of lack of effort that he experienced failure. His inability to achieve the desired results was caused by something revealed in his conversation with Del Burns. Burt couldn't explain to Del why they were reviewing her performance. From his own standpoint, Burt hoped to build morale through free and open discussion of performance. Admirable, yes—but he failed to realize the full impact of performance reviews on the individual. He also failed to take into account the assumptions employees make concerning management's use of performance appraisals.

Burt began using a tool before he knew what he wanted to do with it or what the capabilities of the tool were. No one would pick up a power saw and start cutting lumber without knowing how the saw worked or what dimensions of lumber were wanted. In effect, that's what Burt was doing, and it didn't matter that he really wanted to cut lumber. He had no direction—no purpose to his activities.

The performance appraisal is a management control designed to provide a report of how well individuals are performing to standards. It provides the supervisor with a basis for corrective action. How the evaluation of an individual's performance is used above his or her level should be thoroughly understood by the supervisor and by the employee. This is the only way the supervisor can be fair to subordinates. For example, if Burt knew that his evaluations would be used for determining merit increases by comparing them with those of other employees, his approach might have been entirely different. On the other hand, if both Norm and Del could be certain that the only purpose for the review was for performance improvement and that no comparison would be made either in or out of the department, their concern over Burt's lower ratings would not have been as great. As it was, no one was sure just why he was doing what he was doing.

Does the performance appraisal fit the definition of control that we established? If properly conceived, the performance appraisal defines the standards of performance for each job, and the goal-setting phase of controlling is covered. Measuring performance against predetermined standards is a function of performance appraisal and a management control. The third step in controlling is taking corrective action, and this is accomplished in performance reviews in a number of ways—suggesting areas for improvement, planning for self-development, encouraging good working habits, and granting or withholding wage increases. So we can see that the performance appraisal meets the criteria of a control.

What are some of the uses to which the supervisor puts the performance appraisal? We'll identify a few, but only with the caution that the list cannot be all-inclusive and that we do not suggest that any given performance-appraisal system should have as its purpose every item listed. Obviously some contradict each other. A single program cannot be all things to all people any more than the same micrometer can be used to measure close tolerances and to crack hickory nuts. Here, then, are some of the purposes for using performance appraisal:

Improvement of Performance

A periodic evaluation and review of performance points up areas for improvement in an employee's work. The evaluation is valuable in detecting performance slippage before it becomes a matter for disciplinary action. Supervisor and employee have an opportunity to agree on corrective action that both can take to improve performance. Planning for improvement is done in a positive climate. Because a definite time has been set aside for the review, the supervisor is more likely to feel an obligation to formulate specific improvement plans. The great majority of performance-appraisal programs set forth improvement of performance as their prime objective.

Basis for Personnel Action

Promotion, demotion, transfer, and salary increases are frequently tied to performance appraisals. The appraisal, it is felt, provides a much better basis for taking such actions than off-the-cuff judgments. Whether or not this is true depends, of course, on how accurate, honest, and objective the evaluations have been. Some theories hold that basing personnel actions such as wage adjustments on formalized appraisals is the most effective way of controlling employee performance. We can see the conflicts that are possible in the mind of a supervisor who tries to use the program for wage adjustments and performance-improvement purposes. For example, Burt was apparently conservative in rating some of his best workers because he wanted to leave room for improvement. If he had been using those same ratings to try to justify wage increases for Norm and Del, he would have been at a marked disadvantage in competing with a supervisor who had rated his people very liberally.

Determining Training Needs

Training directors and supervisors alike have found the performance appraisal helpful in spotting areas that require training for groups of employees. Widespread difficulties in performing one phase of a job call for training to be done as quickly as possible. Wherever patterns of similar problems suggest training, the supervisor will want to get help and advice from any staff specialists available. The supervisor may ask them to do the training as a corrective action, or may simply get advice on how to do it personally.

Improving Supervisor-Employee Communication

Properly handled, the performance review can contribute greatly to better communication between supervisor and employee. It sets a definite time for sitting down to talk about the employee's progress. This is something the supervisor wants to know and has a right to know. Undoubtedly, Burt Hall saw his performance reviews primarily in this light—a chance to tell his people how much he appreciated their cooperation and effort. He didn't consider the emotional pressures experienced by his employees, and their reserve threw him. He worked hard on the appraisal but didn't plan the interview. The interview can improve communications, but it must produce real understanding of what the supervisor is trying to accomplish. Half-truths and unanswered questions about the purpose of the appraisal can't possibly contribute positively to relations with subordinates.

Feedback on Standards and Supervision

If two-way communication is encouraged in the performance review and the employee is confident that he or she can speak openly without recrimination, the supervisor can learn a great deal in the appraisal interview about how his or her style of supervision is accepted by subordinates. The employee should be given an opportunity to explain how fair he or she views the standards against which performance is measured. Participation by the employee in setting goals is increasingly being heralded as a motivational technique second to none. Certainly an employee who has participated in setting a performance standard on his or her own job is going to try to exceed that standard.

To come anywhere near being an effective tool, the purpose of the performance appraisal must be clearly fixed. Knowing the purpose gives direction to appraisal efforts. It increases the likelihood that those efforts will result in an effective management control.

OBJECTIONS TO PERFORMANCE APPRAISALS

Performance appraisals do take time, and the payoff for the time required is often difficult to see. Because of the time and the questionable results, supervisors raise many other objections. "There are too many problems." "It's too tough to get consistent ratings." "We don't like to sit in judgment." "People work better if they're not shaken up by ratings." "It just opens the door to unnecessary questions." And so on. To deny that there are problems in appraising and reviewing employees' performance would be dishonest. There are problems—real ones! In striving for a management-minded approach to performance appraisal, the supervisor should look at the problems in terms of how to overcome them. Let's examine a few of the more common problems.

Difficulty in Setting Standards

How can standards of performance be set on jobs where the output either is a service or can't be measured quantitatively? It's difficult in many areas, but it's even more surprising how a little ingenuity on the part of the supervisor and the employee will produce standards that both can accept. The standards need not have the preciseness of predetermined time standards, but they can be an adequate basis for agreement on how well the job is being performed. For example, a stock chaser's performance might be measured in terms of total orders filled—recognizing that over a period of time the one-item orders and the ten-item orders will average out. Performance might be measured in terms of the number of orders held more than twenty-four hours without being filled. An exercise is to pick a job and try to find something that can be used as a standard. A supervisor can ask, "How about my own job? How many measurements are there of how well I'm performing on my own job?"

Inconsistency of Rating by Different Supervisors

How should a supervisor rate his or her people? Some supervisors tend toward high ratings on the theory that since it makes people feel better, there are fewer problems from employees and that high ratings make them seem to be better supervisors. Other supervisors lean toward low ratings because they feel that a high rating removes the incentive to improve, and high ratings leave them open to demands for more money and more privileges. All too often both of these schools of thought have lost sight of the fact that the supervisor is evaluating actual performance and is not using the form simply to nudge, needle, or bludgeon an employee.

The answer to this problem of inconsistency seems in part to be in the training of supervisors as raters. Certainly it would be to the supervisor's benefit to get some guidance from qualified people. A more practical answer to getting some consistency is for the supervisor to base as much of the appraisal as possible on objective standards and goals. There is little ground for disagreement when we can see that John or Jane reached 95 percent of their goal or exceeded it by 5 percent.

Failure of Forms to Cover the Job

If the forms don't fit the job, a supervisor can perhaps take some initiative to correct them. Forms, such as Burt Hall was using, which consider only quantity and quality of production and a few personal characteristics might very well miss the most important aspect of the job in the mind of the employee. Even if a supervisor is required to use a specific form in the company, changes can be suggested to the personnel department and comments added to the evaluation form. A supervisor in a Wisconsin company who had to work with an appraisal form similar to that used by Burt Hall took the initiative by adding a supplement to the usual appraisal with six of his key people. He asked each of the six to make his or her own preparations for the interview. He told the six that there were three things he wanted:

1. A listing of what each considered to be the most important part of the job—production, quality, customer service, new ideas, etc.

2. A list of the problems each felt were keeping him or her from doing as good a job as he or she would like to do.

3. Any ideas each might have on what could be done to solve the problems.

He discussed with each person both the company's form and the answers which had been prepared to his three questions. The result was a far more meaningful interview with his people. Also, the company revised its appraisal form to make it more useful.

Dislike of the Formality Involved

Many supervisors experience the feeling that Burt did in talking with Del and Norm. A warm, friendly relationship often seems to chill in the formality of the appraisal interview. Evaluation and review of performance is a touchy situation and is for many supervisors one of the most difficult aspects of their job. There is nothing wrong with the formality of the appraisal interview. It is a time for serious thought and discussion. Let's look at the situation for what it is—a boss discussing an evaluation of performance with a subordinate. It's an analysis of how the person performs his or her life's work—an analysis that may influence the employee's advancement, the employee's pay, the employee's personal feelings of satisfaction, and the employee's future training. Serious and formal? Of course it is! It's not a time for joking, certainly. The mere fact that we regard it seriously is likely to cause the employee to enter into the discussion constructively.

A brief summary here should take note of the fact that the problems aren't entirely the fault of the program or the control but of how supervisors as individuals administer the controls. A knowledge of what they want to accomplish and how they are going to accomplish it and a desire to make it work can bring positive results even from a poorly conceived appraisal system.

THE "RESULTS" APPROACH VERSUS THE "TRAITS" APPROACH

So many recent problems have been attributed to the fact that appraisal systems have required managers to make subjective judgments about the personality traits of their subordinates. By defining the ideal employee in terms of personality traits and judging that person on those traits, it was felt that supervisors could show how he or she missed fitting the perfect mold and show what modifications would have to be made. Think of the difficulties built into that approach.

What traits are really important? How should a trait be evaluated? How can bias and emotion be removed from the rating? How should supervisors tell an employee that they think the mployee is lazy or that they think his or her judgment is poor? How do supervisors keep their values straight and true after rating twenty employees on twenty or thirty traits? How can they prevent one unpleasant incident from coloring their judgment about an employee? By the same token, can a supervisor be sure that those employees who have been cooperative are more deserving of high ratings than those who have created a problem or two? Of course not—but it always seems to come out that way.

These and hundreds of other problems have given managers no end of trouble in trying to carry out employee-evaluation programs. There has been a change of terminology in the last two paragraphs. We started out by discussing performance appraisal and have now switched to employee evaluation. The difference between employee evaluation and performance appraisal has caused many companies to renew their efforts to make this control constructive. A supervisor should not try to evaluate people by using undefinable traits as a criteria but should instead strive to evaluate their performance by using quantitative measures wherever possible. The supervisor should have much less concern for what kind of personalities the employees have than for how well they perform their jobs. The object of this control is to improve behavior, not to reshape personalities.

One of the reasons that performance is so much more difficult to control is the lack of sound acceptable quantitative standards. If a supervisor is asked how he or she is coming on the budget, the answer can be precise—Running 3 percent over on overhead costs, or direct labor costs are right on the button. But let someone ask how John Jones is doing, and the likely answer is that he seems to be doing all right and that, given a little time, he should be paying his own way. Why the hedging? The supervisor simply doesn't know just how well John Jones is doing, and hopes that Jones might blossom forth in time to save the supervisor the embarrassment of having to make a decision about him.

Today, wherever and whenever possible, many are trying to find objective means of evaluating performance. This is part of the philosophy advocated by Edward Schleh and Peter Drucker—the idea of management by results or by objectives. Supervisors find themselves on much stronger ground when they can discuss performance with an employee in terms of whether or not he or she is meeting a standard. What are some of the measures that are used to evaluate employee performance? Let's look at a few:

Volume of production. How many units, pounds, tons did an employee turn out per day or week on the average? What amount is acceptable? What goal should the employee shoot for in the next period?

Quality of production.   How is quality measured—in percentage of rejects or rework, pounds or tons of scrap, number of complaints by customers? What goals is the worker striving for now and next period?

Attendance.   How many times is an employee tardy or absent against what is normally allowed?

Safety.   Has the worker had any accidents or been the cause of any? Has he or she contributed any ideas for improvement of safety?

Cost.   Is the employee's cost record available? Has he or she contributed any cost-saving ideas? Are there examples of practicing cost-consciousness?

Once goals have been set for an individual employee and he or she has accepted them, performance reviews can be conducted in a much less emotional climate. If production falls short of a goal, the supervisor's concern is with how it can be brought up next time; but there is no basis for argument with employees when the results are there for review. Supervisor and employee may have a problem to solve together, but no emotion-laden charges need fly back and forth.

Another positive result of appraising performance quantitatively has been a self-generated tendency toward improvement. If an individual produced fifty-five units a day on the average, and if that exceeded standard, he or she is more likely to set a higher goal on the next round. Many supervisors attending institutes at the University of Wisconsin have reported experiencing this self-motivation to seek improvement. Some have even expressed concern about how to shut it off because, they say, some of the employees under them have exceeded all reasonable standards and yet keep going to a point where supervisors feel concern for their health.

When company appraisal forms require evaluation of traits, supervisors can still improve the effectiveness of their ratings by backing them up with specific incidents. For example, if the form calls for a rating on cooperativeness, it will help a supervisor make a fair judgment to have several examples of an employee's exhibiting a willingness to be helpful. Conversely, if a supervisor must rate an employee low, it will be easier to convince the employee that the rating is justified if incidents of uncooperativeness can be cited. The same approach will help in rating other traits, such as dependability, initiative, and creativity.

As a management control, performance appraisal will work much more constructively if appraisals can be based on specific results achieved. The farther a supervisor can get away from subjective judgments of personality traits, the better off he or she will be. Many of those traits do make a valuable employee. But until some way to quantify and measure such traits as cooperativeness is established, supervisors are better off evaluating quantity and quality of production.

**THE APPRAISAL
INTERVIEW**

Even a poorly conceived performance-appraisal system can be an effective control if skillful appraisal interviewing is practiced. The make-or-break point in any appraisal program is the review interview with the employee. Essentially the supervisor is seeking two things in the appraisal interview. The first is to move the employee to improve job performance or engage in self-development activities, or both. The second is to create a deeper understanding between the supervisor and the employee. It was the second objective that Burt was seeking, but he had only a fuzzy idea of what he wanted and no plan for accomplishing it in the interview. Simply holding the interview and wanting to do a good job is no guarantee of positive results.

Skillful interviewing takes practice, but unfortunately the adage "Practice makes perfect" doesn't work here. Practice doesn't make perfect unless we practice proven techniques. It should be worth our while, then, to consider some suggestions from personnel specialists. Backing up these guidelines is the experience of hundreds of first-line supervisors who have said, "These guides have helped me."

Prepare for the Interview

Preparations for the interview should cover two factors. The first is the appraisal. Is it based as much as possible on specific results? The supervisor will be on stronger ground and represent management much more effectively if he or she can stick to objective measures of performance. Where company systems call for trait evaluation, the preparation will be more effective if the supervisor can back up the evaluation with illustrative incidents or examples. If this is done, the supervisor and the employee will be more likely to agree on the meaning of words like *dependability, initiative, loyalty,* and *creativity.* Double-checking the appraisal just before the interview is helpful.

The second factor in preparation is the interview itself. Here's where Burt Hall fell down. He did an excellent job of making his appraisals and supporting them with specific results, but he gave no thought to the interview other than hoping it would go well. The interview needs careful planning. There is little chance of a successful interview if a supervisor doesn't begin the preparations by defining his or her objectives. We have noted that as a control the appraisal seeks to correct or adjust. If performance improvement is the objective, the supervisor should recognize it. More important, he or she should know how much improvement is wanted and what approach will be used to gain the employee's acceptance of those same goals.

The supervisor's preparation cannot ignore the personality of the individual whose performance is being reviewed. In view of the appraisal, how is the employee likely to react? Empathy can be extremely helpful. The supervisor should ask, "How would I react if I were in his or her shoes? How can I put the appraisal so he or she will react positively?" If there's little chance of a positive response, can the supervisor at least make the employee understand without a display of emotion? Of course, a person who is on the defensive can't see any viewpoint other than his or her own, and this applies to employees and supervisors equally.

Encourage Preparation by Employees

If the supervisor's objective of creating a better understanding with his or her subordinates is to be realized, the employees should also be thinking about the appraisal. We have already mentioned the example of the Wisconsin supervisor who asked some of his key employees to prepare answers to three questions before the interview. Those who don't feel that preparations by employees should go that far will find value in speaking to an employee two or three days before the interview. The comment might go like this: "Harry, on Wednesday we'll have a chance to review your performance and mine for the past six months. I'd appreciate it if you would give some thought to your job and what we might do to make it more satisfying to you. If you have any problems in doing as good a job as you would like to do, let's discuss those too."

Now the supervisor has told Harry (1) that he will review his performance, (2) that Harry, too, has an opportunity to talk, (3) that the supervisor wants to create an even better working relationship, and (4) that Harry is free to comment on the supervisor's supervision. The chances are that Harry has a better idea of how well he has performed than the supervisor has, and he should come prepared to share his ideas.

Arrange for Uninterrupted Privacy

Since performance review is a touchy situation, the supervisor will naturally want to do everything possible to remove distractions and to protect the feelings of the employee.

Level With the Employee

Stressing the need for seeking positive results from the interview sometimes leads to the mistaken idea that it's best to gloss over any deficiencies in performance. The supervisor is of no help to anyone unless he or she lets employees know exactly where they stand. This can still be done with tact and consideration for the employees' feelings.

Encourage Employees to Talk

As they talk, employees are participating and the supervisor is learning. Many times employees will bring up their own deficiencies and make them easier to discuss. Employees' participation is essential if they are to be motivated to improve performance. The supervisors cannot assume, however, that employees will talk without encouragement. No matter how free and open a climate the supervisor tries to create, the supervisor can't overlook the fact that the boss-subordinate relationship is strongly felt by employees. That feeling may cause even the most talkative employee to become quiet. This is one time, say many experienced supervisors, that supervisors should be prepared to get the employee to open up. They can't accomplish the objective of the appraisal interview unless they do.

Try to Set Goals

Where appraisals have been based on specific results, the job of setting goals is much easier. The self-motivating feature of employee-centered appraisals isn't realized until the employee has participated in the setting of goals for the next period. The setting of goals puts the emphasis of the appraisal interview on tomorrow's performance instead of on yesterday's. Managers seeking to control their departments are much more concerned with what is going to happen than with what has happened. The primary function of controls is to adjust and guide future operations.

Appraise the Interview

To his credit, Burt Hall was preparing to find out what went wrong with his first two interviews. He hadn't done as well as he had hoped he would, and he wanted to take corrective action. Most supervisors will benefit from the same action. A supervisor should ask, "Did I reach the objective of the interview? If not, why not? What did I learn that will help me in future interviews?" Each interview should be a learning experience, but the supervisor should take the time to evaluate what was learned.

Follow Up

In the course of the interview, a supervisor may very well have made suggestions or offered help that should not be forgotten. The effectiveness of the entire performance-appraisal system can be threatened by a failure to follow up on promises made during the interview. Such failure makes the appraisal appear to be a mere formality to be forgotten as soon as the interview is concluded. If the interview resulted in planning for improved performance or in trying to correct a performance deficiency, the supervisor will certainly want to check progress with the employee periodically rather than wait until the next appraisal interview. It's in these follow-up actions that the supervisor demonstrates sincerity in trying to make the appraisal an effective control.

Skillfully handled, the appraisal interview is of great benefit to the employee, the supervisor, and the company. The employee gains a sense of direction and participation in the development of his or her career. Employees find that they have a voice in managing their own jobs. To the supervisor comes the knowledge that he or she is controlling the department by correcting, adjusting, and upgrading.

HIGHLIGHTS

1. The purpose of the control phase of the management process is to assure the supervisor that what he or she has planned and directed is accomplished. Through control a supervisor takes charge of the department.

2. The three essential steps in controlling are:

   a. Setting goals and standards at key points in a process
   b. Measuring performance or progress against standards
   c. Taking corrective action or making adjustments

3. Performance appraisals are management controls which set standards of performance, measure or evaluate performance against accepted standards, and seek to improve employees' performance.

4. Some of the key uses of performance appraisal are:

   a. To improve performance
   b. To provide a basis for personnel actions
   c. To determine training needs
   d. To improve supervisor-employee communication
   e. To gain feedback on performance standards and supervision

5. Appraising employees' performances is avoided by many supervisors. The problems that they cite are:

   a. Difficulty in setting standards
   b. Inconsistency of rating by different supervisors
   c. Appraisal forms that don't cover the job
   d. Dislike for the formality involved

6. The closer a supervisor can come to basing an appraisal on specific results and objective standards, the more effective his or her use of this management control will be.

7. The appraisal interview can make or break the entire program. It can rescue a poorly conceived program or threaten the effectiveness of the most accurate appraisals. The supervisor should:

   a. Prepare for the interview
   b. Encourage preparation by employees
   c. Arrange for uninterrupted privacy
   d. Level with employees
   e. Encourage employees to talk
   f. Try to set goals
   g. Appraise the interview
   h. Follow up

DISCUSSION QUESTIONS

1. Cite some specific goals or standards in your department that provide the basis for control.

2. What are some of the reports supervisors give to staff departments and higher management to help them control the larger operation?

3. What are the main reasons for the establishment of management controls?

4. What are the main limitations of performance appraisal and reviews?

5. Evaluate the "traits" approach versus the "results" approach to appraising employes' performances.

6. How do you explain the statement that a good performance review can overcome a faulty appraisal form or program?

7. Assume that you have evaluated an employee's performance on a company form. What preparations would you make for the appraisal interview?

8. Why is an employee's participation in and contribution to the appraisal interview so important?

CASE PROBLEMS

THE CASE OF ELEANOR BRIDGES

Eleanor Bridges's work in the registrar's office of Hoskins College had always been satisfactory—not distinguished, but satisfactory. In a small but rapidly growing college she was one of the old-timers with over ten years' experience. Lately her work has started to slip badly. In some cases it has taken almost twice as long to complete assignments—and even then numerous errors have crept into her work. These errors have taken more time to rectify, and resulted in considerable grumbling.

Registrar Rex Rehfeldt discussed Eleanor's declining performance with her and soon learned of her keen disappointment at not being named assistant registrar when the position was created. She felt that being the "oldest" person in the department with the greatest experience in registration procedures and student records entitled her to the job.

The position of assistant registrar was created to provide the department with a supervisor of both full- and part-time clerical help. Eleanor, who was regarded as "adequate" in clerical work with no evidence of innovative ability or leadership skills, hadn't even been considered for the job. At best, Mr. Rehfeldt thought of her only as continuing in her present job. Her performance in the last few months cast doubt about even that. What do you do, he wondered, with a person who has aspirations beyond her ability? Obviously something would have to be done to correct the situation.

1. What justification does Eleanor have for thinking she should have gotten the supervisory job?

2. What can Mr. Rehfeldt do to get Eleanor to perform her present job in a satisfactory manner?

3. What should he do about Eleanor's interest in supervisory work?

THE CASE OF GREG GRAY

Greg Gray has worked in the underwriting department of the Capitol Insurance Company for nearly two years. In many ways he is one of the bright young stars on the horizon. His supervisor, John Albright, is preparing to review his performance with him.

The record shows that Greg consistently does more work than is expected of him and usually does it more quickly than anyone else in the department. Greg has been especially helpful with new people in the department. He has cheerfully assumed part of their training and followed up like a good coach. John is especially pleased with Greg's help in this area.

Several special and difficult assignments have been approached cooperatively and handled expertly. Greg has never been hesitant to work extra hours even at personal inconvenience. He just smiles and asks what has to be done. In all his relations with people inside and outside the department Greg is very well liked. His loyalty to the company is noticeable and genuine.

Greg does have one shortcoming. His performance report shows occasional clerical errors. When John mentioned them at the time, Greg's attitude was cooperative and apologetic. But John felt that Greg didn't really take them too seriously when Greg stressed the need to get work done on time.

1. What should John Albright's objective be when planning his appraisal interview with Greg?

2. Outline what John's preparation for the interview should include.

3. How should John handle the one shortcoming that Greg has when he interviews Greg?

THE CASE OF EDITH SHEILD

Edith Sheild, supervisor of applications research for the Glo-Brite Wax and Polish Company, hated performance appraisals more than any other part of her job. "You spend a year building good morale and wipe it out with one round of appraisals. How can anything which is supposed to be good for supervisor-employee relationships have such an opposite reaction?" was the question on Edith's mind as she made preparations for next week's round of reviews.

The problems Edith had had in the past she could see happening again, and short of abdicating her responsibility she didn't know how to avoid them. Personnel had always told supervisors not to get into discussions of salary adjustments, that the primary purpose of appraising and reviewing performance was to let employees know where they stand in their bosses' eyes and to show them how they could improve. The appraisal interviews were supposed to open the lines of communication between supervisors and their employees.

Edith knew it didn't work that way for her. Most of her people seemed disappointed in her evaluations of their performance. How, she wondered, can I stimulate improvement unless I keep my ratings conservative—on the low side? If they see high ratings, they'll just feel no improvement is needed. I want to give them something to shoot for. Instead of wanting to talk about improvement, they want to argue about ratings and they want to know how it's going to affect their wages. I get the feeling that they resent me instead of being motivated to want to improve. I can't even get most of them to talk about improvement. My people always have had lots of ideas for new projects and tests, but for about two months after appraisals those ideas seem to dry up.

It would be easy, she thought, to rate everybody real high and make them feel good. But that would be abdication and wouldn't accomplish anything!

1. What's wrong with Edith's thinking about performance appraisals?

2. Why do Edith's employees react to her appraisal reviews the way they do?

3.   What should Edith do about the next round of appraisal interviews in her department?

SUGGESTIONS FOR FURTHER STUDY

Bittel, Lester R., *What Every Supervisor Should Know*, 3d ed., Chapters 11 and 12, McGraw-Hill Book Company, New York, 1974.

Evans, C. George, *Supervising R & D Personnel*, Chapter 10, American Management Association, New York, 1969.

Shout, Howard F., *Start Supervising*, Chapter 8, Bureau of National Affairs, Inc., Washington, D.C., 1972.

Steinmetz, Lawrence L., and H. Ralph Todd, Jr., *First-Line Management*, Chapter 9, Business Publications, Inc., Dallas, Texas, 1975.

Webber, Ross A., *Management*, Chapters 14 and 15, Richard D. Irwin, Inc., Homewood, Illinois, 1975.

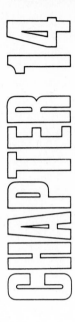

CHAPTER 14

MAKING SOUND DECISIONS

THE CASE OF THE
NEW ASSISTANT

Ray Ford and Burt Hall had been discussing the changes that had taken place in Assembly Department B since Burt became supervisor just fourteen short months before. The work force had grown by 20 percent. Productivity was up over 30 percent. New equipment and new methods were in evidence. And looming on the distant horizon was the possibility of starting a second shift.

"One of these days," Ray said to Burt, "I suppose we'll have to give some thought to getting you an assistant."

He said it casually, without any particular emphasis, but he started Burt thinking about the way his work load had been increasing. He was staying on top of everything. He knew he was growing in the job. No longer did he entertain any thoughts of how much easier it had been back in the ranks. But the realization that he needed help to keep on top was slowly beginning to develop.

Burt knew that delegation was a partial answer. Good delegation could relieve him of some of his growing load. It was also a way of developing some of his key employees. Maybe it was this last factor that made him shy away from delegating more—the appearance of playing favorites or picking an heir apparent after being a supervisor only a little over a year.

If Ray was beginning to think about an assistant for Burt, hadn't he better do some serious thinking himself? Was Ray suggesting that Burt should have a person picked and in the grooming process? If Burt just let it ride until he had authorization from above, would the selection be made for him—possibly of someone from another partment? Burt felt that there were some good people in his department who deserved the opportunity. No doubt about it, the time for a decision had come.

In the days that followed, Burt gave a good deal of thought to which of his key employees he wanted for an assistant. He knew his choice would demonstrate to Ray and Oscar Palmer his own skill in picking workers with management potential. More than an assistant foremanship was involved. The person he picked might very well be the supervisor of the second shift when it started. That person might become Burt's successor if a promotion were ever offered to Burt. Having a capable person ready was just good insurance.

An analysis of potential assistants brought three people to the top of his list. Each had definite assets. Each had some minor drawbacks.

Sam Pitman had been a real problem for Burt when he was first used as a trainer. Both Burt and Sam learned a few things about training from that initial trial. Sam had matured in his understanding of the learning problems of new employees. No longer was he sarcastic. His tendency to show off and become impatient with slow learners seemed to be under control. Results from the people Sam trained were good now. Sam was sharp. He was young—just turned twenty-eight—but still he had over ten years of experience in the department. Few people in the department, even those with much more experience, knew more than Sam about the total operation. No one could top Sam's ability to produce. He took pleasure in taking a tough job and licking it. Although he wasn't an introvert, his superior ability as a producer tended to separate him from the others, and he was regarded as something of a loner. In many ways, Burt thought, Sam was a carbon copy of himself a few years back. Maybe that was why he liked Sam so much.

Clarence "Squeaks" West had distinguished himself as a trainer in Burt's first attempt at delegation. Squeaks was a favorite among new employees because of his helpful attitude, and he was very popular with his fellow workers. Everybody respected Squeaks for his job knowledge, for his ability to produce, and especially for his ability to get along with people.

Squeaks was the most experienced of Burt's three candidates. He had sixteen years in the department and over eighteen years with the company. Squeaks's reputation for being cost- and quality-conscious was well known by both Ray Ford and Oscar Palmer. His knowledge of total departmental operations was equal to if not better than Sam Pitman's. Burt frequently called on Squeaks for troubleshooting assistance and always found him extremely helpful and cooperative.

Squeaks was fifty years old. His intelligence was high, but he had never finished high school. At the beginning of World War II, he had dropped in his senior year to enlist in the infantry. As a sergeant, Squeaks distinguished himself in combat. He was a steady, reliable family man with a wife and three teenage children.

Jane Raymond was a relative newcomer to be given such serious consideration for supervisory responsibility. She had completed two years at the university in mechanical engineering before having to drop out for financial reasons. Determined to get her degree, Jane was taking courses at night. Six to eight years would pass before she could complete her degree work. In the ten months she had worked for Burt, Jane had drawn attention to herself in a number of ways. Constructively inquisitive, she demonstrated a sincere interest in making improvements on every job she worked on. Many of her minor suggestions and two of her major ideas had been implemented already.

Jane confided to Burt that she wanted to get ahead and that she was willing to work at anything that would help her learn the ropes. She demonstrated her sincerity by tackling every assignment Burt gave her with enthusiasm. Being quick to learn, Jane already had a keen understanding of what it took to make a smoothly functioning department. She frequently discussed her university assignments with Burt to get the practical side. Burt enjoyed these discussions with Jane. He noticed, too, that Jane was extremely well liked by everyone she worked with. At twenty-four, Jane had tremendous potential. She was intelligent, popular, anxious to please, a quick learner, and dedicated to her work. To top it off, she wanted to move up into supervision. Burt could only guess about this last factor as far as Sam and Squeaks were concerned.

In maturity, experience, and popularity, Squeaks commanded the greatest respect and probably would be his first choice, Burt thought, but—But he knew that a high school diploma was a minimum requirement of the company for supervisors. Also, fifty years of age was the cutoff point for supervisory appointments. Two years could easily pass before an assistant might make supervisor. On the other hand, Squeaks still had a good fifteen years ahead of him before retirement.

Sam was the number one producer of the three. He was both young and experienced. The only question Burt had about Sam was about his leadership ability. Sam really hadn't had a chance to show what he could do on this score, but there was enough evidence of his being a loner to cause some serious concern.

On the basis of dedication, interest, education, and enthusiasm, Jane Raymond stood out. With a year or two of assistant supervisory experience behind her, Burt did not doubt that Jane would make an excellent supervisor. But there was her youth and lack of experience to consider. Burt also wondered what would happen to morale if he moved such a new person up ahead of those with more experience.

One afternoon when his shift had left for the day, Burt sat in the quiet of his office and wrote down some of the alternatives he had.

1. Do nothing, and wait until the position is authorized.

2. Push Ray Ford to get formal authorization before going any further.

3. Select a person and tell him or her that the position isn't authorized, but start him or her learning some of the jobs to be performed when the appointment is announced.

4. Discuss the merits of each person with Ray Ford and use the discussions to get Ray's evaluation of them. This would also serve to stimulate Ray to think more about formalizing the position.

5. Select the person, but say nothing to anyone. Quietly go about giving him or her assignments to test that person's ability to learn.

6. Start on a program of grooming all three with growth experiences. This way Burt could delegate more, get a better evaluation of each one, and be in a more solid position to recommend the right person when the position is authorized.

7. Wait until the job is formalized, and then recommend all three to higher management, giving the strengths and limitations of each. Then management could make the decision in the light of company policies and their greater experience in making such selections. Since all three were acceptable, Burt could live with any decision management made.

Having written down the alternatives, Burt put them in his desk, turned out the lights, and left. He knew that he might get another idea or two overnight and that he could evaluate the alternatives more clearly in the morning when he was fresh. Whatever he decided, he knew that carrying out his decision would have to be very carefully planned.

1. How can Burt's feeling that the time for a decision had come be explained?

2. A common step in the analysis of a problem is the defining of the problem. How could Burt's problem be defined?

3. Evaluate each of Burt's alternatives. What are the advantages and disadvantages of each one?

4. Are there any other possible solutions?

5. What might Burt have had in mind when he felt that carrying out his decision would require careful planning?

THE MANAGEMENT-MINDED SUPERVISOR AS A DECISION MAKER

When all is said and done, a supervisor is paid to be a decision maker. The supervisor probably makes as many as forty decisions a day. His or her value to the company is in the quality of those decisions. The supervisor's worth to the team is found in his or her batting average. How often does he or she make successful decisions?

The supervisor's position exists because there is a need to make decisions on the frontline. These decisions will require varying degrees of skill and knowledge. Some will be routine. Some will be big decisions that set precedent.

Decisions will concern people, equipment, methods, maintenance, production schedules, use of personal time, etc. Every time a choice is made in the course of a day's operations, a decision is made; and even a seemingly insignificant decision can have far-reaching effects.

Some supervisors find the job of making many decisions a day a challenge to be met with enthusiasm. They find their greatest job satisfaction in improving their decision-making batting average. They see that their effectiveness and future as managers lie in the quality of their decisions. This is the management-minded approach to decision making. On the other hand, we have all seen the supervisor who throws up his or her hands, crying that the job would be all right if it weren't for all the decisions required. Or consider those supervisors who can't make a decision and whose mental or emotional health is adversely affected by the pressure of problems waiting for solutions. They would be better off in nonsupervisory work.

There are many types of supervisors, some of which are discussed below. Supervisors should be able to recognize their weaknesses and try to overcome them by developing a management-minded approach to supervision. Can we recognize decision makers we know among the types discussed here? More important, can we recognize ourselves among them?

THE IMPULSIVE TYPE

This supervisor is not nearly as interested in his or her batting average as in setting speed records. This person gives little consideration to facts, feelings, or funds—he or she makes a decision and moves on to the next one. There are always more decisions to be made. He or she frequently doesn't realize that this impulsiveness creates more problems to solve. His or her pride is in the volume of decisions made and the speed with which they are handled.

THE PIPE SMOKER

This person's philosophy is that most problems will solve themselves if left to incubate long enough. Strictly a low-pressure operator, this person doesn't let anything upset or excite him. Time is the great healer of most management ills. This person sits back, puffs on a pipe, and says, "Let's think about it for a while."

THE BULL IN THE CHINA SHOP

"My job is to make decisions," this supervisor says. No one is to question his or her authority, wisdom, or method of implementing decisions. If feelings get hurt, that's life. The important thing is to get things moving regardless of what people think.

THE FENCE-SITTER

This person is usually unable to make a decision because of an unwillingness to inconvenience anyone. When opinions or feelings are in conflict, he or she is stymied because of wanting everybody to be happy and have his or her own way. The fence-sitter recognizes the need for developing alternative solutions but can never choose between alternatives. It takes forever to make a decision. He or she doesn't like to take risks, and glosses over the fact that not making a decision at all also involves risk. This delay usually results in more crisis-type decisions, thereby making his or her position on the fence more and more uncomfortable.

THE PROFESSOR

This is the analytical type. The professor never makes a decision without all the facts. The catch is that all the facts are seldom available, but that doesn't stop him or her from trying. Like the pipe smoker, the professor can't be hurried. If the problem solves itself before he or she acts, it only proves that there was nothing to get excited about.

There are others—like the worrier, the timid type, and the operator. But our concern is for a constructive management-minded approach to our decision-making responsibility. First, the types of decisions supervisors are called upon to make should be identified. Some problems repeat themselves, and the decisions become routine. Perhaps there are a few variables, but the decisions are geared to past practices, and little judgment is required. Ordering supplies for stock and routing shipments are examples of situations calling for routine decisions. Whenever possible these decisions should be delegated to allow the supervisor to concentrate his or her efforts on situations that can truly be labeled problems and that require a great deal more judgment.

THE ANATOMY OF A DECISION

The purpose of this chapter is to examine how the decision-making process breaks down, what happens in each of the major phases of the process, and how all other chapters in this book relate to this critical responsibility. Knowledge of human relations, communication, discipline, initiating change, and the management process all contribute to the quality of a supervisor's decisions and the skill with which he or she implements them.

When the decision-making process is broken down, three major phases are identifiable—*alert, analysis, action*. In the *alert* phase an awareness develops that a decision must be made. Something goes wrong. A need becomes apparent. A request is made. Having been alerted to the need for decision, the next phase is an *analysis* of the problems that bear on the situation and the possible solutions that form the basis of a decision. Selecting the best decision leads then to the *action* phase, in which the decision is implemented. In major decisions, each of these phases requires the best that the supervisor can give. It's in such situations that the managers are separated from the clerks.

PHASE 1: ALERT

Most supervisors and executives, if pressed for an answer to the question, "How do you make your decisions?" would answer that they don't know. Yet most would also agree that making effective decisions is synonymous with good management. Developing a sensitivity to problems in their embryonic stages—before they become critical—is essential to the supervisor who would avoid being a crisis manager. One can see that problems nipped in the bud require less momentous decisions. We know the truth of the adage that an ounce of prevention is worth a pound of cure. We know, too, that tension and anxiety are less likely to confuse our own and others' thinking if we act quickly.

Management-mindedness for a supervisor is being alert to potential problems, having skill in problem analysis, and being willing to act decisively. Waiting to be pushed into a decision is a failure to accept management responsibility. The result of such failure is a pressure-ridden supervisor jumping from one crisis to another until that supervisor or someone of higher authority decides that the job is too big for such a person.

An analysis of the major problems that demand decisions usually reveals that symptoms had begun to appear long before the situation developed into a problem. Burt Hall demonstrated admirable sensitivity when he determined that the time for a decision had arrived. Even so, there were symptoms long before he became alert to the need to select and groom an assistant. Ray Ford's offhand remark about an assistant simply triggered Burt's decision to get moving. His increasing work load, the departmental changes, an increasing work force, and the growing realization that a second shift would someday materialize all pointed to the fact that a problem was emerging. We could even criticize Burt for not acting sooner, but it seems more appropriate to give him credit for his determination to face the challenge positively. After all, he could have let the situation ride until he was asked to pick an assistant. He chose instead to anticipate the day when the position would be authorized. The day might even be advanced to his advantage.

Every day conditions around a supervisor may be pointing to the development of a problem and the need for action. An operation starts producing a little more scrap than usual. Absenteeism increases slightly. Downtime on a machine starts to exceed reasonable limits. Deliveries of critical materials are late. Accident frequency rates begin to rise. Housekeeping performance slips. Employees complain more than is customary about working conditions. Production bottlenecks develop. A good employee misses deadlines or production quotas. None of these symptoms perhaps is serious in its early stages, but if left unattended, each is a potential crisis. Somewhere between the earliest symptoms and the crisis, a supervisor is alerted to the fact that something is wrong. The more sensitive that supervisor is to a smoothly functioning department, the quicker he or she will be alerted.

The decision-making process begins with the alert, whether subtle symptoms or a crisis bring it about. At the time supervisors become aware of the need for decision, they demonstrate their management-mindedness. They can ignore the symptoms, wait for something more definitive, or start immediately to define and analyze the problem. Most major decisions supervisors make involve some risk, and it's the risk involved that causes them to procrastinate. It should be recognized that not making a decision can also be highly risky. A supervisor might develop a reputation for indecisiveness and jeopardize his or her management future. It is also possible that the decision will be made elsewhere—not always to the satisfaction of the supervisor, who should have made it in the first place.

For example, Burt Hall could have turned his attention to more pressing work until the position of assistant supervisor was formally approved. There are those who would claim that he was sticking his neck out unnecessarily until that time. To follow such a course, however, would be to risk the possibility that the position might never be created or that someone from another department might be assigned to him. In either case Burt would not have the chance to develop and advance one of his own people. By being alert and ready, he stands a much better chance of getting what he wants. He'll also be fulfilling his responsibility to have someone in his department ready to step into his shoes if the need develops.

Decision-making ability is developed by making decisions. Confidence is an important attribute to the successful decision maker. Confidence comes only with making sound decisions repeatedly. On the other hand, shying away from the making of decisions leads to uncertainty for everyone—the supervisor, subordinates, and higher management.

An early definition of the problem is a part of the alert phase of the decision-making process and is the transition into the analysis phase. We seldom question the saying that a problem well defined is half solved. It contains a great deal of truth, but it's likely to be an oversimplification. The first definition of a problem will likely be a statement of the symptoms—something is wrong; a situation needs improvement; a difficulty has been encountered; the boss wants action. Careful analysis of the facts and factors affecting the situation in all probability will call for a redefinition of the problem and give direction to the sound development of alternatives. Once the initial definition of the problem has been verbalized, either mentally or on paper, the decision-making process moves into its second phase, the phase of analysis.

It should be noted that what we are talking about throughout this chapter is a systematic approach to making effective decisions. The impulsive approach is commendable only to the extent that it demonstrates a willingness to take the bull by the horns and make a decision. In all other respects it fails the test of intelligent decision making. For difficult situations, the analysis phase is critical. Sensitivity and thorough understanding of departmental standards alert the supervisor to the need for decisions, but a systematic analysis leads the supervisor to quality decisions.

PHASE 2: ANALYSIS

The alert phase of decision making is inescapable. Sooner or later the existence of a problem or the need for a decision penetrates the awareness of even the dullest supervisor. The analysis phase, however, can be overlooked and frequently is. Problems go unanalyzed, and snap decisions are made every day. The consequences of such actions are familiar. Supervisors who persist in circumventing the analysis phase eventually become the victims of chaotic conditions in their departments. Sound decisions follow intelligent analysis just as guided practice improves a skill.

"Get the facts" is a seemingly overworked phrase. Yet getting the facts that bear on a problem or a decision is so fundamental that the analysis phase cannot be discussed without stressing its importance. For example, Burt Hall possessed many vital facts to help him reach his decision. How could he make an intelligent choice of an assistant without identifying the strengths and limitations of each candidate, as he had done so well? It is also easy to see that he needed more information before making his decision: What is the company's policy with regard to educational requirements? Can job knowledge and experience ever be substituted for formal education? To what extent is seniority a factor? How do Squeaks and Sam feel about accepting supervisory responsibility?

Let's consider some of the factual information a supervisor might want to secure before arriving at decisions. What company policies, procedures, rules, or practices bear on the situation? What is the past production record of the equipment or employee? How do those concerned with the problem feel about it—the boss, the employee, the union? Do contracts with the union or the customer limit the possible alternatives? What costs are involved—either in creating the problem or in recommending a solution? Have solutions to similar problems established precedents that should be evaluated? What company or departmental goals will be affected? These are but a few considerations. Individual situations calling for decisions will undoubtedly point to other sources of desirable information. A questioning attitude is essential in the analytical phase. The planning questions discussed in Chapter 11 provide a solid foundation in our search for the facts—*what, where, when, who,* and *how.*

Hand in hand with getting the facts is the need to identify accurately the real causes of the problem. Exit interviews, for example, may reveal any number of reasons why employees wish to terminate—more money, a job closer to home, more desirable shift, etc. Dealing with these symptoms individually could easily go on for some time until it finally is determined that poor supervision or lack of opportunity is the real cause for the high turnover. Similarly, substandard work may be assumed to be the result of faulty equipment or poor materials, when poorly trained operators are the real cause. Jumping to conclusions by attacking surface symptoms is an easy trap to fall into. Thorough fact gathering and a genuinely questioning attitude contribute significantly to the ability to determine the real cause of problems.

Having identified the exact cause of the problem, the supervisor should reexamine the first definition of the problem. Is it a true statement of the real problem? In some situations a clear statement of the problem may be no more than a restatement of the cause. The supervisor should, however, guard against setting forth the solution in the problem statement lest he or she limit consideration of possible alternatives. In the turnover problem mentioned above, for example, there is a difference between these two versions of the problem: (1) How can we reduce turnover in the department? (2) How can we get rid of the supervisor? To be sure, the supervisor might have been the cause of the turnover, and eliminating this person might be one alternative—but certainly not the only one. The first statement opens the analysis of the problem to a wide range of possibilities, from training the supervisor to transferring this person. The first version allows for the consideration of other causes such as poor working conditions, low pay, and lack of opportunity. The second begins with the decision to get rid of the supervisor as the primary cause and leaves only the question of how this is to be done.

Before being satisfied with a redefinition of a problem, the supervisor should check the possibility of its relationship to other problems. Will putting out this fire leave several others still burning? Is this only a part of a much larger problem? The ability to see the big picture is a distinct asset to the supervisor–decision maker–manager.

At various times supervisors have been given advice like, "Get all the facts" and "Never make assumptions." It sounds good in theory, but realistically it can't always be done. Seldom are all the facts available. To get all the facts would frequently mean that a supervisor would never get around to making a decision. Supervisors have to make assumptions or, more accurately, educated guesses. Intelligent decision making does not rule out making assumptions but does require that the decision maker realize the difference between facts and assumptions. Confusing the difference between assumptions and facts leads to difficulties. When assumptions are made, special consideration must be given to their validity. In view of the available facts, is it a safe assumption?

Short of asking Sam Pitman if he was interested in becoming an assistant supervisor under Burt, the only way Burt could consider him as a prime candidate would be to assume his interest. From previous conversations and from Sam's attitude and performance, Burt could make this assumption with reasonably good prospects of being right. With Squeaks it might be another matter. Why, after all these years of top-notch performance, had West been passed over? Was it because he didn't want the job, or was the lack of a high school diploma the main reason? It's easy to see that an assumption here would be risky without some concrete evidence of interest. When assumptions are necessary, they should be checked against the best information available.

With the facts gathered, the causes of the problem determined, and the problem clearly defined, the supervisor is ready to start what has been the main objective—the development of a solution. All too often the temptation to jump from the alert phase to the first solution that occurs is irresistible. Yielding to this temptation, however, results in a higher percentage of poor decisions than a supervisor would want.

Creative, high-quality decisions are usually not the first ones to pop into a supervisor's mind. For this reason giving special care to developing as many solutions to the problem as possible pays dividends. The creative-thinking specialists have good advice to offer concerning the development of alternatives—avoid judicial thinking, and use only creative thinking until as many solutions as possible have been identified. Judicial thinking inhibits the creative approach. It tends to evaluate the solution and discard that which is unusual or hasn't been tried before. By developing many alternatives, a supervisor goes beyond the obvious. The obvious solution frequently is not the best—whether it is will not be known until several alternatives are explored. Very often in striving to develop a list of alternative solutions, a supervisor will find that a combination of two or three of them gives a more comprehensive answer to the problem.

Burt Hall developed a list of several alternatives to his problem. Any one of them might prove to be workable. It will take additional effort on his part to evaluate each of them, but how much better it is to be able to choose from several possibilities. Combinations of his listed alternatives also reveal still more possibilities.

Confidence and pride in his decisions are more likely to result from a supervisor's having thoroughly explored and evaluated the alternatives. We can say with conviction that this is the best decision we could have reached. When we must defend a chosen course of action, we are in a better position when we can say, "I considered that, and my best judgment points to this decision for these reasons."

Evaluative or judicial thinking follows the listing of possible alternatives. Avoiding evaluation in the listing of alternatives tends to generate more ideas. Now sound decision making requires that the best of the alternatives be selected. Careful appraisal of each alternative is the most practical method of arriving at the decision which represents the supervisor's best judgment.

A few key questions will guide the supervisor in making the evaluation. He or she should consider whether or not the decision will correct the situation or reach the desired goal. If all the alternatives are likely to fall short of accomplishing the purpose, other approaches should be explored. Other criteria against which decisions should be checked are apparent in the following questions: Is the cost justified? How will it affect other people or other departments? Is it in conflict with established policies or contracts? Will it set a desirable precedent? How will it affect production?

The result of this thorough and systematic analysis, of course, is the best possible decision, and the transition into the action phase of the decision-making process begins.

One of the most satisfying experiences a manager can have is to lick a tough problem. The satisfaction increases if he or she has thoroughly studied the problem and if the decision is supported and smoothly implemented by everyone involved. Such satisfaction isn't likely to happen by chance. It follows more often a well-conceived plan for implementing a decision. Failure to plan how an otherwise sound decision will be put into action can easily result in confusion and frustration.

Decisions frequently involve change. Resistance can be expected unless a plan for overcoming it is formulated. Chapter 4 discusses the problems involved when decisions create significant changes. Taking action on major decisions should include these five important considerations: (1) a well-planned procedure for taking action; (2) the participation of those affected; (3) the communication of the decision to all concerned; (4) follow-up during the implementation; (5) the evaluation of results. Each of these considerations is critical in realizing the goal of a successfully implemented decision.

Planning the Procedure for Taking Action

Once the decision has been reached, the decision-making process has not been completed. The supervisor is still faced with the problem of making it work. Many good decisions fail because action was taken at the wrong time or because important details had not been anticipated. In considering several of Burt Hall's alternatives, it's easy to see that the critical factor would not be in what he decided to do but in how he planned to take action. For example, let us consider the possibility that he decided to begin grooming all three candidates without committing himself to any of them. When should he start? What assignments could he give to them? Should Ray Ford and Mr. Palmer be informed? Should assignments be rotated among them, or should each be given a specific area of responsibility? Similar questions would have to be answered for any of the alternatives Burt listed if it were to have a chance of succeeding.

In preparing the implementation of a decision, the planning questions again provide a simple systematic approach. What steps need to be taken and in what sequence? Who should do the work, and who will be affected? When is the best time to start, and how long should it take before the decision is fully operational? What difficulties are likely to crop up, or what could go wrong anywhere along the line? This last question is particularly important to consider in order to avoid unnecessary complications. By anticipating possible trouble spots, the supervisor will plan to avoid them and ensure his or her success.

Participation of Those Affected

We have discussed in previous chapters the importance of participation from those whose cooperation the supervisor needs. No matter how carefully the supervisor analyzes problems and reaches decisions, his or her subordinates will ultimately determine whether or not the plan will work. The degree to which others can be involved in these decisions will have to be an individual determination. In some cases a supervisor might decide that subordinates can profitably help analyze the problem, participate in developing alternatives, and help decide what should be done. This would be a very high degree of participation and would be more likely to gain the full support of subordinates.

Often the decision is one which the supervisor alone must make. It is still possible to outline the decision to those affected and to get their ideas about its workability. If the supervisor is flexible and open-minded, both boss and subordinates can offer suggestions to improve the plan of action. Finally, if the decision is a firm one from which no deviations can be considered, a supervisor can still build in participation by allowing discussion of the best ways to implement it. Support for decisions is much more likely to come from those who have participated and feel that they are a part of them. This applies not only to subordinates, but to the boss and other department heads as well.

Communication to All Concerned

Any supervisor who has ever complained of learning about a management decision from the union steward can appreciate the importance of the proper timing and proper channels for communicating a decision. We defined communication as the creation of understanding. Understanding of what decisions have been made and why they have been made is of vital importance to a supervisor's superiors. Their need to know what is going on in any department is essential if they are to coordinate or manage several departments. The boss should never be surprised by learning of the supervisor's decisions from other sources. Informing the boss promptly of decisions or discussing them with the boss beforehand is just one of the many ways the supervisor can give support to the boss. This support contributes in no small measure to the boss's desire to support the supervisor.

Employees who will have to abide by a supervisor's decisions or who will have to carry them out can make them look silly or sound. Their cooperation is essential and is dependent on the degree to which they understand how the decision will affect them. They will want to know what their responsibilities are, how they are to proceed, what the decision is intended to accomplish, how they will benefit, and how they might be expected to change their behavior. Anticipating these questions and communicating the answers beforehand will help avoid needless difficulties and anxieties.

Other departments should also be considered if their operations are affected. Will the output from a supervisor's department in quantity, quality, or time put additional demands on others? Common courtesy dictates that they be informed of the decision to help them cooperate. For example, in discipline and grievance decisions, the supervisor will want the support of the labor relations department and must keep its members posted. A decision to change a production schedule may affect the shipping department, other production departments, or the sales department, which has promised delivery.

The timing and method of communication will be determined by the individual situation. In relatively minor or routine decisions a verbal instruction or phone call is probably adequate. When other departments are affected, a memo is advisable. Decisions resulting in new procedures should be carefully written, and copies sent to everyone concerned. Decisions which affect company policy or which are likely to set a precedent might combine a spoken explanation to the boss with a written report on how and why the decision was made. Decisions affecting administration of the labor contract should generally be put in writing after discussions with the parties concerned. In those cases where the feelings of a group might be involved, a meeting should be considered so that everyone gets the information at the same time and has a chance to react.

Follow-Up During the Implementation

The best-laid plans, the saying goes, often go awry. To ensure the successful implementation of a decision, the effective decision maker will follow closely the action initiated. In planning the course of action, the decision maker tries to anticipate everything that could go wrong, but knows he or she can't afford to issue directives and forget them. Is everyone performing according to expectations? Has any resistance developed? Is everything on schedule? Are materials up to standard? Is equipment functioning smoothly? Are desired results being realized? Follow-up, if the decision-making process was conscientiously carried out, should be no more than a few routine checks on progress. No one is so perfect, however, that every decision made will be carried out exactly. Catching deviations early may save both time and embarrassment. Slight modifications, accomplished early, can be the difference between succeeding and failing.

Evaluation of Results

Naturally all supervisors are interested in their decision-making batting average. Their primary concern is whether or not their decisions achieved the results expected. Their interest in self-development as managers requires that they periodically look at their decisions and evaluate their effectiveness. "If the desired results were achieved, could I do an even better job next time?" "If I failed, why did I?" They can learn from failure just as surely as they do from successes. Every decision they are called upon to make is a challenge. "How do I meet challenge—with enthusiasm and determination or by turning my back and waiting?" In the final analysis, supervisors are paid and promoted for their decision-making ability—an ability that can be improved with practice. This chapter provides the kind of guidance that leads to better decisions. It's up to each individual to decide how he or she will use it.

Each chapter so far has concluded with a summary of highlights—not so this chapter. Figure 12 diagrams the anatomy of a decision. It not only incorporates the highlights of this chapter, but represents, we hope, the fact that every subject discussed in this book will be reflected in the quality of a supervisor's decisions.

A LOOK AHEAD

A member of management—that's the supervisor in business, government, and industry. Being a member of management involves meeting challenges; shouldering tremendous responsibilities; experiencing satisfactions and frustrations; and bearing the burden of decisions. Looking at the job ahead, the supervisor should be able to see opportunity in every direction. Those

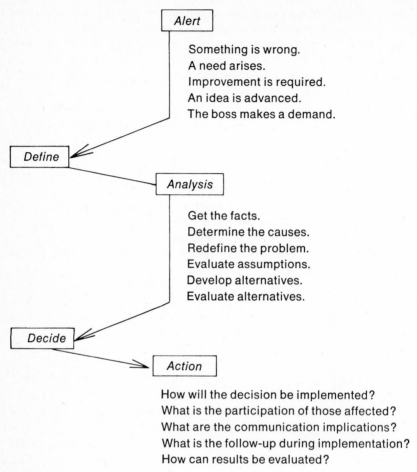

FIGURE 12   The Anatomy of a Decision

opportunities may be labeled problems, challenges, uncertainties, demands, puzzles, and confusions, but they are all a chance to show that the supervisor is worthy of being identified as a member of management.

There are no simple formulas for success in management. No prescription, no formula, certainly no book can ever provide specific answers to specific supervisory problems. An attempt has been made in this book to stimulate thinking about what it means to be a management-minded supervisor. Guidelines have been suggested to give directions to the awesome responsibility of managing human resources in the hope that the supervisor can enjoy the satisfactions of a job well done. The problems of Burt Hall have been presented in the hope that they are typical and will stimulate the study of commonsense approaches to resolving them. Managers can never stop studying and learning.

DISCUSSION QUESTIONS

1. Think of a decision you have made that didn't work out well. Can you trace its failure to overlooking one of the steps discussed in this chapter? What should have been done?

2. Why is so much stress placed on developing many alternatives or possible solutions? Can you cite an example where having several alternatives has paid dividends?

3. How do you account for the fact that many successful executives say they can't explain how they made their decisions?

4. Should a supervisor take a problem to the boss before reaching a decision? If so, under what circumstances? If not, why not?

5. When would the systematic approach to decision making be most helpful? Are there situations calling for decisions when this approach can't or shouldn't be used? Explain your opinion.

6. What are the primary benefits to the supervisor in using the systematic approach to making decisions?

CASE PROBLEMS

THE CASE OF CHARLENE STANTON

"How long can this go on? Mrs. Alexander is the third nurse to quit in two months. And I've never had so much juggling of schedules in my life," Charlene Stanton, supervisor of nursing in pediatrics, was saying to herself. "If this keeps up, we're going to have to do something. I hate to pry into nurses' private lives—suppose it's really none of my business why they're leaving. I've certainly given them plenty of opportunity to tell me, if they wanted to. I don't like to come right out and ask them. Good nurses are hard to find. I haven't found a replacement for that nice Marianne Blake, and now I've got two to look for.

"Three nurses quitting is bad enough, but the absentees are even more of a problem. I've never seen such a rash of minor illnesses and personal problems in my life. You can't blame nurses for complaining about having to change schedules to cover for somebody else and there's been so much of that. They must know it's not my fault. And when I have to ask for so much cooperation, it's hard to discipline people for being late or a little lax now and then. I've got some pretty good nurses—why does everything bunch up like this—never had this much trouble at one time before.

"Maybe we aren't the best-paying, best-equipped hospital in town, but we've got a good reputation in the community. Our little ones get the best care here it's possible to give them—no frills, but good medical care and attention.

"Something's not right, and I don't know what it is. My world is crumbling all around me. What should I do?"

1. What is wrong with Charlene Stanton's approach to her "problem"?

2. How can she find out what's wrong?

3. How should Charlene handle the situation she finds herself in?

THE CASE OF STEVE JOHNSON

"It won't be a popular decision, but I'm certain it's the best one I could have made. When the surprise and hurt feelings subside, Karen Finch will be an outstanding supervisor," Steve Johnson said to himself as he put the finishing touches to a memo nominating Karen to be his replacement. She would be the new supervisor of the accounting section of Tasty Food Stores' home office.

Of the fifteen people in the department, Karen without a doubt was the best qualified. She had graduated with honors from the local business college. In the year and a half with Tasty Foods, she learned exceedingly quickly and could handle any job in the department with ease. She was popular with everyone in the department and all the store managers she dealt with. Higher management had a high regard for her work—so high that Steve was positive his decision would be praised. He knew, too, that he had been very thorough in considering every qualified person in the department. When you have as many facts as Steve, any objective person would have to agree with his nomination. The problem is that not everybody can have all the facts and be as objective as Steve had been.

For example, Jason Evert was sure that he would get the promotion. Most of the people in the department had Jason pegged as the "heir apparent." He had almost six years with Tasty Foods and four years' previous experience with a competitive chain of food stores. Jason was all business—respected but somewhat aloof. He knew that he had earned his promotion and was counting on it.

There were two others considered, both of whom had potential and would probably advance in time, but in the final analysis the choice was between Karen and Jason.

Steve prepared to personally deliver his memo to the controller. As he walked toward Mr. Stein's office he glanced around at his busily working department and thought, "It's a good decision, but it's going to have to be sold."

1. What new problems is Steve going to face as he lets his decision be known?

2. Assuming Mr. Stein's agreement on Karen Finch, what should Steve tell him about his plans for announcing the decision?

3. How should Steve handle Jason Evert?

THE CASE OF BETH DAMRON

Beth Damron just couldn't understand her former friend and now subordinate, Grace Paxton. Beth has been supervising the filing section of the state Environmental Protection Agency for about six months. The agency is relatively new, about six years, and has grown rather rapidly—faster in many cases than the procedures that contribute to an efficiently functioning agency of state government.

At least that's what Grace Paxton felt about her job. Grace and Beth had both started with the agency at its beginning—same grade, same work, same pay. Grace was a few years older than Beth, but they were good friends. Grace always maintained a cooperative attitude with Beth after her promotion, and their friendship also continued. Generally, it was off the job that Grace would occasionally comment in recent months about the amount of idiot work and governmental red tape she had to handle. She was becoming increasingly critical of the antiquated systems she had to work with. Beth would just change the subject.

Yesterday, Grace lost her temper in the office when asked to handle a routine assignment that she was very good at. "It's stupid," she cried. "When are we going to get organized around here? I'm fed up!"

Beth took the outburst personally, feeling it was criticism of the way she was supervising the department or possibly Grace's resentment at having to take orders from her. "Why don't you just do what you're told and stop complaining?" Beth snapped in anger.

"I've got a headache. I'm going home," Grace stated for everyone to hear.

1. Evaluate Beth's handling of her problem with Grace.

2. What might be some of the reasons for Grace's behavior? How can Beth determine what is really wrong?

3. How should Beth handle the situation when Grace comes back?

SUGGESTIONS FOR FURTHER STUDY

Drucker, Peter F., *The Practice of Management*, Chapter 28, Harper & Row, Publishers, Incorporated, New York, 1954.

Kepner, Charles H., and Benjamin B. Tregoe, *The Rational Manager*, McGraw-Hill Book Company, New York, 1965.

Steinmetz, Lawrence L., and H. Ralph Todd, Jr., *First-Line Management*, Chapter 4, Business Publications, Inc., Dallas, Texas, 1975.

Webber, Ross A., *Management*, Chapter 2, Richard D. Irwin, Inc., Homewood, Illinois, 1975.

NEW CENTURY-
NEW DEMANDS

The first decade in our third century as a nation promises to usher in a new revolution. The industrial revolution of the nineteenth century is history. Unbelievable technological advances have been witnessed by our generation. There is no question that advances will continue. But technology will take a backseat to a fomenting unrest in management today, a disturbing restlessness that is permeating all levels of management in almost every type of organization—industry, government, and social and service organizations. We are plunging with nervous agitation into the productivity revolution.

WHAT ARE THE NEW DEMANDS ON MANAGEMENT?

Surfacing signs of discontent have been swept aside or glossed over for two decades. No longer can they be ignored. Consumers are in revolt; taxpayers are in revolt in increasing numbers. Inflation threatens our economic life as a nation. What are these signs of unrest that will create new and heavy demands for skillful management in our organizations? Let's look at a few.

Consumerism

The consumer, first feebly crying in the wilderness, now demands recognition in an organized way. Poor quality workmanship is being challenged. Unsafe design is rejected. "Stop increasing prices while diminishing value or we won't buy" seems to be the battle cry. When the consumer stops buying, our economy falters. Inflation results when productivity does not keep pace with rising prices and wages. Unfortunately, some companies have tried to cut costs by using less expensive substitutes and reducing quality. But inflated costs and narrow profit margins keep raising prices until the consumer says, "I can't buy," or "I won't buy."

Taxpayer Revolts

At all levels of government, the taxpayer is saying, "I've had it." We seem to be perceiving slowly that the government cannot give that which it first must take. Increased government services at the local, state, and federal levels are challenged when executive budgets are presented for approval. At an alarming level, taxpayers are saying "No!" to bonding proposals for schools, highways, health care institutions, and so on. The mushrooming employment levels in government are questioned in light of the satisfactoriness of the productivity of employees in departments and bureaus.

Social Services

Abuses in welfare claims, growing numbers of welfare recipients, and skyrocketing welfare costs are causing taxpayer groups to question how their money is being spent. Unfortunately, overreaction can hurt those who need help the most. Some economists say we are in danger of becoming a welfare society in which a growing segment of nonproductive people increases to a point of collapse the burden on those who are productive.

Even social agencies that depend on contributions are experiencing resistance and are being questioned about how efficiently they utilize their funds. Surprisingly, churches are wrestling with the problem too. Boards of trustees are challenging boards, committees, and paid staff to account for their stewardships.

The intent in looking at the new century is not to paint a doomsday picture, but rather to recognize the new challenges that must be met by our companies and organizations. Opportunities to be a part of the solution exist for every person who wishes to be identified as a *management-minded supervisor.*

HOW CAN WE APPROACH PRODUCTIVITY IMPROVEMENT?

The logical, the pragmatic, answer to the swelling unrest lies in our return to a fundamental principle of economics: to get more of what we want, we must produce more. To get inflation under control, to respond positively to consumer and taxpayer revolts, management must find ways and means to increase the productive output of the organization. "Partners in productivity" could well be the new theme of the management team in every type of organization. Coining slogans, however, is easy. Getting tangible results will not be. A realistic appraisal of where we are and how we can move forward is essential.

Productivity improvement, in general, can be approached two ways. The first approach is by means of improved technology. Our advances here have been tremendously significant and we can expect continued advances. We have passed the point, however, where we can expect technology to cure the problem while we ignore the other approach—improving the productivity of people. Our one great, untapped natural resource is the innovative, creative, productive capacity of our people. We are surely moving into an era of informed human relations —not the misguided, "smother 'em with kindness" human relations that was preached by so many in the fifties and sixties. Instead, human relations in the next decade will be oriented to capitalizing on the desire of men and women to sense a feeling of accomplishment in their work.

It's tragic to see how widespread an ignorance of the need to produce something in return for wages has become. In too many areas, we see the attitude that government, the company, or society owes us a living—a type of economic immaturity that could strangle us as a nation. We are fast becoming a culture conditioned to casual feelings about work, and management must understand and learn how to reeducate society to the economic facts of life.

If we listen to behavioral scientists, we can find the beginnings of a way to reverse this disturbing trend. Great joy and satisfaction in life come from a sense of having produced something worthwhile. The human drive to accomplish may need to be redefined, stimulated, and directed, but it exists within almost all of us. Greater productivity is a source of satisfaction to the employee as well as to the employer. Morale in an organization is necessarily accomplishment-oriented. Thus productivity and morale are as compatible as apple pie and ice cream.

More and more, management will abandon its defensive posture and assume the offense in the battle for increased productivity. We will have to educate our work force concerning what makes our economy tick and be willing to share with them our concerns for survival and growth. In the private sector, we will find new ways for employees to share in the fruits of their labor. In the public sector, we will develop a new sense of stewardship of the tax dollar.

HOW DOES THE HUMAN RELATIONS APPROACH WORK?

"It's too big for me!" any one of us might say. Turning around an entire organization is beyond the ability of a single individual, especially a person at the first level of management. And, certainly, none of us can expect to influence the entire economy. What will happen, however, is a closer and closer scrutiny of the leadership effectiveness of the supervisor—an effectiveness that will be measured in terms of concrete results achieved. The pressure from outside the organization by customer, client, user, or taxpayer reaches the supervisor through internal channels like the boss, higher management, and staff departments. Recognition of supervisors for outstanding achievement will be forthcoming for those who show results in increasing the productive output of their departments. One supervisor can have a very significant impact on an organization and thus enjoy the fruits of accomplishment.

If our main hope for increasing productivity does lie in people, supervisors especially must stop overlooking the obvious. We seem to be engaged in an unending search to find a magic formula for motivating people, ignoring what we've always known or at least have known for the past two decades. When Douglas McGregor suggested that work can be a source of enjoyment and that the individual is self-directing when committed, we nodded with interest but looked for a different answer. When Robert Blake showed us how team management integrated a concern for productivity and a concern for people, we thought it might work in some places, but we needed something that fit *our* organization because we were different. When Fredrick Herzberg suggested that in the job itself we find the greatest potential for motivating people, it just didn't seem practical. Skinner stressing positive reinforcement, McCelland advocating achievement motivation, and Maslow identifying the social, ego, and self-actualization needs of people in the work environment all carry the same message in different words. But still we hope for some new revelation—a button to push to get people tuned in and turned on.

WHAT CAN ONE SUPERVISOR DO?

Each of the behavioral scientists cited above has directly or indirectly stressed benefits to be realized from employee participation in decision making, problem solving, and setting of goals and targets. Our work force today is far better educated, and the trend toward better education will increase in the coming decades. Successful management has to find ways of capitalizing on employees' intelligence, creative ability, and desire to achieve. If we, as management, are willing to share our concerns, rewards, and recognition, we might find a different response from many of our employees. The key to productivity in the organization and in an individual supervisor's department begins with the abandonment of the attempt to manipulate people in favor of real motivation through participation, involvement, and sharing. Instead of prodding and pushing, we might try to make employees partners in productivity.

Here are ten practical tips a supervisor might use to demonstrate how productivity can be improved in his or her department.

Develop an Understanding of the Economics of the Company or Organization

This means, for example, knowing our source of income and capital. Is it federal, state, or city taxes? Is it voluntary contributions or membership dues? Is it customer purchases or investors' savings? No matter what the source, there is an expectation of something in return. When the people who provide revenue question the value received, constraints are imposed on the organization's freedom to operate and grow. A supervisor should have an idea of how much it costs to run his or her department —at least what the major costs are. Can we see materials and supplies used, energy consumed, space occupied, equipment purchased, and labor paid for as dollars that will have to be recovered from our revenue sources?

Help Employees Understand the Economics of the Company or Organization

So often we hear complaints about the lack of concern or lack of job pride on the part of employees these days. Before a supervisor points to poor employee attitudes, he or she might reflect on what has been done to develop a more constructive attitude.

Instead of contributing to the unfortunately familiar adversary relationship between management and employee, the supervisor should recognize that the time is at hand to begin emphasizing the achievement of mission of the organization. Truly sharing with employees our concern for improving productivity, instead of harping, might lead to employees sharing their ideas on improvements.

In order to improve productivity and gain the cooperation of subordinates, the supervisor will have to be a better communicator—a teacher, if you will, of the economic facts of life. This cannot be done in a tongue-in-cheek way. It must be done with enthusiasm, if we are to maintain our credibility. Wherever we seek cooperation, it is essential that we create an understanding of why that cooperation is needed.

Question and Challenge Present Ways of Doing Things

It has been said that all we know is the most up-to-date obsolete ways of doing things. Others have said that there is always a better way to do anything. Still others insist that the way to begin making improvements is "to why the hell out of everything." Why are we performing this operation? Is it necessary? Could it be done a better, more productive way?

Applied to *who* is performing a job, *where* it is being performed, *when* it is being done, and *how* it is being done, this line of questioning leads to many improvement possibilities.The supervisor who is constantly questioning his or her department's operations with a view toward how the department can be more productive, improve quality, or cut costs is going to generate more ideas than the supervisor who accepts the philosophy, "We've always done it this way. Why change now?"

Encourage Employees to Challenge Present Methods and Make Suggestions

Actively seek out employees' ideas and suggestions. Alan Mogenson, founder of the world-famous Lake Placid Work Simplification Conferences, said, "The best qualified person to improve a job is the person doing that job." We give lip service to the concept that our employees' ideas are a gold mine. In practice, however, there isn't much real prospecting being done. If the creative imagination of our employees is our great, untapped natural resource, isn't it time to tap that source of potential productivity improvement?

One of the things that kills most suggestion systems is the failure to give serious consideration to ideas and suggestions when they are presented. A person who gives an idea and feels it was ignored won't give another. If we encourage employees to think, we will have to think and consider along with them.

Encourage Employees in the Setting of Goals and Targets

Not every job offers this potential, but everything we know about motivational theory says employees will produce more if they have been involved in the setting of an objective. Beyond theory, actual practice has proved that, when given the opportunity to suggest a goal, employees will set a higher goal than management would have dared.

Often we will resist a standard or objective set by others but when asked, "What is the best you can do?" will exceed imposed goals. Once committed to a goal, people are self-directing, according to Douglas McGregor. In practice, this is proven every day in organizations across the land.

Provide Feedback on Performance and Recognition for Excellence

Prevalent today is the thought that people are paid for good work and that's all that's really important. If employees are to be real partners in productivity, they must know when they have done well and be told the value of what they have contributed. Employees take the paycheck for granted as a condition of employment. If we are to tap their spirit, their imagination, their motivation, it will take more than a paycheck. How many times will we have to remind ourselves of the value of feedback before we recognize the importance of it?

Enthusiastically Orient New Employees to Their Role in Productivity

The time to build attitudes is the first day on the job; that's when people are the most impressionable. An employee's orientation should include a well-planned explanation of the mission of the organization, the importance of quality work, and the need for serious concern about productivity. Here's the golden opportunity to invite suggestions and stimulate thinking about how to improve productivity.

Sharpen Training of New Employees

The quality of performance in a department is not likely to rise above the level of the training given. Instead of passing off employees to an old-timer for training, the supervisor should exercise care to see that they are taught how to be most productive. We can hardly expect people to show concern if we don't provide them with the training that gives them the best know-how and with the encouragement to use that training.

Use Controls to Monitor Performance

The productivity-minded supervisor will continually ask, "How are we doing? Is our output what it should be, and can it be improved? When costs start getting out of line, what can be done to check them? Is customer or user satisfaction what it should be? Is the taxpayer getting full value from our department? If we are not as productive as we should be, why not? What can we do about it?" Recall that we said that the purpose of control is corrective action. If our monitoring of performance in the department shows that productivity is less than it could or should be, we can quickly take action to get it back in line.

Demonstrate or Discuss Ideas on Productivity Improvement With the Boss

Everything that has been said about sharing our concern about productivity with employees applies up the line to the boss as well. Higher management should know of our concern for improving productivity. Here's a chance for the boss to know of our concern and to help with our attempts to upgrade departmental performance. The boss, as has been said before, has a vested interest in our success. It stands to reason that our demonstrated concern for improving productivity will reflect to our credit. Just call it being wisely selfish.

INDEX